Combination and Conspiracy

Combination and Conspiracy

A Legal History of Trade Unionism, 1721–1906

JOHN V. ORTH

CLARENDON PRESS · OXFORD
1991

Oxford University Press, Walton Street, Oxford OX2 6DP
Oxford New York Toronto
Delhi Bombay Calcutta Madras Karachi
Petaling Jaya Singapore Hong Kong Tokyo
Nairobi Dar es Salaam Cape Town
Melbourne Auckland
and associated companies in
Berlin Ibadan

Oxford is a trade mark of Oxford University Press

Published in the United States
by Oxford University Press, New York

British Library Cataloguing in Publication Data
Orth, John V. 1947–
Combination and conspiracy: a legal history of trade
unionism, 1721–1906.
1. Great Britain. Trade unions. Law, history
I. Title
344.104109
ISBN 0–19–825299–4

Library of Congress Cataloging in Publication Data
Orth, John V.
Combination and conspiracy: a legal history of trade unionism,
1721–1906 / John V. Orth.
Includes bibliographical references and index.
1. Trade-unions—Law and legislation—Great Britain—History.
2. Labor laws and legislation—Great Britain—History.
3. Conspiracy—Great Britain—History. I. Title.
KD3050.078   1991   344.41'0188'09—dc20   [344.10418809]   90–21507
ISBN 0–19–825299–4

Typeset by Hope Services (Abingdon) Ltd.
Printed in Great Britain by
Bookcraft Ltd
Midsomer Norton
Avon

To
Samuel E. Thorne
who summoned a spirit
from the vasty deep

and to
Zachary John
whose name, but for his father's cowardice,
would have been Zachary John Samuel

Preface

Of the making of books on the subject of English Trade Unions and the allied problems of modern industry there is indeed no end.

Edward Cummings (1899)[1]

This is not a book about current law. The combination acts, which are so painstakingly analysed in these pages, were all repealed a long time ago. Conspiracy law as it bears on labour, while by no means a dead letter today, is examined in its early stages; it is described as it was more than a century ago, before many important changes. The modern history of English labour law, superseding combination and conspiracy, began in 1906 with the passage of the Trade Disputes Act which amended and supplemented the Trade Union Act (1871). Several excellent legal textbooks cover the law as it has developed since then and as it is today.

Instead, this is a book about pre-modern labour law. Given the obvious importance of labour in the last hundred years and the number of books devoted to English trade unions, it is surprising how little has been written about the legal history of labour. More than fifty years ago, Sir William Holdsworth published an article on eighteenth-century industrial combinations, now immured in his *magnum opus*, the many-volumed *History of English Law*. In the aftermath of the 1926 General Strike, M. Dorothy George, irked by loose talk about labour's grievances, published her oft-cited reappraisals of the combination acts. In addition, there is a slender volume by R. Y. Hedges and Allan Winterbottom, *The Legal History of Trade Unionism*. Published in 1930, still in the shadow of the General Strike, that work was largely concerned with the era that began in 1871; the law of the previous five centuries was covered in a mere sixty pages.

Why has the legal history of labour attracted so little attention? The answer in part is that until fairly recently little attention was paid to any aspect of the legal history of modern Britain. As G. R. Elton put it in 1970: 'For the post-medieval period, the history of law, law courts and justice remains something of a cinderella . . .'[2] Since then, several fairy godmothers have appeared, most unlikely perhaps, E. P. Thompson, and a 'new' legal

---

[1] Edward Cummings, 'A Collectivist Philosophy of Trade Unionism', *Quarterly Journal of Economics*, 13 (1898–9), 151.
[2] G. R. Elton, *Modern Historians on British History, 1485–1945: A Critical Bibliography, 1945–1969* (Ithaca, NY, 1970), 172. Elton did concede that 'a little more life can be reported . . . than would have been possible twenty-five years ago.'

history has recently been proclaimed.[3] Neglect of legal history in general is, however, only part of the answer. The rest is that law played only a minor role in shaping labour relations in England. The first Industrial Revolution occurred without central planning; in fact, the weakness of national government and traditions of local administration prevented law from playing a more significant role. Later, the ideology of *laissez-faire* denied the value of regulation. Economic relations in general and labour relations in particular were for long on the limits of the law. When dramatic developments in the 1970s put labour law at the top of the political agenda, one commentator drew attention to a 'distinct gap in the literature':[4] the absence of legal historical studies. Perhaps, too, many of the older historians implicitly shared the assumptions of *laissez-faire*. In a survey of trade union historiography, E. J. Hobsbawm, himself a distinguished practitioner, concluded: 'Almost the only question about the state's relations to the unions was, whether governments provided legal freedom for their actions and whether they discriminated in other ways against labour organisations.'[5]

Unlike most preface-writers, who have by this time earnestly assured the reader of the importance of their subjects, I have done just the reverse: I have conceded that law played a relatively minor role in labour history. But however small the role it played, law *did* play a role. In fact, it may have loomed larger in its pre-modern period than later on; its makers certainly intended as much. Holdsworth's gloomy assessment was that near the end of our period law missed the chance to shape labour relations for the better.[6] Whatever the moral of the story, the legal history of labour in the eighteenth and nineteenth centuries defined the terms—literally, as well as in the larger sense—that were used in the eventual settlement. The abstentionism that came to characterize law's relation to labour was suggested by earlier experience and was within a framework inherited from the past.

Having now, after my fashion, asserted the importance of my subject to the reader, I must confess its importance to me. To my eye, it offers a pleasing array of cases and statutes, each with its own intriguing

[3] See e.g. E. P. Thompson, *Whigs and Hunters: The Origin of the Black Act* (New York, 1975) (the Black Act was passed in 1723); Douglas Hay, Peter Linebaugh, John Rule, E. P. Thompson, and Cal Winslow, *Albion's Fatal Tree: Crime and Society in Eighteenth-Century England* (New York, 1975); David Sugarman and G. R. Rubin, 'Towards a New History of Law and Material Society in England, 1750–1914', in Rubin and Sugarman (eds.), *Law, Economy and Society, 1750–1914: Essays in the History of English Law* (Abingdon, 1984), 1–123 (reviewed by John V. Orth, *Law and History Review*, 4 (1986), 210–12). See also 'Note', 'Law and Legitimacy in England, 1800–1832: Bringing Professors Hay and Thompson to the Bargaining Table', 68 *Boston University Law Review* 621–51 (1988).

[4] Roy Lewis, 'The Historical Development of Labour Law', *British Journal of Industrial Relations*, 14 (1976), 1.

[5] E. J. Hobsbawm, 'Trade Union Historiography', *Bulletin of the Society for the Study of Labour History*, 8 (Spring 1964), 33.

[6] William S. Holdsworth, *A History of English Law*, 17 vols. (1903–76), xv., ed. A. L. Goodhart and H. G. Hanbury (London, 1965), 86.

complexities of language and meaning. While parliament legislated on combination, the courts elaborated the common law of conspiracy. Historians have sometimes written as if the two were quite distinct: those inclined to criticize the legislation have been told that, compared to conspiracy, it was mild indeed; critics of conspiracy, on the other hand, have pointed the finger at the statutes. In fact, as this study will show, combination and conspiracy were always closely related.

Not only were the combination acts related to the developing law of conspiracy, they were also organically related to one another. From the first recognizable combination act in 1721, regulating the London tailoring trade, until the Trade Union Act (1871) and the Trade Disputes Act (1906), the legislation on combination formed a connected series. Concepts appeared, were modified, extended, sometimes rejected. The Trade Union Act (1871), which itself marked a new beginning, was also marked by what went before. Historians have again tended to overlook the connections. A. V. Dicey may innocently have caused some of the trouble. Invited to lecture at the Harvard Law School in 1898 on the development of English law 'during the nineteenth century', Dicey commenced his survey precisely at 1800. Since there happened to be a combination act that year, he used it to begin his history of the right of association, disregarding what went before. With touching literalness, he even noted that the nineteenth century did not really begin in 1800. (There being no year 0 in the Christian calendar, the first century began with AD 1; each succeeding century should begin accordingly at hundred-year intervals.) Dicey justified using 1800 as the first year of the new century by reference to 'popular phraseology'.[7] Historians have perhaps too readily assumed that he treated 1800 as the beginning of combination law as well as the beginning of a new century.

To recognize the connectedness of the combination acts one must look at each act as a whole, its procedural as well as its substantive sections. This means breaking with established traditions of legal analysis. By the mid-nineteenth century, lawyers distinguished sharply between rules that the courts enforced and rules of procedure, dismissingly labelled by Jeremy Bentham 'adjective law'. In the legal history of labour this manifested itself as exclusive concern with the rules of law—the 'nouns', as it were, of legal discourse. But the eighteenth century drew no such sharp distinction: each combination act contained a miniature code of procedure as well as a rule (or rules) of law. The development of combination law and many of the disputes that swirled around the statutes concerned proper procedure, what may be called, in a phrase made famous by the American Bill of Rights (1791), 'due process of law'. To dismiss this aspect of combination law is to ignore what contemporaries of all classes thought most important about it.

---

[7] A. V. Dicey, *Lectures on the Relation between Law and Public Opinion in England during the Nineteenth Century* (2nd edn., London, 1914), 62 n. 1.

In the nineteenth century the more familiar pattern of substantive rules emerged from the thicket of procedure. Having solved the not inconsiderable problem of how to do things the right way, law moved on to the grander question of what was to be done by means of the newly perfected procedures. Due process eventually acquired a substantive meaning of its own: that all were to be treated alike. Proper procedures, formal legal equality, and *laissez-faire* melded to form a powerful jurisprudential system. Labour reaped many of the gains of even-handedness in forms and rules but suffered from an ideology of individualism informed by economic hostility. The more obvious debates have long been well known to historians, but concealed in seemingly technical rules of contract and tort were policy choices of equal significance to labour. To overlook these doctrinal developments is to miss an important part of the story, and to lose the opportunity to examine the preconceptions of modern labour law.

Writing about legal history risks irritating both lawyer and historian. The first looks for and fails to find the analytical method of a modern legal treatise; the second keeps trying to see society apart from its laws (as if that were possible). The dual premises of this study are that it is worth while to examine law chronologically and that a thorough examination of law in its own terms will assist future historians of society. However much (or little) history lawyers may read, one thing is certain: historians rarely read and almost never properly cite the law. An astounding number of reputable historians, when they refer to law at all, seem to prefer newspaper accounts to legal sources, although the latter are readily available in every law library, even in America.

Both law and labour are too important to be left to lawyers and historians. So that this book might be accessible to educated lay persons as well, I have tried to explain legal terms and describe the legal system in adequate detail in the text; a glossary of legal terms is provided at the back. I would frankly rather annoy ninety-nine learned lawyers and historians than lose one of those 'gentle readers'.

J.V.O

Chapel Hill, NC
March 1990

Acknowledgements

Now and then, over the last dozen years, I have published articles on various aspects of the history of labour law. Although in a couple of cases I seem to have retained the copyright, in a few instances I gave it to others. My article on 'English Combination Acts of the Eighteenth Century', which appeared in *Law and History Review*, 5 (1987), 175–211, and which forms the basis of Chapter 2, is copyrighted by Cornell University. A paper entitled 'The Law of Strikes, 1847–1871', presented to the Bristol Legal History Conference and published in *Law and Social Change in British History* (1984), 126–44, belongs to the editors of that volume, J. A. Guy and H. G. Beale; part of it is reprinted, in modified form, as Chapter 8 of the present work. Two other articles that no longer belong to me dealt with subjects that are also covered here, albeit in substantially different form. 'The Legal Status of English Trade Unions, 1799–1871', a short paper presented to the Edinburgh Legal History Conference and published in *Law-Making and Law-Makers in British History* (1980), 195–207, is copyrighted by Alan Harding, the editor of that volume; and 'English Law and Striking Workmen: The Molestation of Workmen Act, 1859', which appeared in *Journal of Legal History*, 2 (1981), 238–57, is apparently owned by the publisher, Frank Cass & Co. To these owners of my intellectual property, acknowledgement is due for permission to reuse parts of it.

To the best of my belief, no permission is required in three other cases, either because I retain title or because no substantial part is reused. I refer first to 'The English Combination Laws Reconsidered', which began under a somewhat different title as a paper presented to an international conference at the University of Warwick on the History of Law, Labour, and Crime and which appeared in Francis Snyder and Douglas Hay (eds.), *Labour, Law, and Crime: An Historical Perspective* (1987), 123–49. A shortened version of this paper was read at the Carolinas Symposium on British Studies and (I am proud to say) was awarded the Symposium Prize for 1985. Two other articles, I believe, are also still mine: 'Doing Legal History', 14 NS *Irish Jurist* 114–23 (1979) and 'The British Trade Union Acts of 1824 and 1825: Dicey and the Relation between Law and Opinion', 5 *Anglo-American Law Review* 131–52 (1976). In the event I am mistaken, I sincerely apologize to any and all whose right is hereby infringed.

Finally, acknowledgement must be paid to the Law Center Board of the University of North Carolina at Chapel Hill for financial support during the Summer of 1987, while I worked on Chapter 3.

Intellectual debts are, to my way of thinking, more important than others because they can never be repaid. I hereby acknowledge outstanding obligations to Richard A. Cosgrove, Richard Price, and Christopher L. Tomlins, each of whom read this work in manuscript and commented on it candidly and constructively. As ever with debtor and creditor, any misuse of the assets by the former is not attributable to the latter.

Contents

List of Figures

List of Tables

Note on Citations

In citations to legal periodicals I follow the convenient legal form: volume number first, then title, page numbers, and finally the date in parentheses. If the periodical has no volume number, the date takes its place.

The masters are these: nobles, rich men, the prosperous generally. These few, who do no work, determine what pay the vast hive shall have who *do* work. You see? They're a 'combine'—a trade union, to coin a new phrase—who band themselves together to force their lowly brother to take what they choose to give. Thirteen hundred years hence—so says the unwritten law—the 'combine' will be the other way, and then how these fine people's posterity will fume and fret and grit their teeth over the insolent tyranny of trade unions! Yes indeed! the magistrate will tranquilly arrange the wages from now clear away down into the nineteenth century; and then all of a sudden the wage earner will consider that a couple of thousand years or so is enough of this one-sided sort of thing; and he will rise up and take a hand in fixing his wages himself. Ah, he will have a long and bitter account of wrong and humiliation to settle.

Mark Twain, 'Sixth-Century Political Economy', in
A Connecticut Yankee in King Arthur's Court (1889)

1

Introduction

[T]hough anciently it was usual to rate wages, first by general laws
extending over the whole kingdom, and afterwards by particular orders
of the justices of peace in every particular county, both these practices
have now gone entirely into disuse . . . Particular acts of parliament,
however, still attempt sometimes to regulate wages in particular trades
and in particular places.

Adam Smith (1776)

Ever since 'Adam delved and Eve span'[1] the world has faced the problem of
work. Whether all able-bodied persons must work, whether those in work
are entitled to the whole produce of their labour, whether those willing and
able to work have a right to do so—the answers to these questions have
shaped society from earliest times to the present. They have prompted
searching inquiries into the nature of work as well as into its corollary,
leisure. Once these grand preliminaries have been more or less settled, the
struggle has narrowed to the particularities that shape the everyday
experience of working people: how long must they labour, under what
conditions, and—most momentous of all—how much will they be paid? Of
almost equal moment to society as a whole has been the question: who will
decide?

In all settled communities the distribution of power and wealth expresses
itself in terms of law. Constitutional law reflects the organization of society,
the distribution of political power, while property law allocates rights to
material things, economic power. The law of contract authorizes binding
agreements to exchange things of value. Tort provides the legal definition of
private wrong, and criminal law sets the outer limits of publicly tolerated
behaviour. The legal history of labour implicates many aspects of law.
Before the triumph of democracy, law was made by those whose most
significant contact with manual labour was collecting its rents and profits.
In eighteenth- and nineteenth-century England, the aristocracy was increasingly allied with the commercial middle class, apparently endlessly on the

---

[1] From the text used by the itinerant priest John Ball for an incendiary sermon during the
Peasants' Revolt (1381). See Thomas Walsingham, *Historia Anglicana, 1272–1422*, ed. Henry
Thomas Riley (1863–4), ii. 32 (altered to common form). The text concludes with the
rhetorical question: 'Who was then a gentleman?'

rise. By statute and case, the ruling élite created labour law—at first (as it created the British Empire) in a seeming 'fit of absence of mind' but later (as economic struggle concentrated that mind) with greater deliberateness.

Labour law was made of many elements. A revolutionary reconceptualization of property was eventually one of them: labour, it was discovered, was not only a (or the) source of wealth; it was wealth itself, 'the poor man's capital'.[2] Contract meanwhile played a smaller role than might have been expected: labour was for long thought of primarily as a status to which rights and duties were attached rather than as the performance of one side of an agreement. Indeed, until property in labour was clearly recognized, a bargained-for exchange of it could not be readily thought about. Tort entered into the regulation of workmen trying to exert pressure on one another or on their employers, who were called throughout most of our period their 'masters'. But it was in terms of criminal law—the instinctual resort of élites confronted with new and unsettling realities—that the state first grappled with the labour problem.

The earliest legal memory of labour in England dates to the aftermath of the Black Death in 1348. That terrible winnowing of human life resulted in a drastic shortage of labour. Long before Adam Smith demonstrated how supply and demand set prices, the powers that be felt the pinch caused by a straitened labour market. Few workers were willing to follow the example set by the pious Piers Plowman and toil on as if nothing had changed;[3] most sought better status, higher wages, or simply more leisure. Criminal law registered the response of England's rulers. Custom could no longer be trusted to determine economic relationships, and surrender to the 'natural law' of supply and demand was unacceptable. Positive law, legislation, was instead wheeled into place to impose a solution. The Statutes of Labourers,[4] among the first entries in the English statute book, compelled work at wages that had prevailed before the catastrophe. All men and women under the age of sixty and without land or a trade sufficient for self-support had to serve whoever required their labour, although lords had the first right to the service of their tenants. To enforce the rules, the Crown named 'justices of

---

[2] See e.g. *Hansard*, 2nd ser., vol. 12, col. 1292 (29 Mar. 1825) (speech by William Huskisson, president of the Board of Trade).

[3] William Langland, *Piers the Plowman*, ed. Walter W. Skeat, 4 vols. (1886), i. 222 (B vi. 314–24) (composed in the last half of the 14th cent.).

[4] 23 Edw. 3 (1349) in *Statutes at Large*, ed. Danby Pickering (1762–6), ii. 26–30; 25 Edw. 3, st. 1 (1350), ibid. ii. 31–5. See Bertha Haven Putnam, *The Enforcement of the Statutes of Labourers during the First Decade after the Black Death, 1349–1359* (New York, 1908) (reprinting in an appendix the Latin texts of the enactments); Elaine Clark, 'Medieval Labor Law and English Local Courts', *American Journal of Legal History*, 27 (1983), 330–53; L. R. Poos, 'The Social Context of Statute of Labourers Enforcement', *Law and History Review*, 1 (1983), 27–52. The first enactment is commonly called an ordinance rather than a statute since it was issued by the king without the concurrence of parliament, unable to meet because of the plague.

labourers', one of the roots from which eventually sprang the justices of the peace.[5]

The primitive economics that motivated the legislators has been aptly caricatured in a historical novel written six hundred years later; as expressed by the fictional Prior of Etchingdon: 'Though there should be but one labourer left, man and loaf should be as cheap as before.'[6] The legislative attempt to set back the clock met inevitable failure, but not before it had provoked widespread hostility, not only from labourers but also from landowners who wanted to compete for labour. The Peasants' Revolt of 1381, which included the statutes among its targets, reunited the wealthy, but wrenching practical accommodations were required before the medieval mechanism of custom got going again.

The next great legislative impulse came two centuries later, in the Tudor period. The Elizabethan Statute of Artificers (1563),[7] which repealed the medieval Statutes of Labourers, set the framework for labour law until well into the eighteenth century; Blackstone was obliged to refer to it often in his *Commentaries*. Under the statute, wages were to be set locally by justices of the peace, laymen appointed for each county. For more than two centuries the justices of the peace had been assembling regularly four times a year for quarter sessions, the dates of which were tied by statute to convenient feast-days, one in each season of the year: Michaelmas (29 September), Epiphany (6 January), Easter (a movable feast between 22 March and 25 April), and the Translation of Saint Thomas[8] (7 July).[9] Reliance on the religious calendar later prompted a pointed observation from Benjamin Disraeli: the English gentleman, he said, is governed by 'Arabian laws and Syrian customs' and 'regulates the quarterly performance of his judicial duties in his province by the advent of the sacred festivals'.[10]

---

[5] William S. Holdsworth, *A History of English Law* (London, 1903–72), x. 195; see also ibid. i. 26*–27* (introductory essay by S. B. Chrimes).

[6] Sylvia Townsend Warner, *The Corner that Held Them* (1948), in *Four in Hand* (New York, 1986), 629. For another literary reference see T. H. White's poignant short story, 'Not Until Tomorrow', repr. in *The Maharajah and other Stories* (New York, 1983), 155–6.

[7] 5 Eliz. 1, c. 4 (1563). (Pickering dated the Statute of Artificers 1562, but it became effective in 1563.) See S. T. Bindoff, 'The Making of the Statute of Artificers', in S. T. Bindoff, J. Hurstfield, and C. H. Williams (eds.), *Elizabethan Government and Society: Essays Presented to Sir John Neale* (London, 1961), 56–94; Donald Woodward, 'The Background to the Statute of Artificers: The Genesis of Labour Policy, 1558–63', *Economic History Review*, 2nd ser., 33 (1980), 32–44.

[8] St Thomas à Becket had been murdered at the urging of King Henry II on 29 Dec. 1170. While his feast is still the anniversary of his death, a second was also observed in the Middle Ages on 7 July, the date in 1220 when his relics were translated from his tomb to an impressive shrine in Canterbury Cathedral.

[9] 2 Hen. 5, st. 1, c. 4 (1414). The Statute of Labourers, 25 Edw. 3, st. 1, c. 7 (1350), contains the earliest regulation of the dates of quarter sessions: Michaelmas (29 Sept.), St Nicholas (6 Dec.), the Annunciation (25 Mar.), and St Margaret (20 July). Other dates were tried (see 36 Edw. 3, st. 1, c. 12 (1362)) before the fifteenth-century statute settled the dates that were to be maintained until quarter sessions were abolished in 1971.

[10] Benjamin Disraeli, *Tancred: or, The New Crusade* (1847) (1877), i. 153.

The Statute of Artificers broke with the medieval practice of wage regulation by 'general laws extending over the whole kingdom'; instead, the justices of the peace in every county were authorized to set wages by 'particular orders'.[11] Empowered by the statute to confer with 'discreet and grave persons' and paying special attention to the 'plenty or scarcity of the time', the justices of the peace were required to set annual wages at the quarter sessions next after Easter.[12] Concomitant with wage regulation went a legal code of behaviour for workmen, the foundation of the long-lived law of master and servant. A principal provision of this code forbade leaving work unfinished. So long as labour was viewed as a status and wages were regulated, this simply spelled out one of the workman's duties. When wage regulation faltered and labour was reconceptualized in terms of contract, the law of master and servant survived as an increasingly anomalous aspect of criminal law concerning breach of contract. Still later, as workmen forged the strike into a major weapon of economic warfare, this law added to the employers' arsenal.

Further clauses of the Statute of Artificers, giving rise to the misnomer the 'Statute of Apprentices', regulated the training of skilled labour.[13] Before practising any craft, a workman had to serve an apprenticeship of at least seven years. Thereafter he became a journeyman, qualified to work for a master and eligible, if he could assemble the necessary capital, to graduate into a master himself. In course of time the grades of master and journeyman (or 'man', for short) tended to become permanent, and apprenticeships, originally a device to assure quality, came to be regarded— as labour was reconceptualized as a commodity—as a throttle on the supply of skilled men.

In the eighteenth century, as Adam Smith observed, wage regulation by justices of the peace, like that by general legislation, went 'entirely into disuse', although it received a renewed lease of life in 'particular acts', regulating wages 'in particular trades and in particular places'.[14] Incident to regulating wages, these acts forbade combination to alter the prescribed wages or working conditions. It is with these combination acts that our story begins.

---

[11] Adam Smith, *An Inquiry into the Nature and Causes of the Wealth of Nations*, ed. Edwin Cannan (New York, 1937), 141 (1st edn., 1776) (epigraph of the present chapter of this book).

[12] 5 Eliz. 1, c. 4, § 15.

[13] Ibid. §§ 26–33. See Margaret G. Davies, *The Enforcement of English Apprenticeship: A Study in Applied Mercantilism, 1563–1642* (Cambridge, Mass., 1956).

[14] Smith, *Wealth of Nations*, 141. See W. E. Minchinton, *Wage Regulation in Pre-Industrial England* (New York, 1972), 9–36, 206–35.

2

Combination: 1721–1799

One is inclined to call the last century the century of *privilegia*. It seems afraid to rise to the dignity of a general proposition . . .

F. W. Maitland (1888)

'Combination' first entered the statute book in 1721 as the legal name for labour organizations.[1] Earlier statutes had labelled their precursors 'conspiracies'[2] or 'confederacies'.[3] All the names were bad. Conspiracy, perhaps the worst of all, was predominantly used to describe the common-law crime that was coming to be recognized when a group agreed to injure an individual, but combination was bad enough. As Dr Johnson noted in his famous *Dictionary* at mid-century, it was 'generally used in an ill sense'.[4] Soon thereafter, Burke pointed the contrast: 'When bad men combine, the good must associate.'[5] Later on, some workmen tried to redeem the word: 'By combination we shall succeed', proudly proclaimed the Amalgamated Society of Journeymen Cloggers.[6] But it came too late: the semantic struggle was already lost. Although the word was to shed its ill sense late in the period covered by this book,[7] combination was in the mean time too freighted with negative connotations and was finally dropped. A better future called for a new name. The United Society of Brushmakers recognized the need: 'United to protect, not combined to injure.'[8] In

---

[1] 7 Geo. 1, st. 1, c. 13 (1721). (Pickering dated the statute 1720, but it became effective in 1721.)

[2] E.g., 2 & 3 Edw. 6, c. 15 (1548) (conspiracies of victuallers and craftsmen).

[3] E.g., 3 Hen. 6, c. 1 (1424) (confederacies of masons).

[4] Samuel Johnson, *Dictionary* (1755), s.v. 'combination'.

[5] Edmund Burke, *Thoughts on the Cause of the Present Discontents* (1770), repr. in *Writings and Speeches*, ii. ed. Paul Langford (1981), 315. Cf. an apparently inadvertent paraphrase sixty-four years later: Anon., 'Combinations and Combination Laws', *Law Magazine*, 11 (1834), 147 ('when bad men conspire, good men must combine').

[6] R. Frow, E. Frow, and Michael Katanka, *The History of British Trade Unionism: A Select Bibliography* (London, 1969), front cover (illustration of membership card).

[7] *Oxford English Dictionary* (1st edn., 1884–1928), s.v. 'combination' ('formerly used almost always in a bad sense, as conspiracy, self-interested or illegal confederacy'); *Webster's Third New International Dictionary* (Springfield, Mass., 1966), s.v. 'combination' ('formerly often to achieve a result contrary to law or public welfare but now usu. to achieve a legitimate social, political, or economic end').

[8] Frow, *et al.*, *Bibliography*, 12 (illustration of membership card); see also John Batt, ' "United to Support but not Combined to Injure": Public Order, Trade Unions and the Repeal

union—in which there is strength—lay the answer, but 'trade union', both as a popular name and as a legal appellation, did not arrive until well into the nineteenth century. In the mean time the law had found a bad name for labour organizations, although it still lacked a coherent approach to them. Over the course of the eighteenth century statute after statute regulated wages and forbade combination in particular trades and places. Only at the very end of the century did parliament hazard a 'general proposition'.

The history of the combination acts begins, appropriately enough, with a work stoppage, what would in time be called a strike. In 1720 speculation in shares of the South Sea Company ended disastrously when the bubble burst. The sharp downturn in the economy 'beggared half the nation', as Blackstone later recalled;[9] in fact, John Gay composed *The Beggar's Opera* (1728) in an attempt to recoup his losses. Master craftsmen who depended on the prosperity of the well-to-do suffered along with their clients; journeymen in turn felt the pinch.[10] Tempers flared in the tailoring trade,[11] a vulnerable consumer industry whose workmen had long been hard pressed. (In *A Midsummer Night's Dream* more than a century earlier, Shakespeare had given his rustic tailor a significant name: Robin Starveling.) The dispute that ensued was the occasion for the enactment of the first combination act,[12] as well as for an early prosecution of journeymen for criminal conspiracy.[13]

The tailors' combination act began with a preamble reciting the recent unrest and proceeded to enact a comprehensive scheme for labour relations in the metropolis—or, in the old-fashioned language of the law, 'within the weekly bills of mortality'.[14] These bills, dating from the last visitation of the plague in the seventeenth century, were records of burials kept by the Company of Parish Clerks; they gave their name to greater London and Westminster. The act proceeded on the legal assumption that journeymen tailors in the area had previously agreed on a course of action; so, to stamp out their combinations, it voided all existing 'contracts, covenants or agreements' for raising wages or reducing hours and imposed two months' imprisonment on those who made such agreements in future.[15] At the discretion of the justices of the peace, imprisonment could be either in the common gaol or at hard labour in the house of correction. The latter institution, popularly known as a bridewell because the first example had

---

of the Combination Acts of 1799–1800', *International Review of Social History*, 31 (1986), 185–203. T. J. Dunning used 'United to support, but not combined to injure' as the epigraph of his book, *Trades' Unions and Strikes: Their Philosophy and Intention* (1860).

[9] William Blackstone, *Commentaries on the Laws of England* (1765–9), iv. 177.
[10] John Carswell, *The South Sea Bubble* (Stanford, Calif., 1960), 197–8.
[11] See *Select Documents Illustrating the History of Trade Unionism: 1. The Tailoring Trade*, ed. Frank W. Galton (1896), pp. xiii–xxvi, 1–22.
[12] 7 Geo. 1, st. 1, c. 13 (1721).
[13] R. v. *Journeymen-Taylors of Cambridge*, 8 Mod. 10, 88 Eng. Rep. 9 (KB 1721).
[14] 7 Geo. 1, st. 1, c. 13, § 1.   [15] Ibid.

been established in a disused royal palace of that name,[16] had originally been intended as a reformatory where habits of industry would be taught.[17] By the eighteenth century they had become simply gaols; whatever labour was done in them was for the profit of the master of the house.[18] At mid-century Henry Fielding, novelist and justice of the peace in London, exposed the horrors of the gaols in *Amelia*,[19] and in *Tom Jones* commented ironically on the house of correction: 'that house where the inferior sort of people may learn one good lesson, viz. respect and deference to their superiors; since it must show them the wide distinction Fortune intends between those persons who are to be corrected for their faults, and those who are not'.[20] That house also awaited those tailors who departed from service before the end of their terms of employment, who left work unfinished, or who refused employment without just cause.[21]

Prosecution was to be by summary procedure, without the time-consuming steps of indictment, pleading, and trial by jury. At common law, apart from statutes, such expedited proceedings were permitted only in cases of contempt committed 'in the face of the court'.[22] Medieval legislation had given justices of the peace power to punish offences committed in their view out of court, and Tudor–Stuart acts had greatly expanded it, conferring on them the same power with respect to offences discovered by 'examination'.[23] In the eighteenth century the justices' power of summary conviction was continually augmented, each combination act adding to it. The county justices were, as we shall see, substantial citizens, but those in the metropolitan area were far beneath them socially. The justices for Middlesex, in which lay London and the weekly bills of mortality, were often corrupt; Justice Gobble in Smollett's *Launcelot Greaves* (1761) is the standard caricature of a Middlesex 'trading justice'.

Under the tailors' combination act, the examination was to be conducted by two of these justices within three months of the offence, and conviction had to rest on confession or the sworn testimony of at least one witness.[24] Appeal lay to quarter sessions, the decision of which was said to be 'final'.[25] (In fact, as we shall see, the Court of King's Bench continued to exert a supervisory power by means of the writ of *certiorari*.) Those punished under the act were granted immunity from further punishment for the same

---

[16] Johnson, *Dictionary*, s.v. 'bridewell'.

[17] See Joanna Innes, 'Prisons for the Poor: English Bridewells, 1555–1800', in Francis Snyder and Douglas Hay (eds.), *Labour, Law, and Crime: An Historical Perspective* (London, 1987), 42–122.

[18] See John Howard, *The State of the Prisons in England and Wales* (1777), 68–77.

[19] Henry Fielding, *Amelia* (1751); see also B. M. Jones, *Henry Fielding, Novelist and Magistrate* (London, 1933), 208–19.

[20] Fielding, *Tom Jones* (1749) (London, 1959), 112–13.

[21] 7 Geo. 1, st. 1, c. 13, § 6.

[22] Blackstone, *Commentaries*, iv. 283.

[23] J. H. Baker, *An Introduction to English Legal History* (2nd edn., London, 1979), 419.

[24] 7 Geo. 1, st. 1, c. 13, § 1.   [25] Ibid. § 9.

offence 'by authority of any law now in force'.[26] Offending tailors were, as the last clause plainly recognized, also liable to prosecution under other laws, particularly those governing the relationship of master and servant, the subject of a later chapter. 'Leaving work unfinished', to name only one offence under the tailors' combination act, was (as we have seen) already punishable under the Elizabethan Statute of Artificers (1563).[27] Over and above various statutes applicable to their case, however, loomed the common law—the *lex non scripta* or unwritten law, as it was still called, to which legal theorists continued to give pride of place.[28] Combination was, it seemed, also punishable as common-law conspiracy: coincidental with the tailors' combination act came a criminal prosecution in Cambridge, to be described in the next chapter.

To settle the dispute in London, the tailors' combination act fixed wages and hours in the trade. Wages were to be no more than 2s. a day during the busiest season, from 25 March (Lady Day[29]) to 20 June, and no more than 1s. 8d. a day at other times.[30] Regular working hours were to be from 6 a.m. to 8 p.m. with an hour off for dinner,[31] although those with the stamina were permitted to eke out their statutory wages with overtime work.[32] Journeymen were provided a special process for collecting unpaid wages. The justices of the peace were empowered to proceed by distress and sale of the defaulting master's goods; in other words, they could seize personal property and sell it to raise the necessary funds. If the defaulter had insufficient means, he was to be imprisoned until satisfaction was made.[33] With wages and hours determined by legislation, there naturally arose the risk of evasion by economically motivated masters and men. To prevent such violations, criminal penalties were provided: masters paying too much would be fined £5, and journeymen taking too much would be set to hard labour in the house of correction for two months.[34] Setting wages by statute ran the further risk of being outdated by economic developments. To permit the necessary flexibility, the act echoed the Statute of Artificers and delegated to the justices of the peace in quarter sessions the power to alter wages and hours according to the 'plenty or scarcity of the time'.[35]

Almost a half-century after the tailors' combination act, unrest in the trade coincided with disturbances surrounding the turbulent John Wilkes.[36] In 1768 a second statute was passed to improve the functioning of the

[26] Ibid. § 10.

[27] 5 Eliz. 1, c. 4, § 13 (1563).

[28] E.g., Blackstone, *Commentaries*, i. 63–84.

[29] Lady Day, officially the feast of the Annunciation of the Blessed Virgin, commemorated the day on which Jesus Christ was conceived; it was, until 1752, the first day of the new year in England and its overseas colonies.

[30] 7 Geo. 1, st. 1, c. 13, § 2.   [31] Ibid.   [32] Ibid. § 8.

[33] Ibid. §§ 3–4. On distress and sale, see Blackstone, *Commentaries*, iii. 6–15.

[34] 7 Geo. 1, st. 1, c. 13, § 7.   [35] Cf. ibid. § 5 with 5 Eliz. 1, c. 4, § 15.

[36] See George Rudé, *Wilkes and Liberty: A Social Study of 1763 to 1774* (Oxford, 1962), 94–5; *Select Documents*, pp. xl–xlv, 57–65.

earlier one.[37] Although the justices of the peace within the weekly bills of mortality had from time to time adjusted wages and hours, the preamble to the later statute declared that 'doubts and difficulties' had arisen and 'many subtil devices' been practised to evade the regulations.[38] The act established a new schedule of wages and hours, registering apparent improvement in the journeymen's economic condition. The maximum wage was set at 2s. 7d. a day all the year round, except during a time of general mourning when high demand for black clothing[39] caused a rise of more than double in the maximum, to 5s 1½d. a day.[40] A modern historian has wryly wondered 'how many church-going tailors . . . prayed with all their hearts for the health of the royal family'.[41] Regular working hours were somewhat shorter under the new act: from 6 a.m. to 7 p.m. with an hour off for refreshment.[42] Punishment for violating the act was the same as that laid down forty-seven years earlier: two months' imprisonment either in the common gaol or in the house of correction at hard labour.[43] In keeping with the statute's purpose, elaborate provisions were included to reduce the opportunity for procedural delay. Reluctant witnesses for the prosecution could be compelled to appear by a summons served personally or left at their usual place of abode, and those who refused to testify could be locked up.[44] Appellants were required to provide security for their later appearance.[45]

The English were a litigious people, and the draftsman of the statute anticipated suits against those enforcing the law. Ever since Tudor–Stuart legislation had devolved many of the responsibilities of local government on the justices of the peace, special procedures had been provided for suits against them and those who aided in local law enforcement.[46] In the absence of supervision by the central government, such suits were the principal means of ensuring the discharge of local duties and preventing abuse of power. In the second tailors' act such counteractions were limited to six months after the fact.[47] Since these suits would be tried by common-law courts, not using the summary procedure of the justices of the peace, a special procedural provision was necessary to authorize defendants to plead

---

[37] 8 Geo. 3, c. 17 (1768). (Pickering dated the statute 1767, but it became effective in 1768.)

[38] Ibid. preamble.

[39] For the costume required for mourning, see C. Willett Cunnington and Phillis Cunnington, *Handbook of English Costume in the Eighteenth Century* (Boston, 1957), 218, 317–19. For a contemporary analysis of the economic impact of mourning on the clothing industry, see Adam Smith, *An Inquiry into the Nature and Causes of the Wealth of Nations*, ed. Edwin Cannan (New York, 1937), 59, 116.

[40] 8 Geo. 3, c. 17, § 1.

[41] John Rule, *The Experience of Labour in Eighteenth-Century English Industry* (New York, 1981), 179.

[42] 8 Geo. 3, c. 17, § 1.   [43] Ibid. § 2.   [44] Ibid. § 3.

[45] Ibid. § 8.

[46] William S. Holdsworth identified the original Poor Law, 43 Eliz. 1, c. 2 (1601), as the first statute to include special provision for suits against local officials (*A History of English Law* (London, 1903–72), x. 157).

[47] 8 Geo. 3, c. 17, § 9.

the general issue, that is, to deny plaintiffs' claims in general, on both the facts and the law,[48] the effect of which was to cast the burden of proof on plaintiffs. If defendants prevailed, they were to be awarded full costs.[49]

The act expressly declared itself a 'public act' (as opposed to a private one), the principal effect of which was, as the clause itself spelled out, to require all judges and justices of the peace to take official notice of it without special pleading.[50] Public acts were printed in full ('at large') in the volumes of the Statutes at Large while private acts were listed only by title. Although not expressly so named, the first tailors' act had also been public. The distinction loomed larger in the eighteenth century than today because special fees were then payable to parliamentary officers during the passage of private acts.[51] On the theoretical level, as Blackstone formulated it: 'A general or public act is an universal rule, that regards the whole community . . . Special or private acts are rather exceptions than rules, being those which only operate upon particular persons, and private concerns.'[52] Private acts, in other words, conferred *privilegia*, exceptions to ordinary law, rather than formulating general propositions.[53] One can see how particular acts for tailors within the weekly bills of mortality might require explicit labelling.

To keep the regulations of wages and hours current, justices of the peace were again empowered to alter them 'as the exigencies of the times may require'.[54] In the past, variations had occurred within the metropolitan area: in 1751–2 working hours in the City of London had been one hour shorter than those in Middlesex.[55] To provide uniformity the mayor, aldermen, and recorder[56] of the City were to set the tailors' wages and hours not only for the City itself but also for the area five miles round about.[57] To provide sufficient notice of proposed changes, advertisements were to be placed three times in any two daily newspapers in the capital.[58]

In its enforcement provisions the act was aimed primarily at masters rather than men. The section concerning witnesses singled out 'any clerk, foreman, apprentice, servant, or other person or persons *employed or*

---

[48] 8 Geo. 3, c. 17, § 10. Concerning pleading the general issue, see Blackstone, *Commentaries*, iii. 305–6.

[49] 8 Geo. 3, c. 17, § 10.   [50] Ibid. § 11.

[51] On the distinction between public and private acts in the 18th century, see Holdsworth, *History of English Law*, xi. 292–310.

[52] Blackstone, *Commentaries*, i. 85–6.

[53] See Maitland, *Constitutional History of England*, ed. H. A. L. Fisher (Cambridge, 1908), 383 (lectures delivered 1887–8) (epigraph of the present chapter of this book); Holdsworth, *History of English Law*, xi. 325.

[54] 8 Geo. 3, c. 17, § 4.

[55] See C. R. Dobson, *Masters and Journeymen: A Prehistory of Industrial Relations, 1717–1800* (London, 1980), 66.

[56] The recorder of London, appointed by the mayor and aldermen, was the official spokesman for the City. He was also usually a justice of the peace and a judge at the criminal court adjoining Newgate prison, known as the Old Bailey.

[57] 8 Geo. 3, c. 17, § 4.   [58] Ibid. § 5.

retained by such person so suspected to have offended'.[59] And although the statute carefully exempted foremen and overtime work from its coverage, it expressly provided that such exemptions might not be used to elude the prescribed wage and hour regulations.[60] Such evasions would require at least acquiescence by the master. Finally, a special provision was aimed at masters who tried to elude the act by paying more than the allowed wages to journeymen outside the London area: they were subject to the extraordinary fine of £500![61] To make discovering such violations worth while, an informer would be rewarded with half that huge amount.[62] Informers have a long history in law enforcement: Edward Gibbon found them in Roman law and remarked in a characteristic aside on the 'ignominy which, in every age and country, has attended the character of an informer'.[63] In England their use dated from Elizabethan times.[64] The 'common informer', not a hired servant of the Crown but a private person seeking a reward, was provided a special form of action known as a *qui tam*, Latin for 'who as well', since he sued as well for the king as for himself: '*qui tam pro domino rege, etc. quam pro seipso*'.[65]

The emphasis on violations by masters shows that the legislation was designed as much to maintain employer solidarity in face of economic temptation as to keep workmen down; as Adam Smith observed, the statute 'enforces by law that very regulation which masters sometimes attempt to establish by . . . combinations'.[66] Smith went on to endorse a criticism he attributed to journeymen: 'The complaint of the workmen, that it puts the ablest and most industrious upon the same footing with an ordinary workman, seems perfectly well founded.'[67] This objection to wage regulation—whether by government, employers, or trade unions—was to become an oft-repeated tenet of liberal orthodoxy in the next century. It was to be repeated in passing in John Stuart Mill's world-famous essay *On Liberty* (1859).[68]

Soon after the first tailors' combination act, strikes and violence by weavers[69] precipitated legislation in 1726 covering the venerable woollen trade throughout the country.[70] After reciting recent events, the act voided

---

[59] Ibid. § 3 (italics added).   [60] Ibid. § 6.   [61] Ibid. § 7.   [62] Ibid.

[63] Edward Gibbon, *The Decline and Fall of the Roman Empire* (1776–88), ed. J. B. Bury (London, 1909), ii. 100.

[64] See Maurice W. Beresford, 'The Common Informer, the Penal Statutes and Economic Regulation', *Economic History Review*, 2nd ser., 10 (1957–8), 221–38.

[65] Blackstone, *Commentaries*, iii. 160; see also ibid. iii. 261–2; iv. 303–4.

[66] Smith, *Wealth of Nations*, 142.

[67] Ibid.

[68] John Stuart Mill, *On Liberty* (1859), (Indianapolis, Ind., 1978), 85–6. See Chap. 8, n. 44.

[69] See *Commons Journal*, 20 (1725–6), 598–9, 602, 627, 647–8; Ephraim Lipson, *Economic History of England*, iii. *The Age of Mercantilism* (6th edn., London, 1956), 392–5.

[70] 12 Geo. 1, c. 34 (1726). (Pickering dated the act 1725, but it became effective in 1726.) Principally directed at woolcombers and weavers, ibid. § 1, the act was extended by its last section to cover combers of jersey, framework knitters, and stockingers, ibid. § 8.

all contracts by journeymen weavers to regulate trade and prices, to raise wages, or to reduce hours; journeymen entering into such agreements in future were to be imprisoned for three months either in the common gaol or at hard labour in the house of correction.[71] Subject to similar punishment were those who departed before the end of their terms or who left work unfinished.[72] In case work was damaged, the journeyman was liable to the owner for double its value; if the forfeiture went unpaid, he could be imprisoned for three months.[73]

To eliminate a cause of dissension in the trade, masters were prohibited from paying wages 'by way of truck'.[74] The truck system, payment in goods rather than money, although of uncertain economic impact,[75] was strenuously objected to by workmen. A perennial issue in industrial relations, the truck system was finally outlawed by general acts in the nineteenth century.[76] In the mean time it (like combination) was legislated against piecemeal. Individual masters, while not necessarily committed to the system, feared to abandon it lest they be disadvantaged with respect to competitors; abolition by act of parliament had the advantage of excluding the practice by everyone. The weavers' combination act punished payment in truck by a fine of £10, half of which went to the informer.[77] It also empowered two justices of the peace to collect overdue money wages by distress and sale; in case of insufficiency, the offending master weaver was to be imprisoned for six months.[78] Appeals from convictions under the act were to be heard by quarter sessions, whose decisions were said to be 'final'.[79]

Unlike the legislation concerning tailors which applied to the trade only within the weekly bills of mortality, the weavers' act blanketed the country. It was only one of many statutes in the eighteenth century that increased the power of the county justices of the peace. Unlike the trading justices of Middlesex, the county justices were substantial citizens. When the weavers' act was passed, the legal qualification, dating from the fifteenth century, was the possession of lands yielding at least £20 a year.[80] Inflation, as Blackstone

---

[71] 12 Geo. 1, c. 34, § 1.

[72] Ibid. § 2 (imprisonment in house of correction at hard labour).

[73] Ibid. (imprisonment in house of correction at hard labour).

[74] Ibid. § 3. For earlier truck acts, see 1 Anne, st. 2, c. 18 (1703) (expired 1707); 9 Anne, c. 30 (1711) (revived earlier act and made it perpetual); 10 Anne, c. 16 (1712) (penalty for truck payment 20s.); 1 Geo. 1, st. 2, c. 15 (1715) (increasing penalty for truck payment to 40s.).

[75] See George W. Hilton, *The Truck System: Including a History of the British Truck Acts, 1465–1960* (Cambridge, 1960), 1–60.

[76] 1 & 2 Will. 4, cc 36–7 (1831).

[77] 12 Geo. 1, c. 34, § 4. A limitation period of three months for prosecutions under this section was added a year later. 13 Geo. 1, c. 23, §§ 16–17 (1727).

[78] 12 Geo. 1, c. 34, § 3.

[79] Ibid. § 5.

[80] 18 Hen. 6, c. 11 (1440).

recognized, had greatly lowered that threshold,[81] so within a few years the qualification was raised to £100 a year.[82]

In what amounts to a distinct act within the weavers' combination act, Draconian punishments were imposed for violence to person or property. Assaulting or threatening a master was made a felony, punishable by seven years' transportation,[83] a form of exile to remote parts of the British Empire; until 1776 the destination was usually one of the North American colonies, later Australia was used. Transportation was actually an improvement on the common law which routinely sentenced felons to death, subject only to the sovereign's prerogative of mercy. By another section of the weavers' combination act, for example, breaking into a workshop with intent to destroy goods or tools was made a felony, this one punishable by death 'without benefit of clergy',[84] that is, on the first offence. Passed within a few years of the notorious Black Act,[85] this section added yet one more to the steadily lengthening list of capital crimes.[86] Because of the harsh penalties, the new felonies were not triable by justices of the peace using summary procedure; instead, prosecution was by common-law forms. What was lost in speed of conviction was presumably made up by solemnity of trial and severity of punishment.

Like the tailors' combination act, that for weavers also required modification in light of practical experience,[87] although the sections specifically dealing with combination remained unchanged. In particular the provisions prohibiting payment of weavers in truck had not proved effective. The preamble to the new act in 1756 recited 'several prosecutions' of masters that had been dropped because of expense: wealthy defendants had removed their cases from the justices of the peace to the higher courts.[88] Although the decisions of quarter sessions had been legislatively declared 'final' in such cases, the higher judiciary continued to exercise a supervisory power over the justices of the peace by means of the writ of *certiorari*, an order requiring that the record of a proceeding be certified and sent to the higher court. While not in form an appeal, *certiorari* provided a means for review. In the seventeenth century, before the Glorious Revolution and especially before the Civil War, agencies of the executive had monitored the

---

[81] Blackstone, *Commentaries*, i. 341.

[82] 5 Geo. 2, c. 18 (1732); see also 18 Geo. 2, c. 20 (1746) (requiring justices to take oath concerning qualification).

[83] 12 Geo. 1, c. 34, § 6.

[84] Ibid. § 7. This section was extended to silk manufacture by 6 Geo. 3, c. 28, § 15 (1766). For an eighteenth-century explanation of the anachronistic 'benefit of clergy', see Blackstone, *Commentaries*, iv. 358–67. See generally L. C. Gabel, *Benefit of Clergy in England in the Later Middle Ages* (New York, 1928).

[85] 9 Geo. 1, c. 22 (1723). See E. P. Thompson, *Whigs and Hunters: The Origin of the Black Act* (New York, 1975).

[86] See Leon Radzinowicz, *A History of English Criminal Law and its Administration from 1750*, i. *The Movement for Reform, 1750–1833* (London, 1948), 236 n. 15.

[87] 29 Geo. 2, c. 33 (1756).

[88] Ibid. preamble.

organs of local government, but the rout of the powers of centralism had created a vacuum that the common-law courts moved to fill.[89] In 1760, only a few years after the second weavers' act, the Court of King's Bench solemnly announced: 'The jurisdiction of this Court is not taken away, unless there be express words to take it away.'[90] Merely declaring a decision 'final' was not enough.

To make effectual the prohibition of truck, the new statute doubled the fine from £10 to £20.[91] Since half, as in the 1726 act, went to the informer,[92] a substantial incentive existed to set a summary prosecution in motion. In addition, the new act dangled still more lucrative bait: a plaintiff willing to put up with the common law's delay could collect the entire £20 by suing directly for it.[93] Since the appeals provisions of the earlier act had been found wanting, the succeeding act tightened the procedure. Appeal was conditioned on entering into a recognizance 'with sufficient security';[94] that is, the appellant obligated himself to pay a certain sum of money unless he prosecuted his appeal in good faith.[95] Decisions of quarter sessions were again declared 'final', but this time removal by *certiorari* 'or other forms or process of law' was expressly prohibited.[96]

Not only did the second weavers' act strengthen the ban on truck, it also responded to the weavers' call for public regulation of wages.[97] An act passed in 1727, the year after the weavers' combination act, had required payment by the yard on pain of a £5 fine.[98] The preamble to the 1756 act recited the requirement and declared it ineffectual because of the expense of prosecution and the want of 'proper powers' to regulate the wages to be paid to weavers.[99] To remedy the situation the new act empowered the justices of the peace to set rates for weaving[100] and directed that notice of the rates be posted on church and chapel doors.[101] At the first exercise of the new power, however, the masters protested that the order was impossible to obey because of the various shapes in which cloth was made.[102] The wage regulation section of the 1756 act was promptly

---

[89] Holdsworth, *History of English Law*, x. 156, 244–5.

[90] *R.* v. *Moreley*, 2 Burr. 1042, 97 Eng. Rep. 697 (KB 1760) (per curiam).

[91] 29 Geo. 2, c. 33, § 3. The outlawry of truck was repeated the next year, 30 Geo. 2, c. 12, § 3 (1757), and employers were required to pay wages within two days of completion of work on pain of a 40s. fine (ibid. § 4).

[92] 29 Geo. 2, c. 33, § 5.

[93] Ibid. § 4.

[94] Ibid. § 7.

[95] For a brief statement of the law on recognizances together with the form of words used, see Blackstone, *Commentaries*, ii. 341–2, 464.

[96] 29 Geo. 2, c. 33, § 7.

[97] See W. E. Minchinton, 'The Petitions of the Weavers and Clothiers of Gloucestershire in 1756', *Transactions of the Bristol and Gloucestershire Archaeological Society*, 73 (1954), 216–27.

[98] 13 Geo. 1, c. 23, § 9 (1727).

[99] 29 Geo. 2, c. 33, preamble.   [100] Ibid. § 1.   [101] Ibid. § 2.

[102] See Dobson, *Masters and Journeymen*, 76.

repealed,[103] although a provision that anticipated later legislation declared wage agreements between masters and journeymen 'good, valid and effectual, to all intents and purposes'.[104] In the Webbs' trenchant phrase, parliament was in the process of exchanging 'its policy of medieval protection for one of "Administrative Nihilism" '.[105]

At mid-century the statutory ban on combination was expanded to include trades other than tailoring and weaving.[106] The immediate cause of legislation in 1749 was dispute in the hat-making industry over embezzlement.[107] By custom in many trades workmen augmented their wages by keeping for their own use some of the leftover raw material. As production was rationalized in the eighteenth century, cost-conscious masters tried to stop the practice.[108] The common law proved unable to handle the problem since it refused to find an unlawful taking when goods were intentionally delivered to a person; as Blackstone flatly declared: 'no delivery of the goods from the owner to the offender, upon trust, can ground a larciny [*sic*]'.[109] After responding to that problem by extending an earlier anti-embezzlement statute,[110] the act went on, almost as an afterthought, to extend the first weavers' combination act (1726) to many other trades, most of them also in the clothing industry.[111] Dyers and hot-pressers, felt-makers and hatters, and all persons employed in the manufacture of silk, mohair, fur, hemp, flax, linen, cotton, fustian, iron, and leather—all were subjected to the anti-combination and anti-truck provisions that had earlier applied only to weavers.[112] Although weavers and woolcombers were themselves already covered, the extension reached as well all persons employed 'in or about any of the woollen manufactures'.[113] The felony of assaulting or threatening employers, punishable by seven years' transportation, was also extended,[114] although the capital offence in weaving of breaking into a workshop with intent to destroy goods or tools[115] was not. Given the large number of workmen involved or soon to be involved in the enumerated trades, especially in the cotton industry, the coverage of the combination law was

---

[103] 30 Geo. 2, c. 12, § 1 (1757).   [104] Ibid. § 2.

[105] Sidney Webb and Beatrice Webb, *The History of Trade Unionism* (rev. edn., London 1920), 51.

[106] 22 Geo. 2, c. 27, § 12 (1749).

[107] See Rule, *Labour in Eighteenth Century*, 131.

[108] See Craig Becker, 'Property in the Workplace: Labor, Capital, and Crime in the Eighteenth-Century British Woolen and Worsted Industry', 69 *Virginia Law Review* 1487–515 (1983); John Styles, 'Embezzlement, Industry and the Law in England, 1500–1800', in Maxine Berg, Pat Hudson, and Michael Sonenscher (eds.), *Manufacture in Town and Country before the Factory* (Cambridge, 1983), 173–210.

[109] Blackstone, *Commentaries*, iv. 230. For a modern overview see George P. Fletcher, 'The Metamorphosis of Larceny', 89 *Harvard Law Review* 469–530 (1976).

[110] 22 Geo. 2, c. 27, § 1 (extending 13 Geo. 2, c. 8 (1740)). See also 17 Geo. 3, c. 56 (1777).

[111] 22 Geo. 2, c. 27, § 12.

[112] 12 Geo. 1, c. 34, §§ 1–5 (extended by 22 Geo. 2, c. 27, § 12).

[113] 12 Geo. 1, c. 34, §§ 1–5.

[114] Ibid. § 6 (extended by 22 Geo. 2, c. 27, § 12).

[115] 12 Geo. 1, c. 34, § 7 (repealed and replaced by 22 Geo. 3, c. 40 (1782)).

greatly expanded at a stroke. For exactly half a century, until the general Combination Act (1799), there was to be no comparable expansion of coverage. In the mean time, legislation against combination continued in particular trades, for example, the second tailors' act (1768), discussed earlier, and still-to-be described acts concerning Spitalfields silk-weavers (1773; 1792), hatters (1777), and papermakers (1796). That further legislation was required for silk-weaving and hat-making suggests that it was too soon for a general proposition to be effective.

In 1773 distress in Spitalfields, the London district where silk-weaving had been concentrated since the settlement of Huguenot craftsmen a century earlier, led to further legislation in favour of wage regulation and against combination.[116] Two justices of the peace in the area[117] were empowered to set wages, notice of which was to be published three times in two daily newspapers.[118] Masters who paid other than the set wages were to be fined £50;[119] journeymen who took other than the set wages were to be fined 40s.[120] A further clause imposed the same penalty on journeymen who combined to raise wages, who intimidated others to quit work in order to raise wages, or who assembled in groups of more than ten to demand higher wages—except by petitioning the justices of the peace assembled in quarter sessions.[121] As Holdsworth observed, the exception supports the proposition that 'combinations to present petitions to the King or to Parliament were regarded as legal'.[122] Fines of both masters and workmen were payable to the Weavers' Company to be used for the relief of 'distressed journeymen weavers'.[123] In case of default in paying their fines, masters were liable to distress and sale of their goods,[124] while workmen were liable to imprisonment at hard labour for three months.[125] Should a master evade the act by employing workmen outside the regulated area, he could be sued in a common-law court for £50, which the Crown divided with the informer.[126] Bona fide foremen were exempt from the act,[127] as in the second tailors' combination act (1768). To limit the supply of labour—and

---

[116] 13 Geo. 3, c. 68 (1773). For the background of the legislation, see J. H. Clapham, 'The Spitalfields Acts, 1773–1824', *Economic Journal*, 26 (1916), 459–71 and Alfred Plummer, *The London Weavers' Company, 1600–1970* (London, 1972), 315–28.

[117] The act covered the county of Middlesex, the cities of London and Westminster, and the liberty of the Tower of London. 13 Geo. 3, c. 68, § 1.

[118] Ibid.   [119] Ibid. § 2.   [120] Ibid. § 3.   [121] Ibid.

[122] William S. Holdsworth, 'Industrial Combinations and the Law in the Eighteenth Century', 18 *Minnesota Law Review* 383 n. 85 (1934) (repeated in *History of English Law*, xi. 489 n. 14). On the right to petition, see *History of English Law*, x. 696–700. In 1799 the Duke of Portland, then Home Secretary, conceded that it was not illegal for an association of workmen to petition parliament (*The Early English Trade Unions: Documents from the Home Office Papers in the Public Record Office*, ed. Arthur Aspinall (London, 1949), 26). Cf. US Const., amend. I (1791) ('Congress shall make no law . . . abridging . . . the right of the people peaceably to assemble, and to petition the government for a redress of grievances'). See 'Note', 'A Short History of the Right to Petition Government for the Redress of Grievances', 96 *Yale Law Journal* 142–66 (1986).

[123] 13 Geo. 3, c. 68, §§ 2–3.

[124] Ibid. § 2.   [125] Ibid. § 3.   [126] Ibid. § 5.   [127] Ibid. § 6.

presumably to put upward pressure on wages in the long run—the act limited the intake of apprentices to two per master; a fine of £20 was imposed on violators.[128] Ever since the Statute of Apprentices in 1563 weavers had been permitted three apprentices for the first journeyman and one for each additional journeyman.[129] Apprenticeship may have been what G. M. Trevelyan once called it, 'the old English school of craftsmanship and of character',[130] but in the eighteenth century its economic aspect was uppermost.

In its procedural sections the Spitalfields Act followed the lines laid down in earlier statutes concerning other trades. As in the second tailors' act (1768), two justices of the peace were empowered to summon witnesses; in case of non-appearance a witness was subject to arrest, and in case of refusal to testify he was subject to one month's imprisonment.[131] As in the second weavers' act (1756), appeal lay to quarter sessions, the appellant first finding 'sufficient security'.[132] As in the second tailors' act (1768), actions against persons enforcing the act had to be brought within six months.[133] Defendants in such actions were permitted to plead the general issue and to recover full costs in case of judgment in their favour or nonsuit[134]—the latter a judicial order in favour of defendant discontinuing suit when plaintiff failed to establish a legal cause of action or to support his pleadings with admissible evidence. Finally, the Spitalfields Act, like the second tailors' act (1768), was expressly declared a public act,[135] presumably to rebut the presumption that since it applied to only one trade and place, it was not what Blackstone called 'an universal rule'.

After almost two decades of experience with the Spitalfields Act it was extended in 1792 to include weavers in the same area who mixed other materials with silk.[136] Simply because blended fabrics were produced, the weavers did not escape regulation. At the same time minor amendments were made in procedures under the act. A standard 'form of conviction' was provided,[137] to be filed with the records of quarter sessions, kept by the clerk of the peace who was appointed by the principal justice, nominally the *custos rotulorum* or 'keeper of the rolls'.[138] As in the second weavers' act (1756), the common-law courts were expressly prohibited from removing

[128] Ibid. § 7.

[129] 5 Eliz. 1, c. 4, § 33 (1563).

[130] G. M. Trevelyan, *English Social History: A Survey of Six Centuries, Chaucer to Queen Victoria* (London, 1943), 322. For a less rosy assessment, see Rule, *Labour in Eighteenth Century*, chap. 4.

[131] 13 Geo. 3, c. 68, § 4.

[132] Ibid. § 8.

[133] Ibid. § 9.

[134] Ibid. § 10.

[135] Ibid. § 11.

[136] 32 Geo. 3, c. 44, § 1 (1792).

[137] Ibid. § 2.

[138] On the office of the *custos rotulorum*, see Blackstone, *Commentaries*, iv. 269.

the case by writ of *certiorari*.[139] In distinct provisions, earlier acts punishing embezzlement of materials were extended to silk-manufacture.[140]

In 1777 parliament legislated for the hatters.[141] The new law addressed two topics of crucial importance to workmen: apprenticeship and combination. Tudor–Stuart statutes designed to protect the trade against competition from immigrant labour had restricted hat-making to native-born workmen who had served full apprenticeships; they had, in addition, limited masters to two apprentices at a time.[142] Similar restrictions applied in the colonies.[143] Restricted entry had meant smaller numbers, which had in turn translated into economic advantage for workmen. Although the restrictive policy had been applied only four years earlier in the first Spitalfields Act, the new act repealed the old legislation in the hat-making trade,[144] but in a modest concession still required masters to employ one journeyman for each apprentice.[145]

The new law against combination among hatters followed a preamble reciting the extension of the weavers' act (1726) to hatters in the omnibus act (1749) and declaring that it had been rendered ineffectual by delay because no recognizance had been required for appeal. The same complaint had earlier been heard in the woollen industry where prosecutions of employers for paying in truck had also been rendered ineffectual and in the tailoring trade where wage regulation had been evaded by 'many subtil devices'. In those cases the remedy had been to require a recognizance 'with sufficient security' for appeal; in the hatters' combination act the requirement became still more explicit: appeal was conditioned on a recognizance with two sureties of £5 each.[146] In addition the act outlawed hatters' combinations. To attend an illegal meeting, to solicit attendance or money, to endeavour to persuade another to quit work, to give money to an illegal club—all were made punishable by three months' imprisonment either in the common gaol or at hard labour in the house of correction.[147] Examination was to be by two justices of the peace,[148] and appeal lay to

---

[139] 32 Geo. 3, c. 44, § 3.

[140] Ibid. §§ 4–5 (extending 22 Geo. 2, c. 27 (1749) and 17 Geo. 3, c. 56 (1777)). The first act had in addition to outlawing embezzlement in certain trades also extended the weavers' combination act, 12 Geo. 1, c. 34 (1726), to the same trades. The second act was a companion to the hatters' combination act, 17 Geo. 32, c. 55 (1777).

[141] 17 Geo. 3, c. 55 (1777). See also 17 Geo. 3, c. 56 (1777) (concerning embezzlement).

[142] 8 Eliz. 1, c. 11 (1565); 1 Jac. 1, c. 17 (1604).

[143] 5 Geo. 2, c. 22 (1732). Jack P. Greene has recently included this statute on a list of eleven that evidenced parliament's willingness to pass mercantilist legislation while refusing to confront constitutional issues within the Empire (*Peripheries and Center: Constitutional Development in the Extended Polities of the British Empire and the United States, 1607–1788* (Athens, Ga., 1986), 61 (reviewed by John V. Orth, *Journal of American History*, 74 (1987), 1041–2)).

[144] 17 Geo. 3, c. 55, § 1. The apprenticeship clauses of the Statute of Artificers were also repealed as applied to hatters, ibid. § 5. General repeal of the clauses came in 1814, 54 Geo. 3, c. 96.

[145] 17 Geo. 3, c. 55, § 2.　　[146] Ibid. § 3.　　[147] Ibid. § 4.　　[148] Ibid.

quarter sessions.[149] Actions against persons enforcing the act were limited to three months after the event,[150] and defendants in the latter actions were allowed to plead the general issue and to recover double costs in case of judgment or nonsuit.[151] The penalty was twice that allowed in the second tailors' act (1768) or the first Spitalfields Act (1773). A final section, by now routine, declared the act a public one.[152]

A new provision, at once a concession to the hatters and to procedural fair play, excluded masters who were also justices of the peace from acting in their official capacity under the act.[153] Presumably it would always have been viewed as a violation of natural justice for a master to judge a dispute with his own journeymen. Years earlier Sir Edward Coke had made famous the maxim: '*Iniquum est aliquem suae rei esse judicem*' ('It is wrong for a man to be a judge in his own case'),[154] and Blackstone thought it 'one of the evils that civil government was intended to remedy'.[155] The hatters' act carried the idea one step further: master hatters as a class were disqualified from judging journeymen hatters.[156] It was as if parliament had accepted Adam Smith's dictum, uttered only the year before, that '[m]asters are always and every where in a sort of tacit, but constant and uniform combination'.[157] The reality of class interests was registered in the statute book.

In 1796 the last of the limited combination acts was passed. Disputes about wages in the paper-making industry had led the masters to petition parliament for a legislative resolution.[158] Based on provisions in various earlier acts, the papermakers' act[159] was itself the inspiration for the famous Combination Acts that followed in 1799 and 1800. After a preamble reciting recent combinations in the trade, the act voided all contracts to raise wages, to reduce hours of work, to hinder employment of other workmen, or 'in any way whatever' to affect masters in their conduct of business.[160] Parties to such contracts after passage of the act were liable to two months at hard labour in the house of correction.[161] The same punishment awaited journeymen paper-makers who endeavoured directly or indirectly to prevent others from taking work or to prevail on others to quit work, who

---

[149] Ibid. § 8. [150] Ibid. § 9. [151] Ibid. § 10. [152] Ibid. § 11.

[153] Ibid. § 6.

[154] Dr Bonham's Case, 8 Co. Rep. 118b, 77 Eng. Rep. 654 (CP 1610). See Samuel E. Thorne, 'Dr. Bonham's Case', 54 *Law Quarterly Review* 543–52 (1938).

[155] Blackstone, *Commentaries*, iv. 8; see also i. 91; iii. 301 n. n. Cf. *The Federalist* 80 (Alexander Hamilton): 'No man ought certainly to be a judge in his own cause, or in any cause in respect to which he has the least interest or bias.'

[156] Cf. 2 Jac. 1, c. 6, § 9 (1604) (forbidding clothiers who were also justices of the peace from regulating wages of weavers, spinners, etc. under Statute of Artificers).

[157] Smith, *Wealth of Nations*, 66 (referring to a combination 'not to raise the wages of labour').

[158] See D. C. Coleman, *The British Paper Industry, 1495–1860: A Study in Industrial Growth* (Oxford, 1958), 262–4, 272.

[159] 36 Geo. 3, c. 111 (1796).

[160] Ibid. § 1. [161] Ibid. § 2.

attempted to prevent masters from hiring other workmen, or who refused to work with them.[162] Two months' imprisonment also awaited anyone who attended or solicited attendance at an illegal meeting, who gave or collected money for an illegal purpose, or who used intimidation in order to induce another to quit work.[163] In an effort to settle at least one aspect of the dispute that had led to the statute, working hours in the industry were set legislatively: 'vat men' were to spend half an hour on each 'post' and to be assigned twenty posts; 'dry workers' were to labour twelve hours a day.[164] The rapid pace of the Industrial Revolution soon outmoded the legislatively imposed settlement: mechanization, represented by patents beginning in 1801, transformed the techniques of paper-making.[165] The section regulating hours was, however, disposable; without it, there remained the blueprint for a general combination act.

Examinations under the papermakers' act were to be held within one month of the offence, and one justice of the peace (rather than two, as in earlier statutes) was to preside.[166] The justice was empowered to summon offenders and witnesses;[167] he was further empowered, if he saw fit, to arrest offenders without prior summons.[168] Although the second tailors' act (1768) had earlier authorized the summoning of witnesses to assist the prosecution, the papermakers' act was the first in this series explicitly to authorize the summoning of witnesses 'for any of the parties'.[169] It was also the first expressly to provide for the summoning of offenders, by process served personally or left at the person's usual place of abode. From early in the century, the common-law courts in their supervision by writ of *certiorari* over the summary jurisdiction of the justices of the peace had insisted on the principle of natural justice that the accused be summoned and given a chance to defend himself.[170] As Blackstone waspishly put it: 'the courts of common law have thrown in one check upon them, by making it necessary to *summon* the party accused before he is condemned.'[171] Since the practice had begun of excluding *certiorari*, it may have been thought necessary to spell out the requirement of a summons.

To secure the witness necessary to convict, one offender could be compelled to testify against another,[172] even if his testimony would incriminate himself. This provision trenched upon an emerging tenet of

---

[162] 36 Geo. 3, c. 111, § 4.

[163] Ibid. § 5.

[164] Ibid. § 3. For a description of the early techniques of papermaking including an explanation of the statutory terms, see Coleman, *Paper Industry*, 29–33.

[165] Coleman, *Paper Industry*, 179–93.

[166] 36 Geo. 3, c. 111, § 2.   [167] Ibid. § 7.   [168] Ibid. § 9.

[169] Ibid. § 7. Cf. US Const., amend. VI (1791) ('the accused shall enjoy the right . . . to have compulsory process for obtaining witnesses in his favor . . .').

[170] See *R* v. *Dyer*, 6 Mod. 41, 87 Eng. Rep. 803; 1 Salk. 181, 91 Eng. Rep. 165; 1 Holt 157, 90 Eng. Rep. 985 (QB 1703).

[171] Blackstone, *Commentaries*, iv. 279 (italics in original).

[172] 36 Geo. 3, c. 111, § 6.

English constitutionalism. The oath ex officio requiring a person to testify against himself had been earlier abused by the Court of High Commission, an ecclesiastical court that bore the same relation to the Church as the Court of Star Chamber bore to the state. The defeat of Stuart absolutism in the Civil War had created a consensus against such inquisitorial proceedings in any court, religious or lay.[173] The provision in the papermakers' act was squared with the constitution by granting the witness immunity from prosecution.[174]

Convictions were to be recorded on forms specified by the act and filed with the records of quarter sessions,[175] as in the second Spitalfields Act (1792). Appeal lay to the same sessions, but the appellant was first required to enter a recognizance with two sureties for £20; if the appeal failed, he had to pay the appellee's costs.[176] The writ of *certiorari* was denied by express words[177] and with it the usual means for removal of the case to the common-law courts. Actions against persons enforcing the act were limited to six months after the fact; defendants were permitted to plead the general issue and, in case of judgment in their favour or nonsuit, to recover double costs,[178] as in the hatters' act (1777). In a final section the papermakers' act was declared a public one.[179]

At the end of the eighteenth century parliament was to hazard a general proposition regarding combination. Unlike the omnibus act (1749) with its long list of covered trades, this one was to apply to workmen in general. Although applicable to all trades, the Combination Act of 1799 had its origin, like earlier statutes, in a dispute in a particular trade and place. The journeymen millwrights of London, who worked the great mills that supplied the capital's bread, had formed a well-organized combination seeking higher wages.[180] Unable to win the economic struggle and mindful of the various combination acts passed in the course of the century, the master millwrights petitioned parliament to legislate 'for the better preventing of unlawful combinations of workmen employed in the millwright business, and for regulating the wages of such workmen'.[181] Not covered by any of the eighteenth-century statutes, such combinations were

---

[173] See 13 Car. 2, c. 12 (1661). See John H. Wigmore, 'The Privilege against Self-Crimination; Its History', 15 *Harvard Law Review* 610–37 (1901–2); repr. (with brief review of subsequent literature in id., *Wigmore on Evidence*, rev. John T. McNaughton (Boston, 1961) § 2250). Cf. US Const., amend. V (1791) ('No person . . . shall be compelled in any criminal case to be a witness against himself . . .').

[174] 36 Geo. 3, c. 111, § 6. The privilege against self-incrimination in America had early been held not to apply when immunity from prosecution was granted. See Leonard W. Levy, *Origins of the Fifth Amendment: The Right against Self-Incrimination* (Oxford, 1968), 328, 495.

[175] 36 Geo. 3, c. 111, § 8.

[176] Ibid. § 10.   [177] Ibid. § 8.

[178] Ibid. § 11.

[179] Ibid. § 12.

[180] See Dobson, *Masters and Journeymen*, 138–9. See also the slightly later 'Rules Adopted by the Journeymen Millwrights, for the Well-Governing of their Society' (1801).

[181] *Commons Journal*, 54 (1798–9), 405.

unlawful because they were regarded as criminal conspiracies at common law. But the masters found common-law procedures unsatisfactory:

the only method of punishing such delinquents, under the existing laws, is by preferring an indictment, at the [quarter] sessions or assizes, after the commission of the offence, but, before that time arrives, the offenders frequently remove into different parts of the country, so that, even if their places of residence should be discovered, it would be a long time before they could be brought to trial, and the expence of apprehending, and bringing them back, by *habeas*, to the place where the offence was committed, is so heavy to the masters, whose businesses have been stopped by the desertion of the journeymen, that (aware of these difficulties) the journeymen carry on their combination with boldness and impunity.[182]

The petition was referred to a committee which reported, through Sir John Anderson, in favour of a bill on the subject.[183] At this point William Wilberforce, the campaigner against African slavery, made his historic contribution to English labour history:

These combinations he regarded as a general disease in our society; and for which he thought the remedy should be general; so as not only to cure the complaint for the present, but to preclude its return. He thought the worthy mover of this subject deserved praise for what he was doing, as far as the measure went; but if it was enlarged, and made general against combinations, he should be better satisfied with it, and then it would be a measure that might be of great service to society.[184]

Wilberforce's proposal was, however, ruled out of order, and the millwrights' bill passed the Commons and was sent on to the Lords.[185] Two months later the prime minister himself intervened: apparently responding to Wilberforce's suggestion, William Pitt spoke in favour of a bill applicable to all workmen. Ignoring the millwrights, whose bill was abandoned, he referred to more powerful combinations—particularly among cotton-weavers in Lancashire who, incidentally, were already covered by the omnibus act (1749)—and proposed general legislation modelled on the papermakers' act (1796).[186] The next day George Rose, secretary to the Treasury and an expert on workmen's associations, introduced the act that opened a new chapter in labour's legal history. Only six years before, Rose had sponsored the first Friendly Societies Act,[187] which ironically was to provide a cover for combination in the dark days ahead.

Before turning to the general legislation, we should first review the 'particular acts', in which regulatory and anti-combination provisions were joined. Their coverage was, as Adam Smith observed, restricted to

---

[182] *Commons Journal*, 54 (1798–9), 405.
[183] Ibid. 412–13.   [184] *Parliamentary Register*, 8 (1799), 323.
[185] Ibid. 687.   [186] *The Times* (18 June 1799).
[187] 33 Geo. 3, c. 54 (1793). See P. H. J. H. Gosden, *The Friendly Societies in England, 1815–1875* (Manchester, 1961), 5.

particular trades and places. A map of England showing the effect of the eighteenth-century combination acts would reveal their emphasis on London and the clothing trade. Of the eight combination acts described in this chapter,[188] four applied only to the metropolis: tailors within the weekly bills of mortality and silk-weavers in Spitalfields were covered by two acts apiece. Of the four national acts, three were limited respectively to weavers, hatters (many of whom were in the London area), and paper-makers. Only the omnibus act (1749) covered a variety of trades; in that case, an assorted collection mostly concerned with textiles.

The combination acts evolved over the course of the eighteenth century. The first tailors' act (1721) contained a simple definition of the crime and modest arrangements for wage regulation. While the crime came to be more comprehensively described and regulation of the particular trade never wholly disappeared, the greatest development affected neither of these. Instead, it was procedure that received more and more attention as time went on. Provisions for summoning offenders and witnesses, for compelling the latter to testify, concerning the qualifications of justices of the peace and suits against them or other local officials, for record-keeping, and above all for appeals were steadily elaborated. This emphasis on procedural rules— one is tempted to say, on the rule of law—is not surprising in the eighteenth century. The earlier struggles against Stuart absolutism had often taken legal forms, and the victors had learned sound lessons in constitutionalism. In America the revolutionary generation, its familiarity with the seventeenth-century arguments refreshed by recent experience, made 'due process of law' the hallmark of the new Constitution and Bill of Rights.[189] Respect for proper procedure was hypertrophied, while knowledge of political economy was only slowly developing.

Worth noting too is the contractarian nature of legal thinking about labour organizations. Ignoring the social and experiential origins of combinations, their roots in the work-place, neighbourhood, and public house, the parliamentarians conceptualized the nascent trade unions as simple aggregates of individuals bound together by 'contract, covenant or agreement'. Perhaps one should have expected nothing else from the century that made the social contract famous. Positing a contract at the back of combination, the legal draftsman proceeded with impeccable logic, first to void the contract, rendering it unenforceable, then to make criminal the attempt to form it. However mechanical and unrealistic such thinking, it was to mark labour law for years to come.

What moved parliament to pass a combination act in the eighteenth century was always a dispute; what the parliamentarians wanted was social

---

[188] A ninth statute, the second weavers' act (1756), while amending some provisions of the weavers' combination act (1726), did not affect the sections concerning combination.

[189] US Const., amend. V (1791) ('No person . . . shall . . . be deprived of life, liberty, or property, without due process of law . . .').

peace rather than distributive justice. While not ignoring the workmen's grievances, their sympathies lay more with the masters. As Adam Smith astutely warned: 'Whenever the legislature attempts to regulate the differences between masters and their workmen, its counsellors are always the masters.'[190] There can be no mistaking the fact that the instinctual response of England's élite (both legislative and, as we shall see, judicial) to insubordinate workmen was repression. But concern for procedure almost predominated over interest in the result; it monopolized legislative time and clothed the product in legitimacy. Workmen too, as we shall see, believed in the importance of proper form and engaged their betters in a legalistic controversy concerning the details of the general Combination Acts. Before we can examine these statutes, however, we must first consider another 'general proposition', the one that eighteenth-century judges formulated in their decisions in particular cases.

[190] Smith, *Wealth of Nations*, 142.

3

Conspiracy: Criminal Law

> People of the same trade seldom meet together, even for merriment and
> diversion, but the conversation ends in a conspiracy against the public,
> or in some contrivance to raise prices.
>
> Adam Smith (1776)

Conspiracy is a very old crime, its name even older than any one meaning.
So old is conspiracy, in fact, that its earliest definition in the English statute
book is written in Law French, a legacy of the Norman Conquest. A statute
from the early fourteenth century entitled 'Who be Conspirators' answers
its own question:

Conspiratours sount ceux qi se entrelient per serement covenant ou per autre
alliaunce qe chescun eidera & sustendra autri emprise de fausement & maliciouse-
ment enditer ou faire enditer ou fausement mover plees ou maintenir.[1]

In the traditional English translation, that is:

Conspirators be they that do confeder or bind themselves by oath, covenant, or
other alliance, that every of them shall aid and bear the other falsely and maliciously
to indite [i.e., indict], or cause to indite, or falsely to move or maintain pleas.[2]

In other words, conspiracy was originally an agreement to abuse the legal
system by maliciously indicting an innocent person. The crime dated from
the days before the state assumed the duty of prosecuting criminals. The
office of Director of Public Prosecutions was not created until 1880, not
long before the close of the period covered by this book.[3] Although justices
of the peace and, in the nineteenth century, policemen instituted criminal
proceedings on behalf of the public, private prosecutions were once the rule
and long remained common. When the state's chief contribution to law
enforcement was providing courts open to private prosecutors, it was
perhaps inevitable that the remedy for abuse would be the recognition of yet
another crime.

---

[1] 33 Edw. 1, st. 2 (1304) ('Who be Conspirators'; also known as *Ordinatio de
Conspiratoribus*). This was the third attempt in a dozen years to deal with the problem of
conspiracy as it was then understood. See 20 Edw. 1 (1291) (in *Statutes at Large*, ed. T. E.
Tomlins (1811), 399) and 28 Edw. 1, st. 3, c. 10 (1300) (one of the *Articuli Super Chartas*).

[2] 33 Edw. 1, st. 2, in *Statutes at Large*, ed. Danby Pickering (1762), i. 307–8.

[3] 42 & 43 Vict., c. 22 (1897) (commencing 1 Jan. 1880).

Despite its definition in a Plantagenet statute, conspiracy was in time taken over by the common law, expounded in judicial decisions in particular cases. Whenever the common law made such acquisitions, statutes tended to be dismissed as concerned only with isolated instances or, if apparently comprehensive, as merely 'declaratory of the [pre-existing] common law'. Although a past master at subordinating statute to case law, Sir Edward Coke in the early seventeenth century worked no particular magic on conspiracy. At the time he composed his magisterial *Institutes of the Laws of England*, the crime was still recognizable. Although predictably dismissing the medieval statute as 'but in affirmance of the common law',[4] Coke defined the offence in similar terms: 'a consultation and agreement between two or more, to appeale, or indict an innocent falsely, and maliciously of felony.'[5] By this time the logical conclusion had been drawn that since agreement was of the essence, conspiracy could not be committed by one person acting alone, and, it had been decided, the prosecution had to be for the more serious class of offences, that is, for felony. Even so late as Blackstone's *Commentaries* in the mid-eighteenth century that was apparently all it still was: one of a host of 'offences against public justice'.[6]

Between Coke and Blackstone, however, things had begun to change; in this, as in some other matters, the Commentator was a bit *en retard*. When William Hawkins described the crime in 1716, he confidently opined: 'There can be no doubt but that all confederacies whatsoever, wrongfully to prejudice a third person, are highly criminal at common law.'[7] Beginning as criminal abuse of process, conspiracy had mushroomed during the seventeenth century. Two or more still had to enter into an agreement, but the purpose was no longer limited to malicious prosecution: any 'prejudice' would suffice. Even Blackstone occasionally used conspiracy in a secondary sense to mean an agreement to do something unlawful.[8] In popular parlance

---

[4] Edward Coke, *Second Institute* (1641), 562 (composed before 1634).

[5] Id., *Third Institute* (1641), 143 (composed before 1634). 'Appeal' is used here not in its usual sense of complaint to a superior court concerning an injustice done by an inferior tribunal but to refer to a suit brought by one private person against another for damages occasioned by a private wrong. An indictment lay for the offence against the public. Appeals of felony were rare by the eighteenth century and were abolished in 1818. Coke's definition went on to conclude that the innocent party was in fact appealed or indicted and afterwards acquitted. But the Court of Star Chamber, as Coke himself reported, had earlier held that the gist of the offence was the agreement rather than the subsequent appeal or indictment and acquittal (*Poulterers' Case*, 9 Co. Rep. 55b, 77 Eng. Rep. 813 (Star Ch. 1611)). The common-law courts later adopted the same position.

[6] William Blackstone, *Commentaries on the Laws of England* (1765–9), iv. 136 (listing conspiracy as the fifteenth of twenty-two 'offences against public justice'); see also ibid. iii. 126 (covering tort of malicious prosecution). For the history of the original form of the offence, see Percy H. Winfield, *The History of Conspiracy and Abuse of Legal Procedure* (Cambridge, 1921).

[7] William Hawkins, *A Treatise of the Pleas of the Crown* (1st edn., 1716; 7th edn., 1795 (ed. Thomas Leach)), bk. 1, chap. 72, sec. 2. Pleas of the Crown, as opposed to common pleas (claims between private persons), generally concerned crimes.

[8] See e.g. Blackstone, *Commentaries*, iv. 6 ('treason . . . involves . . . conspiracy against an

the word had long had this expansive meaning. In the late sixteenth century Shakespeare used the verb-form in its modern sense: in *A Midsummer Night's Dream*, for example, Helena asks Hermia: 'Have you conspired, have you with these contrived   To bait me with this foul derision?'[9] Early in the next century the translators of the King James Bible used the word in the same sense: Joseph's brothers 'conspired against him to slay him'.[10] In the calculating eighteenth century Adam Smith could denounce price-fixing as 'a conspiracy against the public'.[11]

All the while conspiracy was strictly limited at common law to 'offences against public justice', parliament was legislating haphazardly against conspiracies for various other purposes: to disturb markets,[12] to commit treason,[13] to raise the price of food,[14] to raise wages or alter hours of work.[15] The last purpose, found in a Tudor statute primarily concerned with the cost of provisions, would in time be used to support the argument that combinations had never been criminal conspiracies at common law, apart from statutes. Although eighteenth-century legislators shied away from general propositions, contemporary judges were prepared to venture a few. Conspiracy was only the latest of many notable offences that had begun as offences against public justice and that were later generalized to apply in other contexts. Forgery, perjury, and deceit had already made the transition.[16] As the economy quickened and the Elizabethan system of wage regulation broke down, conspiracy was ready to hand for use against combinations of workmen. As confederacies to raise wages—and thereby to prejudice the masters—they were apparently criminal at common law.

Stating the common law of conspiracy is not, however, so straightforward as stating the statute law of combination. For one thing, common law lacks a single authoritative source comparable to the statute book. While there may be disputes about what a statute means, there are not often disputes about what it says. The common law, on the contrary, was discovered by the judges, the 'oracles of the law', in their decisions in particular cases. No matter how high an authority, and Hawkins stood very high in his day, the common law was not as he stated it unless the oracles agreed. Authorities like Hawkins gathered the law from reported cases, from professional treatises, and from personal experience in court. While his use of old reports

individual, which is also a civil injury'); iv. 12 ('conspiracies to do an injury'); iv. 14 ('crimes that are incomplete, which consist merely in the intention, and are not yet carried into act, as conspiracies and the like'); iv. 15 ('a treasonable conspiracy'); iv. 82 ('conspiracy to levy war').

[9] Shakespeare, *A Midsummer Night's Dream* (c.1595), III. ii. 196–7. A modern editor assumed that 'conspired' needed no explanation, but defined the parallel 'contrived' as 'plotted, conspired' (ibid. ed. Madeline Doran (Baltimore, 1959), 76 n.).

[10] Gen. 37: 18 (1611).

[11] Adam Smith, *An Inquiry into the Nature and Causes of the Wealth of Nations*, ed. Edwin Cannan (New York, 1937), 128 (1st edn., 1776) (epigraph of the present chapter of this book).

[12] 27 Edw. 3, st. 2, c. 25 (1353) (section of Statute of the Staple).

[13] 3 Hen. 7, c. 14 (1486).   [14] 2 & 3 Edw. 6, c. 15 (1548).   [15] Ibid.

[16] See William S. Holdsworth, *A History of English Law* (London, 1903–72), xi. 545.

has been questioned,[17] he proved an accurate prophet of the behaviour of his contemporaries on the bench.

Sometimes it is even difficult to discover what the oracles said in their decisions because the law reports lack the reliability of the Statutes at Large. (By the eighteenth century the various editions of the statutes were reasonably accurate in reprinting contemporary enactments; reliability as to earlier eras was lessened as competing editors inserted dubious material in order to advertise ever more comprehensive editions.) The leading early case on criminal conspiracy as applied to labour, for example, the 1721 prosecution of journeymen tailors in Cambridge, was reported in the self-styled *Modern Reports*.[18] While the precedent seems clear enough, it is worth noting that Chief Justice Holt had damned earlier volumes in the series as 'scambling reports' that 'will make us appear to posterity for a parcel of blockheads'.[19] Produced like the Statutes at Large for sale by private individuals with an eye to profits, law reports varied greatly in quality. Doubting the reports was a well-recognized way for judges to add flexibility to the law. Not until Lord Mansfield's reforms later in the century were reliable reports produced; the truly modern, semi-official series did not begin until 1865.

Beyond the absence of an authoritative statement of common law in general, there are special problems with common-law conspiracy. Since Hawkins's day it has been a peculiarly ill-defined offence. Matters have not been helped by the fact that conspiracy charges have been used against unpopular or seditious groups, as well as to implement contested economic policies. The judiciary has sometimes seemed deliberately vague, keeping conspiracy in reserve, as it were, for cases not plainly encompassed by better defined crimes. A modern judge, paraphrasing Voltaire's famous quip about the Deity, conceded: 'If the offence of conspiracy did not exist, it would have to be invented.'[20] The unlawful purpose has proved particularly elusive, leading to calls in the nineteenth century to eliminate conspiracy as a separate offence altogether. If the unlawful purpose were limited to an already recognized crime, then conspiracy would be no more than the first step towards the commission of that crime by two or more; it would be, in other words, merely an extension of the law concerning attempts. But eighteenth-century judges (to say nothing of their successors) were far from accepting that simple solution.

[17] See R. S. Wright, *The Law of Criminal Conspiracies and Agreements* (1873), 10; Francis Bowes Sayre, *A Selection of Cases and other Authorities on Labor Law* (Cambridge, Mass., 1922), 42 n. 5.

[18] *R. v. Journeymen-Taylors of Cambridge*, 8 Mod. 10, 88 Eng. Rep. 9 (KB 1721).

[19] *Slater* v. *May*, 2 Ld. Raym. 1072, 92 Eng. Rep. 210 (KB 1705) (Holt, CJ) (referring to 4 Mod.). For a careful evaluation of the various volumes of *Modern Reports*, see John William Wallace, *The Reporters* (4th edn., 1882 (ed. Franklin Fiske Heard)), 347–90. Wallace himself reported US Supreme Court decisions from 1863 to 1874.

[20] *Hansard*, HL, 5th ser., vol. 378, col. 811 (Earl Mansfield) (14 Dec. 1976). Cf. Voltaire, *Épîtres*, xcvi ('*Si Dieu n'existait pas, il faudrait l'inventer*').

In 1721 some journeymen tailors in Cambridge, perhaps caught up in the same maelstrom of prices surrounding the South Sea Bubble that led to the first tailors' combination act, were indicted 'for *a conspiracy* amongst themselves to raise their wages'.[21] After being tried with the full panoply of common-law procedure—from indictment through pleading to trial by jury[22]—and found guilty, they secured a writ of error, an order by a higher court to send the record for review for errors of law.[23] (Resembling the writ of *certiorari*, used to secure the record from an inferior tribunal such as quarter sessions, the writ of error was directed to a lower common-law court.) In the Court of King's Bench defendants' counsel moved to arrest judgment because of five errors in the record. Three were dryasdust technicalities, the staple of English legalism: the Latin words *domini Regis* ('of our lord the King') were omitted from the caption of the case; the county in which the offence was alleged to have been committed was not named; it was inconsistent to describe the defendants both as yeomen and as journeymen tailors. The court quickly brushed aside these complaints. While as capable of hypertechnicality as their predecessors, eighteenth-century judges were more reluctant to let form get in the way of substance. Common law had supplied the ideology of the winners in the Civil War and the Glorious Revolution, and its oracles emerged supremely confident of their ability to govern the forces of change. Early in the century Chief Justice Holt had set a new and admired standard of fairness and rationality in the common law; by the end of the century with economic change accelerating Lord Mansfield encountered criticism for carrying too far his wide-ranging quest for 'substantial justice'.[24]

The last technicality in the Cambridge Tailors' Case is now barely understandable. 'Yeoman' usually denoted the most successful of those who worked the land, ranking below gentlemen and above husbandmen. Although legal status counted for less and less in England, a statute from the early fifteenth century still required that all indictments had to set forth, in

[21] 8 Mod. 10, 88 Eng. Rep. 9 (italics in original).

[22] For a detailed and contemporary description of all stages of a common-law criminal trial, see Blackstone, *Commentaries*, iv. 286–399; for a briefer modern account, see J. H. Baker, 'Criminal Courts and Procedure at Common Law, 1550–1800', in J. S. Cockburn (ed.), *Crime in England, 1550–1800* (Princeton, NJ, 1977), 15–48.

[23] For a sample writ of error, see Blackstone, *Commentaries*, iii. pp. xxi–xxvi (App. 3, § 6).

[24] See e.g. *Alderson v. Temple*, 4 Burr. 2239, 98 Eng. Rep. 167 (KB 1768) (Lord Mansfield: 'the most desirable object in all judicial determinations, especially in mercantile ones . . . is, to do substantial justice'). For contemporary criticism, see e.g. Junius, Letter 41 (14 Nov. 1770) in *The Letters of Junius*, ed. John Cannon (Oxford, 1978), 209–10 ('Instead of those certain, positive rules, by which the judgement of a court of law should invariably be determined, you have fondly introduced your own unsettled notions of equity and substantial justice'); Thomas Jefferson, Letter to Philip Mazzei (Nov. 1785), repr. in *The Papers of Thomas Jefferson*, ed. Julian P. Boyd (Princeton, NJ, 1954), ix. 71 ('The object of former judges has been to render the law more and more certain, that of this personage [Lord Mansfield] to render it more incertain under pretence of rendering it more reasonable: no period of the English laws, of whatever length it be taken, can be produced wherein so many of it's settled rules have been reversed as during the time of this judge').

addition to the name of the accused, his 'estate and degree'.[25] Any mistake in the name or 'addition', as it was called, was a technical misnomer and grounds for quashing the indictment.[26] It is difficult to see how journeymen tailors, whose wages in towns and villages, as Adam Smith observed, scarcely equalled those of 'common labour',[27] could have been mistaken for yeomen. Yet there was also an ill-defined category of yeomen in various occupations—recall the 'yeomen of the guard'—ranking below masters and above journeymen.[28] In the Cambridge Tailors' Case the nice question arose whether the defendants could be both yeomen and journeymen. Whatever the etiquette in the trade, the court found no legal error in using both additions.

Two other challenges raised more substantial issues. First, '[n]o crime appears upon the face of this indictment, for it only charges them with a conspiracy and refusal to work at so much *per diem*'.[29] This is insufficient, it was claimed, because under the Statute of Artificers the wages of tailors (and other craftsmen) were set by the year rather than by the day.[30] Second, it was alleged, 'this indictment ought to conclude [with the Latin words] *contra formam statuti* [i.e., contrary to the form of the statute]; for by the late statute 7 Geo. 1, c. 13, journeymen-taylors are prohibited to enter into any contract or agreement for advancing their wages, etc.'. 'And', counsel concluded, 'the statute of 2 & 3 Edw. 6, c. 15 [the Tudor statute concerning conspiracies to raise wages or alter hours of work referred to earlier], makes such persons criminal.'[31] On these allegations also the court held against the defendants: '[I]t is not for the refusing to work, but for conspiring, that they are indicted, and a conspiracy of any kind is illegal, although the matter about which they conspired might have been lawful for them, or any of them, to do, if they had not conspired to do it.'[32] With these words even the renowned Hawkins was left behind. The object of the agreement ('the matter about which they conspired') need not be wrongful; the agreement to act in concert is the gist of the offence. The Statute of Artificers is therefore irrelevant, as indeed are all statutes. Put in the technical terms of the early eighteenth century: 'This indictment need not conclude *contra formam statuti*, because it is for *a conspiracy*, which is an offence at common law.'[33]

The 'late statute' cited by counsel, the first tailors' combination act (1721), is literally irrelevant because, as we have seen, it regulated tailors only within the weekly bills of mortality. Yet it would be a mistake to

[25] 1 Hen. 5, c. 5 (1413).
[26] Blackstone, *Commentaries*, iv. 328; iii. 302.
[27] Smith, *Wealth of Nations*, 104.
[28] See Peter Laslett, *The World we have Lost* (3rd edn., New York, 1984), 43–4.
[29] 8 Mod. 10, 88 Eng. Rep. 9.   [30] 5 Eliz. 1, c. 4, § 3.
[31] 8 Mod. 11–12, 88 Eng. Rep. 10 (per curiam).
[32] 8 Mod. 10–11, 88 Eng. Rep. 10. Refusing to work was a crime under the Statute of Artificers and other statutes comprising the law of master and servant, discussed in Chap. 8.
[33] 8 Mod. 12, 88 Eng. Rep. 10 (italics in original).

dismiss the citation as merely a lapse by careless counsel: the combination act was probably on everyone's mind. Passed only a few months before the Cambridge Tailors' Case was decided, the statute had been an impromptu legislative response to the crisis caused by the bursting of the South Sea Bubble. While limited to a particular trade in a particular place, it had made criminal an agreement to seek higher wages, an act that would not have been wrongful if done individually. Using the common law of conspiracy, the judges simply extended the crime to the area 'without' the weekly bills of mortality.

Later historians, who have ignored the connections between combination and conspiracy, have sometimes argued that the statutes were negligible because what they punished was already criminal at common law.[34] This is to put the cart before the horse. The crucial development in the Cambridge Tailors' Case was the recognition that the agreement could be criminal despite the lawfulness of the object if pursued individually. The tailors' combination act which had made such an agreement the gist of the offence in the metropolis doubtless encouraged the judges in their decision. Other scholars, with even less excuse, have taken the judges to task for an expansive reading of the common law, which was unnecessary (they say) in light of the statute.[35] This badly misses the point. The statute did not apply outside the London area, nor did the Cambridge tailors conspire to violate it. But to have waited for further legislation extending the tailors' act would have been uncharacteristic of eighteenth-century judges. As Lord Mansfield later exclaimed in response to a similar suggestion: 'What! pass a judgment to do mischief, and then bring in a bill to cure it?'[36] In the days before separation of powers *à la* Montesquieu became a tenet of the constitution, judges were far less reluctant to legislate from the bench.

Judges and parliamentarians acted in concert, exchanging advice and encouragement. None the less, the extension of common-law conspiracy along the lines of the tailors' combination act did entail a further significant development, one perhaps not appreciated because not relevant to the case in hand. Within the weekly bills of mortality, tailors' wages were set by the justices of the peace who were enjoined to consider the 'plenty or scarcity of the time'.[37] Hours were also set, and journeymen were provided a special process for collecting unpaid wages. Beyond London and Westminster—in

[34] E.g., M. Dorothy George, 'The Combination Laws Reconsidered', *Economic Journal* (Supp.), Economic History Ser., 2 (May 1927), 217; A. E. Musson, *British Trade Unions, 1800–1875* (London, 1972), 22.

[35] E.g., Francis Bowes Sayre, 'Criminal Conspiracy', 35 *Harvard Law Review* 403–4 (1921–2); Robert Spicer, *Conspiracy: Law, Class and Society* (London, 1981), 28.

[36] *Bishop of London* v. *Ffytche* (HL 1783), reported in T. Cunningham, *The Law of Simony* (1784), 174. Mansfield's query was later quoted by Best, CJ, in *Fletcher* v. *Lord Sondes*, 3 Bing. 580, 130 Eng. Rep. 637 (HL 1826). For a report of *Ffytche*, not including Lord Mansfield's speech, see 2 Brown 211, 1 Eng. Rep. 892.

[37] 7 Geo. 1, st. 1, c. 13, § 5. See Chap. 2, n. 35.

Cambridge, for example—the protection did not extend, only the prohibition. The judges had begun to concoct their own 'general remedy' for
combination, one that parliament would adopt as its own at the end of the
century in general Combination Acts.

Sixty years later another group of tailors outside London, this time in
Liverpool, were embroiled in a trade dispute that also ended in a
prosecution for conspiracy. Booth was the victim, and Eccles and six others
the defendants.[38] The indictment, which was in two counts, alleged that
defendants 'fraudulently, maliciously and unlawfully did confederate,
conspire, combine, and agree among themselves, by wrongful, and indirect
means to impoverish the said H. Booth, and to deprive and hinder him from
following and exercising his aforesaid business of a taylor in Liverpool'.[39]
The first count charged that they did in fact prevent him from working; the
second that they conspired to that end. It is worth remarking that one
cannot tell from the report whether the defendants were masters or
journeymen. It is possible that Eccles *et al.* were a cartel of master tailors
trying to drive a competitor out of business.[40]

The defendants were convicted at the Summer Assizes for Lancaster in
1783, but the record was removed by writ of error to King's Bench, where
their counsel moved to arrest judgment. The first error alleged was
technical: although seven defendants were named, only four had actually
been before the court. This was peremptorily dismissed. Judicial patience in
the Age of Mansfield with this sort of legalism was notably short. The
second error could not be disposed of so quickly. The indictment, it was
contended, was flawed because it failed to detail the means, alleged merely
to be 'wrongful and indirect', used to prejudice Booth. This argument would
seem to test the holding in the Cambridge Tailors' Case, in which the court
had upheld the conviction although the object was lawful. Could it have
been because the means were unlawful? Counsel was presumably trying to
establish the absurdity of upholding a conviction for conspiracy when both
means *and* end were lawful. As applied to this case, if the unlawfulness of
the means formed an essential part of the crime, then they should have been
specified in the indictment. The judges, however, disagreed. According to Mr
Justice Buller, 'the means are matter of evidence to prove the charge, and not
the crime itself.'[41] Lord Mansfield, the famous Chief Justice, concurred
and elaborated on the crime of conspiracy: 'the offence does not consist in
doing the acts by which the mischief is effected, for they may be perfectly
indifferent, but in conspiring with a view to effect the intended mischief *by
any means*'.[42] In the present case this meant that 'every man may work at

---

[38] *R.* v. *Eccles*, 1 Leach 274, 168 Eng. Rep. 240; 3 Dougl. 337, 99 Eng. Rep. 684 (KB 1783).
[39] 1 Leach 275, 168 Eng. Rep. 240.
[40] This was R. A. Wright's suggestion, see *Criminal Conspiracies*, 36.
[41] 1 Leach 277, 168 Eng. Rep. 241.
[42] 1 Leach 276, 168 Eng. Rep. 241 (italics added).

what price he pleases, but a combination not to work under certain prices is an indictable offence'.[43] It is worth noting that his lordship's conclusion— that 'every man may work at what price he pleases'—was contrary to the Statute of Artificers and most of the eighteenth-century combination acts, which provided for some form of wage regulation. As in so many other areas of the law, the forward-looking Chief Justice was anticipating a general proposition that had not yet been adopted. Since the conviction was found to be in due form, the court proceeded to judgment. The defendants were sentenced to six months in Liverpool's insalubrious gaol,[44] four months longer than the maximum under the tailors' combination acts.

The eighteenth century's last reported trial of workmen for criminal conspiracy, *Rex* v. *Hammond and Webb*,[45] took place on 18 February 1799, less than two months before William Wilberforce issued his call for a general remedy for combination. The defendants were journeymen shoe-makers in London, whose trade was not covered by any of the eighteenth-century combination acts, unless the omnibus act (1749) included them among those employed in the manufacture of leather. In any event, the shoemakers were not tried by summary procedure for combination but at common law for conspiracy. The trial was held at Westminster before Chief Justice Lord Kenyon sitting at *nisi prius*. At issue in the case was a question of evidence: the admissibility of the rules of the journeymen shoemakers' society which had been printed a few years earlier.[46] The law of evidence was at this time just emerging from the shadows. As Dean Wigmore, the well-known American legal scholar, later observed: 'In the Nisi Prius reports . . . centering around the quarter-century from 1790 to 1815, there are probably more rulings upon evidence than in all the prior reports of two centuries.'[47] The explanation for this spate of rulings was simple: extensive reporting of trials (as opposed to appeals) was beginning at this time, and disputes about the admissibility of evidence are a major preoccupation at trial. In *Hammond and Webb*, since the offence lay in the agreement,

---

[43] 1 Leach 276–7, 168 Eng. Rep. 241. For other, unreported statements of his lordship's view of the law, corroborating that quoted in the text, see *Unpublished Legal Papers of Lord Mansfield*, ed. James Oldham (Chapel Hill, NC, forthcoming).

[44] For a contemporary description of Liverpool gaol, see John Howard, *The State of the Prisons in England and Wales* (1777), 440 ('out of repair'; 'apartments close and dirty'; in Nov. 1775 almost half the prisoners had gaol fever).

[45] 2 Esp. 719, 170 Eng. Rep. 508 (Nisi Prius 1799). Espinasse's Reports (Esp.) were criticized as inaccurate. See *Small* v. *Nairne*, 13 QB 844, 116 Eng. Rep. 1486 (QB 1849) (Lord Denman, CJ) (Because of their 'want of accuracy' Espinasse's Reports 'were never quoted without doubt and hesitation; and a special reason was often given as an apology for citing that particular case'). With respect to the present case, the report is substantially confirmed by the documents in the Public Record Office cited in the following notes.

[46] A copy of the rules referred to may be found in the Public Record Office, originally forwarded by a government spy. *The Early English Trade Unions: Documents from the Home Office Papers in the Public Record Office*, ed. Arthur Aspinall (London, 1949), 80–2.

[47] John H. Wigmore, 'A General Survey of the History of the Rules of Evidence', in *Select Essays in Anglo-American Legal History* (Boston, 1907–9), ii. 696 (repr. in id., *Wigmore on Evidence*, rev. Peter Tillers (Boston, 1983), § 8 (i. 609–10)).

attention naturally focused on the proof that the defendants had in fact agreed. Kenyon admitted the rules into evidence over the objection of the shoemakers' brilliant advocate, Thomas Erskine, but only on condition that the prosecution later prove that the defendants were members of the society. The showing was subsequently made, and they were found guilty.[48]

A hint about the extent of common-law conspiracy was also dropped in this case. When Lord Kenyon was told that the journeymen's conspiracy had been prompted by the fact that some master shoemakers were paying higher wages than usual, he warned: 'masters should be cautious of conducting themselves in that way, as they were as liable to an indictment for a conspiracy as the journeymen.'[49] The Statute of Artificers and most of the eighteenth-century combination acts envisioned the setting of maximum wages. (The first Spitalfields Act (1773) was an exception: it fined masters who paid more *or less* than the set wages.[50]) In such circumstances it was possible for a conservative jurist such as Kenyon[51] to believe that a combination of masters to raise wages would be indictable. In the Combination Act (1800), as we will see in the next chapter, the statute law too was generalized to include masters as well as men, although it was then more realistically assumed that their object would be to lower rather than to raise wages.[52]

Despite the general Combination Acts of 1799 and 1800, which added to and did not supersede the earlier legislation, conspiracy prosecutions continued to be mounted in the nineteenth century. Prosecutions at common law had to be for conspiracy since the combination acts all

[48] Further information about the background and result of this prosecution may be found in the Public Record Office in the affidavit of the government spy, Thomas Hudson, dated 9 Aug. 1804: 'in or about the year 1792 this informant was applied to to become one of the Society [of Journeymen Boot and Shoe Makers] . . . the violence and injustice of such Society . . . induced a prosecution in 1799 when several were tried and found guilty, but the Court, on motion of Mr. Erskine, permitted the defendants to be bound in their own recognizance to appear to receive the judgement of the said Court when called on, the cause of such mercy being extended was a promise that such combination should in future be done away . . . but . . . the same system of combination, so far from being abated by the mercy of the Court, did exist within a few months after, if not a few weeks . . .' (*Early English Trade Unions*, 71).

[49] 2 Esp. 720, 170 Eng. Rep. 508. His lordship referred vaguely to 'a case where a master, from shewing too great indulgence to his men, had become himself the object of a prosecution'. I have been unable to locate this case. It is perhaps relevant in this connection that it was reported of Kenyon that 'at *nisi prius* he never brought a book with him into court to refer to' (George T. Kenyon, *Life of Lord Kenyon* (1873), 391).

[50] 13 Geo. 3, c. 68, § 2. See Chap. 2, n. 119.

[51] For Kenyon's famous decisions upholding common-law prosecutions for regrating and engrossing (i.e., for interfering with the free market in foodstuffs), although the statutory offences had been abolished in 1772, see *R v. Rusby*, 1 Peake Add. Cas. 189, 170 Eng. Rep. 241 (Nisi Prius 1800) and *R. v. Waddington*, 1 East 143, 102 Eng. Rep. 56 (KB 1800). For a discussion of these cases, see P. S. Atiyah, *The Rise and Fall of Freedom of Contract* (Oxford, 1979), 363–5.

[52] Even before the 1800 Act was passed in July, it was coming to be recognized that a 'combination of masters' to lower wages might be 'contrary to law'. See J. North, 'State of the Poor in the Parish of Ashdon, Essex' (letter from rector dated May 1800), *Annals of Agriculture*, ed. Arthur Young, xxxv. (1800), 466.

provided summary proceedings. In 1804 at the Lent Assizes at Kingston, *Rex* v. *Salter*[53] was argued before Baron[54] Hotham. The indictment charged some journeymen hatters with a conspiracy and alleged

that the defendants endeavoured to extort from one Walter Kearns, a journeyman hatter, the sum of a guinea; and on his refusal, that they endeavoured to cause and procure him to be discharged from the service of one Walls, a master hatmaker, by whom he was employed in his trade and business of a hatter: the said guinea being a fine for his having broken certain rules alleged to have been made for the regulation of journeymen hatmakers, and upon his refusal to pay it, in order to prevent the said Kearns from being employed, that they, in order to compel Walls to discharge him, unlawfully absented themselves, and refused to work for Walls.[55]

At the trial Kearns testified that he had been called before a meeting of journeymen on 20 November 1802 and told that he must pay the fine. He was then asked if he had heard any of the persons present at the meeting say anything respecting the appointment of delegates, presumably to convey the threat to the master. Like *Hammond and Webb* (1799), *Salter* concerned the evidence necessary to prove a conspiracy: the brief report is taken up wholly with arguments about whether Kearns should answer the question or whether the information it elicited was irrelevant. This debate ended when Baron Hotham ruled the question in order. The case stands in the reports, therefore, for the proposition summed up in its headnote that 'where there is evidence of several persons having engaged in a conspiracy, what is said by any of them, at another time and place, respecting the object of the conspiracy, is evidence against the others'.[56] Apparently Kearns answered in the affirmative because the report curtly concludes: 'The defendants were convicted.'[57]

No information is provided on the precise infraction of the rules by the unlucky Kearns, but in view of the strong organization of the hatters, which appeared in testimony before a parliamentary select committee in 1824, it is possible that he had worked in a shop, known in the trade as a 'foul' shop, which employed men who had not served customary apprenticeships. (It may be recalled that the law concerning apprenticeship in the hat-making trade had been changed by the hatters' combination act (1777); ever since that statute, master hatters were permitted to take as many apprentices as they pleased but required to employ at least one journeyman per apprentice.[58] 'Foul' men were often fined before 'fair' ones would agree to

---

[53] 5 Esp. 125, 170 Eng. Rep. 760 (Nisi Prius 1804). On the unreliability of Espinasse's Reports (Esp.), see n. 45, above.

[54] Judges of the Court of Exchequer, one of the three common-law courts, were known as barons. The Exchequer anciently handled financial matters so when in 1215 Magna Carta (c. 21) required that noble offenders could be fined only by judgment of their 'peers', the judges had been perfunctorily ennobled.

[55] 5 Esp. 125–6, 170 Eng. Rep. 760.

[56] 5 Esp. 125, 170 Eng. Rep. 760.

[57] 5 Esp. 127, 170 Eng. Rep. 761.

[58] 17 Geo. 3, c. 55, § 2. See Chap. 2, n. 145.

work with them.[59] Be that as it may, there can be no doubt that Salter and his fellow hatters could have been prosecuted summarily under the unrepealed hatters' combination act or, as we shall see, under the general Combination Act (1800).

In 1810 nineteen printers at *The Times* were indicted for 'combining and conspiring together maliciously to injure their masters and employers[60] by quitting their work on account of their demands for an increase of wages not being acceded to'.[61] Evidence was presented that the London printers were well organized, that *The Times* paid lower wages than other newspapers, that the printers at a competitor had persuaded those at *The Times* to seek a rise in wages, and that the latter, after being turned down, had given two weeks' notice and left. The common serjeant,[62] Sir John Sylvester, who presided at the trial in the Old Bailey, summed up the case for the jury in words reminiscent of Lord Mansfield:

It has been urged by the counsel for the compositors . . . that the giving of notice regularly showed there was no intention of conspiracy. To what end, however, was that notice given, when it was proved that the whole trade was so combined, that there was no chance whatever of having successors to the situations which were thus vacated? It was true that every man had a right to demand what wages he thought his services deserved; this was the law of the land, and the law of reason; but still the manner of making such demand was everything—it could not legally be thus made in a body.[63]

Reviewing the evidence, he told the jury that 'he would not insult their understanding so far as to suppose they could be so blinded by the advocates as to believe all the defendants innocent'.[64] Obligingly, the jury found all guilty, although it recommended eleven of the nineteen to mercy.

The common serjeant immediately remanded the prisoners to Newgate to await sentencing at the next session. When they appeared a month later, he explained that the respite had been ordered 'under the expectation that some symptoms of contrition and amendment on their part, and on that of the journeymen-printers in general, engaged in similar combinations, might have appeared to justify a mitigation of their punishment'.[65] Seeing no such symptoms, however, he ordered the following punishment: two men were sentenced to two years in gaol, three were given eighteen months, three others twelve months, and the eleven who had been recommended to mercy received nine-month sentences. The time already spent in gaol was not to be taken into account. Like *Salter* (1804), the *Times* Printers' Case could have been brought before two justices of the peace under the Combination Act

---

[59] *Parliamentary Papers* (1824), 5, 79–81 (testimony of George Ravenhill, hat-manufacturer).
[60] Note this early use of the word 'employers' in addition to the older term 'masters'.
[61] *The Times* (9 Nov. 1810) (Nisi Prius).
[62] The common serjeant of London, like the recorder, was a legal official in the City who also served as a judge.
[63] *The Times* (9 Nov. 1810) (Nisi Prius).   [64] Ibid.   [65] Ibid.

(1800), but like *Salter* it was brought instead before a common-law court as an illegal conspiracy. The maximum sentence under the act would have been three months.

In 1819 *Rex* v. *Ferguson and Edge*[66] also involved an indictment for a conspiracy. The dispute that led to the charge had begun when two master engravers in Manchester, Samuel Davenport and Robert Fayle, attempted to increase the number of their apprentices. It was suggested earlier that *Salter* may have originated as a dispute about apprenticeship in the hat-making trade, where special rules had applied since the hatters' combination act (1777). Apprenticeship became a common source of contention in skilled trades and generated a number of leading cases after 1814 when the enthusiasts of *laissez-faire* secured the repeal of the apprenticeship clauses of the Statute of Artificers as to all trades.[67] Thereafter, workmen had to bring economic pressure to bear in an attempt to maintain the regime formerly required by law. Davenport and Fayle had originally employed sixteen journeymen and eight apprentices. When they added an extra apprentice, workmen including Ferguson and Edge refused to work. Edge left the firm. Whether he handed in his notice or was fired it is impossible to tell: according to the report, his 'agreement was given up to him, and he went away'.[68] Ferguson and the rest returned to work when the masters caved in and discharged the added apprentice. Davenport and Fayle had not despaired, however, of finally upsetting the customary ratio of two journeymen to one apprentice, so they soon took an additional apprentice. Ferguson and the others again left, and this time the masters initiated a prosecution.

The indictment, which was in three counts, alleged that Ferguson and Edge on and after 29 September 1818 at Manchester in the county of Lancaster

[1.] did conspire, combine, confederate, and agree together, to prevent, hinder, and deter their said masters and employers from retaining and taking into their employment any person as an apprentice . . .
[2.] maliciously intending to hurt, injure, and impoverish their said employers, and to prevent them from retaining any other journeymen and workmen, and retaining and instructing apprentices in the said occupation, did conspire, combine, confederate, and agree to quit, leave, and turn out from their said employment, at one and the same time together . . .
[3.] maliciously intending to controul, injure, terrify, and impoverish their said employers, and force and compel them to dismiss from their said employment divers persons then and there retained by them, as journeymen, workmen, and apprentices therein, unlawfully did conspire, combine, confederate, and agree, to quit, leave, and

---

[66] 2 Stark. 489, 171 Eng. Rep. 714 (Nisi Prius 1819).
[67] 54 Geo. 3, c. 96 (1814). See T. K. Derry, 'Repeal of the Apprenticeship Clauses of the Statute of Apprentices', *Economic History Review*, 1st ser., 3 (1931–2), 67–87 (Statute of Artificers sometimes called Statute of Apprentices).
[68] 2 Stark. 491, 171 Eng. Rep. 714.

turn out from their said employment, until the said last-mentioned journeymen, workmen, and apprentices should be dismissed by their said masters and employers . . .[69]

The indictment reveals the steady advance of conspiracy law in the previous
century. While malice and prejudice to a third person—in this case the
masters—are carefully alleged in the second and third counts, the first
starkly asserts the criminality of the mere agreement to interfere in
employment decisions. Tried at the Lancaster Spring Assizes in 1819 before
Baron Wood, the case came to turn on the sufficiency of the indictment.
Form rather than substance was challenged: counsel for defendants objected
that while the indictment alleged a conspiracy to prevent the masters from
taking *any* apprentices, the evidence merely showed a conspiracy to prevent
them from taking *more* apprentices. Baron Wood rejected the claim, and the
defendants were accordingly found guilty. When they were brought before
the Court of King's Bench for judgment, the objection was renewed, but the
court held that the indictment was sufficiently proved. According to the
report, the defendants received sentence of 'fine and imprisonment'.[70]

In *Rex* v. *Connell*,[71] another case decided by King's Bench in 1819, the
indictment alleged that journeymen coachmakers had combined to lessen
the workday by two hours, to retain the same wages for the shorter day, to
prevent the taking of more than a certain number of apprentices, and to
prevent piece-work. The defendants were convicted without much ado, and
the case is chiefly interesting as an illustration of the use of a conspiracy
prosecution as a deterrent. The prosecutor admitted that the defendants had
been selected out of 'a large body of individuals' engaged in the conspiracy
and that each was a member of a different branch of the trade.[72] All but
Connell were discharged on their own recognizances because Chief Justice
Abbott believed they would behave themselves 'if the judgment hung over
their heads, and they were told that it might be put in force against them in
case of a relapse'.[73]

Why would a prosecutor choose to proceed at common law rather than
under one of the combination acts? The latter were certainly simpler and
more expeditious. From offence to sentencing under summary procedure
could easily be a matter of days; at common law the process took months,
often stretching beyond a year. So, too, they avoided the cost and
uncertainties incident to common-law procedure and lessened the danger,
which the master millwrights had stressed in 1799, of defendants
absconding. In favour of a prosecution for conspiracy, on the other hand,

[69] 2 Stark. 489–91, 171 Eng. Rep. 714.
[70] 2 Stark. 492, 171 Eng. Rep. 715.
[71] *The Times* (10 July 1819) (KB).
[72] Ibid.
[73] Ibid. It appears that a similar result was reached in *Hammond and Webb* (1799); see
n. 48, above.

were the greater solemnity of proceedings and the greater severity of
sentences. Such a choice was not unique to labour law; the law of sedition
offered it as well. The Unlawful Societies Act (1799), passed in response to
fears of French influence, expressly permitted two forms of prosecution with
two degrees of punishment: if offenders were convicted 'in a summary way'
by one justice of the peace, they could be imprisoned for three months or
fined £20; if convicted 'upon indictment by due course of [common] law',
they were liable to seven years' transportation or two years' imprisonment.[74]
Penalties under the labour laws were comparable: in place of the three
months maximum under the acts, conspiracies were punishable by 'fine and
imprisonment', although the two years awarded in the *Times* Printers' Case
(1810) is the harshest of which a record remains. In addition, prosecutions
for conspiracy, even if unsuccessful, certainly involved defendants in greater
expense. As Mr Peachem so melodiously put it in *The Beggar's Opera*: 'If
lawyer's hand is fee'd, sir | He steals your whole estate.'[75]

The exact number of workmen prosecuted for criminal conspiracy will
never be known. Although earlier legal historians of trade unionism asserted
that there were 'many cases of trials for conspiracy',[76] they instanced only
two: a prosecution of Glasgow weavers in 1812[77] and a prosecution of
Coventry silk-weavers in 1819.[78] The former certainly involved a trial for
conspiracy, but took place under Scottish rather than English law;[79] the
latter involved a prosecution for conspiracy but no trial, since charges were
dropped.[80] It would, of course, be a mistake to suppose that the
effectiveness of a law is to be measured only by the number of successful
prosecutions for its violation. Unsuccessful prosecutions, as already
remarked, may involve defendants in extra-legal ruin; threatened prosecutions may deter as effectively as actual ones; selective prosecutions—one
defendant from each branch of a trade, as in *Connell*—may deter 'a large
body of individuals'. Law is not merely, in the once famous phrase, 'what

---

[74] 39 Geo. 3, c. 79, § 8 (1799).

[75] John Gay, *The Beggar's Opera* (1728), i. viii. air 11.

[76] R. Y. Hedges and Allan Winterbottom, *The Legal History of Trade Unionism* (London, 1930), 29.

[77] Ibid. 29 n. 5 (citing Sidney Webb and Beatrice Webb, *The History of Trade Unionism* (rev. edn., London, 1920), 58–9, 82).

[78] Ibid. (citing J. L. Hammond and Barbara Hammond, *The Skilled Labourer, 1760–1832* (London, 1919), 215–16). Hedges and Winterbottom misprint the date of the Coventry prosecution as 1816.

[79] For the development of conspiracy law in Scotland, see David Hume, *Commentaries on the Law of Scotland, Respecting Crimes*, 2 vols. (4th edn., 1844), i. 493–7. The combination acts, including the general legislation, did not apply to Scotland (*Parliamentary Papers* (1824), 5, 486 (testimony of Sir William Rae, Lord Advocate of Scotland)). In his legal capacity the Lord Advocate of Scotland corresponds roughly to the English Attorney General. In the last half of the eighteenth century and throughout much of the nineteenth, in the absence of a Secretary of State for Scotland, the Lord Advocate also participated in the management of Scottish affairs.

[80] Hammond and Hammond, *Skilled Labourer*, 215–16.

officials do about disputes';[81] it is also what ordinary people do (or refrain from doing) because of their worries about what might happen to them otherwise.

As we have seen in this chapter, the passage of general Combination Acts in 1799 and 1800 did not arrest the development of common-law conspiracy. In fact, the statutes probably strengthened the judges' certitude that they were on the right path. As we shall see in a later chapter, however, parliament did once briefly interrupt its development. A statute in 1824 actually suspended prosecutions, but the parliamentarians soon repented. Barely a year later, the 1824 Act was repealed and conspiracy reinstated, although with an exemption for workmen who combined to raise wages or lessen hours. Further consideration of conspiracy will, therefore, have to be postponed until after an analysis of that legislation.

Towards the end of the nineteenth century and on into the twentieth, legal scholars reassessed the history of conspiracy. The process began in 1873, in the midst of the epochal trade-union legislation, when a brilliant young classical scholar and lawyer, R. S. Wright, published a slim volume on the *Law of Criminal Conspiracies and Agreements*.[82] Wright's audacious thesis was simply that workmen's combinations had not been illegal at common law before 1825; instead, he argued, as late as the first quarter of the nineteenth century conspiracy had not yet outgrown a 'seventeenth-century rule' by which combinations to violate statutes were punishable as conspiracies at common law. In other words, Wright denied that any of the cases in this chapter, properly understood, were prosecutions for conspiracy apart from statutes. The report of the Cambridge Tailors' Case (1721) he dismissed as 'untrustworthy',[83] while the rest he reinterpreted; those after the adoption of the Combination Act (1800) he labelled prosecutions for conspiracy to violate that act.

Wright was able to capitalize on uneasiness in legal circles about the exact reach of criminal conspiracy. Just as the relationship between law and morality had been emphasized during the eighteenth century by men like Lord Mansfield, so in the nineteenth century lawyers came to stress the logical rigour of the law. An early attempt to define conspiracy (in a prosecution not involving workmen) had produced Lord Denman's famous antithesis: 'The indictment ought to charge a conspiracy, either to do an unlawful act, or a lawful act by unlawful means.'[84] We have seen

---

[81] K. N. Llewellyn, *The Bramble Bush: On our Law and its Study* (Dobbs Ferry, NY, 1930), 3. In their day, these words, the trumpet call of Legal Realism, signalled a greatly expanded concept of law.

[82] R. S. Wright (1839–1904) had published 'Golden Treasuries' of Greek Poetry (1866) and Prose (with J. E. L. Shadwell, 1870). At Oxford Wright had been a favourite pupil of Benjamin Jowett, the influential classical scholar. He remained Jowett's close friend until the latter's death, 'which took place at Wright's house Hadley Park, in 1893' (*Dictionary of National Biography*, s.v. 'Wright, Robert Samuel').

[83] Wright, *Criminal Conspiracies*, 42.

[84] *R. v. Jones*, 4 B. & Ad. 349, 110 Eng. Rep. 487 (KB 1832).

defendants' lawyers fruitlessly striving for just such a definition in order to confine the offence, and his lordship later worried aloud that he had stated the law incorrectly.[85] While Denman himself had not equated 'unlawful' with 'illegal' in the sense of 'criminal', and may simply have been referring to agreements that were unenforceable in court, Wright argued strenuously for the equation with criminal law. Tying conspiracy to crime, whether defined by statute or case, would yield greater definiteness. It also would eliminate conspiracy as a separate offence. Stating a wish as a fact, Wright simply announced that 'the modern law of conspiracy is in truth merely an extension of the law of attempts, the act of agreement for the criminal purpose being substituted for an actual attempt as the overt act'.[86]

Wright's book was a scholarly success. James Fitzjames Stephen promptly incorporated its argument in his influential *History of the Criminal Law*,[87] published a decade later. In the 1920s Professor Francis Bowes Sayre expounded the position to his labour law classes at Harvard.[88] In their legal history of trade unionism R. Y. Hedges and Allan Winterbottom substantially accepted Wright's argument, only antedating the break with the seventeenth-century rule. While agreeing with him that prosecutions for conspiracy apart from statute had not occurred before the nineteenth century, they were forced to concede that starting with the *Times* Printers' Case (1810) combination was viewed as criminal without regard to the statute book.[89] Quite recently it was asserted that Wright's book has never been superseded,[90] yet his thesis has been persistently criticized by legal historians. Dicey thought it a statement of 'what the law of conspiracy ought to have been', rather than what it was,[91] while Holdsworth magisterially pronounced it not 'the correct view of the attitude of the common law'.[92]

Whether or not conspiracy properly formed a distinct offence was matter for academic debate in England. After all, combination and conspiracy coexisted from 1721 to 1824. But there was another country, also heir to the common law, in which the question could not be finessed. In the United States the first labour case, a prosecution for criminal conspiracy, was tried

[85] See *R. v. Peck*, 9 A. & E. 690, 112 Eng. Rep. 1373 (QB 1839) (Lord Denman: 'I do not think the antithesis very correct').
[86] Wright, *Criminal Conspiracies*, 48; see also ibid. 29.
[87] James Fitzjames Stephen, *A History of the Criminal Law of England*, 3 vols. (1883), iii. 209–10.
[88] See Sayre, 'Criminal Conspiracy', 35 *Harvard Law Review* 393 n. 1.
[89] Hedges and Winterbottom, *Legal History*, 31 ('In [*The Times* Printers' Case] it would seem that combination to cause impoverishment or injury to the employer, and to trade in general, by impeding the employer in some phase of his management, was part at least of the ground of liability . . .').
[90] A. W. B. Simpson (ed.), *Biographical Dictionary of the Common Law* (London, 1984), s.v. 'Wright, Robert Samuel'.
[91] A. V. Dicey, *Lectures on the Relation between Law and Public Opinion in England during the Nineteenth Century* (2nd edn., London, 1914), 97 n. 2.
[92] Holdsworth, *History of English Law* (1938), xi. 483.

in the mayor's court in Philadelphia in 1806.[93] The defendants were shoemakers like those in *Hammond and Webb* (1799), although the Americans were better known as 'cordwainers', a name derived from the cordovan leather they worked.[94] The rule at common law apart from statute was crucial to the case. Before the American Revolution, parliament had occasionally legislated for the colonies; in the last chapter a restriction on the number of apprentices in colonial hat-making was mentioned.[95] After the Revolution, British statutes were obviously inapplicable, but English common law survived; indeed, the revolutionaries insisted that they were 'entitled to the common law'[96] and the prosecutor of the cordwainers, citing the Journals of Congress, hailed it as 'the best birthright and noblest of inheritance'.[97] The courts of the newly independent states continued to apply common-law rules—except, of course, for those specifically rejected or those repugnant to republican institutions.[98] The holding in the Cordwainers' Case was that common law still governed and that conspiracy was criminal apart from statute. Hawkins and King's Bench (both of them cited) were, it seemed, no less authorities in post-Revolutionary Philadelphia than in Georgian England.

[93] *Comm.* v. *Pulis* (Philadelphia, Pa., Mayor's Court, 1806), pamphlet report repr. in *A Documentary History of American Industrial Society*, 10 vols. (New York, 1910–11), iii., ed. John R. Commons and Eugene A. Gilmore, 60–248. For a scholarly discussion of the case, see Walter Nelles, 'The First American Labor Case', 41 *Yale Law Journal* 165–200 (1931).

[94] The name was also known in England. See e.g. 'Articles of the Friendly and United Society of Cordwainers' (1792), repr. in *Early English Trade Unions*, 82–90, and *R.* v. *Dixon*, 6 Car. & P. 602, 172 Eng. Rep. 1383 (Nisi Prius 1834) (Bosanquet, J.) (referring to the 'late Cordwainers' Union of Cambridge'). For the latter case, see Chap. 7, nn. 31–3.

[95] 5 Geo. 2, c. 22 (1732). See Chap. 2, n. 143.

[96] *Journals of the Continental Congress, 1774–1789*, i. (1904), 69.

[97] *Documentary History*, iii. 222.

[98] See e.g. Act of 1778, ch. 133 [Potter's Revisal], codified at *North Carolina General Statutes*, § 4–1 ('so much of the common law as is not destructive of, or repugnant to, or inconsistent with, the freedom and independence of this State and the form of government therein established . . . are hereby declared to be in full force . . .').

4

Combination: 1799–1824

These two Acts [of 1799 and 1800], the second modifying the first, prohibiting all common action in defence of their common interests by workmen, remain the most unqualified surrender of the State to the discretion of a class in the history of England.

> J. L. Hammond and Barbara Hammond (1917)

Whatever the motive for the Act [of 1800] it was in practice a very negligible instrument of oppression.

> M. Dorothy George (1935)

In 1799, near the end of the eighteenth century, parliament ventured its first general proposition concerning labour law, the notorious Combination Act.[1] As recounted in an earlier chapter, this statute, like the particular acts since 1721, had begun with a dispute in a particular trade at a particular place, in this case among the millwrights in London. Dissatisfied with the delay and expense of the common law, as well as with the opportunities it offered for evasion, the master millwrights had petitioned parliament for tailor-made legislation 'for the better preventing of unlawful combinations of workmen employed in the millwright business, and for regulating the wages of such workmen'.[2] The petition, part of which was quoted earlier, provided in its recital a circumstantial, if unfriendly, account of the workmen's *modus operandi*:

That a dangerous combination has for some time existed amongst the journeymen millwrights, within the metropolis, and the limits of twenty-five miles round the same, for enforcing a general increase of their wages, preventing the employment of such journeymen as refuse to join their confederacy, and for other illegal purposes, and frequent conspiracies of this sort have been set on foot by the journeymen, and the masters have as often been obliged to submit, and that a demand of a further advance of wages has recently been made, which not being complied with, the men, within the limits aforesesaid, have refused to work; and a compliance with such demands of an advance of wages hath generally been followed by further claims, with which it is impossible for the masters to comply, without occasioning so considerable an advance in the price of mill work as most materially to affect the

---

[1] 39 Geo. 3, c. 81 (1799).
[2] *Commons Journal*, 54 (1798–9), 405. See Chap. 2, n. 181.

said business, and the different manufactories connected therewith; and that, in support of the said combination (notwithstanding they complain of the insufficiency of their wages) the journeymen have established a general fund, and raised subscriptions, and so regular and connected is their system that their demands are made sometimes by all the journeymen, within the above limits, at the same time, and at other times at some one particular shop, and, in case of non-compliance, the different workshops (where their demands are resisted) are wholly deserted by the men, and other journeymen are prohibited from applying for work until the master millwrights are brought to compliance, and the journeymen, who have thus thrown themselves out of employ, receive support in the mean time from their general fund.[3]

Apparently responding to a friendly suggestion from the evangelical Wilberforce, Prime Minister William Pitt had proposed legislation modelled on the papermakers' act (1796) but applicable to all workmen. In any general proposition on combination, the regulation of wages would raise immense administrative difficulties; the choice of the papermakers' act as a model made not thinking about them that much easier. As we have seen, that act regulated hours rather than wages, and in terms specific to one industry.

In short order, the bill that was to become the Combination Act had been introduced. In the debates that followed, the proposal was attacked, not for the absence of regulation but for its excess: Benjamin Hobhouse, an advanced radical, inveighed against what he saw as an attempt to regulate the labour market by outlawing combination. He also made the pertinent suggestion that a better remedy for the ills complained of would be a bill to render common-law trials more speedy. Recognizing that his auditors were determined to go ahead, Hobhouse quickly switched from *avant-garde* economics and untimely law reform to old-fashioned Whiggery and moved an amendment in favour of the liberty of the subject: since trial by jury would be taken away, two justices of the peace instead of one, as in the papermakers' act, should be required to hear each case. His motion was rejected without division, and the bill was subsequently passed and sent to the Lords.[4] In the upper chamber a major speech against it was made by Lord Holland, the brilliant nephew of Charles James Fox, who followed Hobhouse's lead: 'the great and peculiar feature of the bill was', he declared, 'that it changed the trial by jury for a summary jurisdiction.'[5] This emphasis on the ancient right of trial by jury, which the workmen were soon to echo, deserves remark: juries were no more open to all classes than any other legal institution. Although the qualifications were not standardized until 1825, juries were always drawn from the propertied.[6] For workmen

---

[3] *Commons Journal*, 54 (1798–9), 405–6.
[4] *Parliamentary Register*, 9 (1799), 65–6.
[5] Ibid. 562.
[6] 2 Hen. 5, st. 2, c. 3 (1414); 19 Hen. 7, c. 13 (1503); 23 Hen. 8, c. 13 (1531). For reform see 6 Geo. 4, c. 50 (1825).

this meant that a jury of their 'peers' was always made up of their social superiors.

For the motive behind the bill his lordship pointed to contemporary fear of French revolutionary ideas:

On the part of the workmen, they laboured under the disadvantage arising from a certain degree of dread, that pervaded all the upper ranks of mankind, lest the lower ranks should be seduced by principles, supposed to be particularly afloat at this period, and subversive of society . . . Was it not possible also that the masters, conscious of this temporary advantage, had availed themselves of this period, rather than any other, to enforce their views, and render their workmen more dependent than they had hitherto been, and that in all fairness and equity they ought to be.[7]

Dispassionate analysis of the social situation, however penetrating, was of no avail: the Lords speedily approved the bill,[8] and it became law on 12 July 1799.

After reciting the existence of numerous combinations and the inadequacy of 'the laws at present in force against such unlawful conduct', the new Combination Act promised 'more speedy and exemplary justice'.[9] As had been the case with the earlier particular legislation, the key substantive provision of the 1799 Act was the definition of an illegal contract: one made by workmen

[1.] for obtaining an advance of wages of them, or any of them, or any other journeymen manufacturers or workmen, or other persons in any manufacture, trade, or business, or
[2.] for lessening or altering their or any of their usual hours or time of working, or
[3.] for decreasing the quantity of work, or
[4.] for preventing or hindering any person or persons from employing whomsoever he, she, or they shall think proper to employ in his, her, or their manufacture, trade, or business, or
[5.] for controlling or anyway affecting any person or persons carrying on any manufacture, trade, or business, in the conduct or management thereof.[10]

Such a contract if in existence at the passing of the act was void;[11] to enter into it in future was criminal;[12] to combine for such purposes was also criminal.[13] In addition, one could not directly or indirectly endeavour to prevent a workman from agreeing to work or endeavour to prevail on a workman already hired to leave work; nor could one endeavour to prevent

---

[7] *Parliamentary Register*, 9 (1799), 562–3.
[8] *Lords Journal*, 42 (1798–1800), 307, 314, 325.
[9] 39 Geo. 3, c. 81, preamble.
[10] 39 Geo. 3, c. 81, § 1. Throughout the eighteenth century the word 'manufacturer', true to its Latin roots, meant a person who produced goods manually. In the nineteenth century the word crossed the divide between capital and labour and became the common name of one who employed hand-workers. In the 1825 Act, discussed in the next chapter, it was still *en route*: in a single section it was used to mean both a 'person hired or employed' and a 'person carrying on any trade or business'.
[11] Ibid.   [12] Ibid. § 2.   [13] Ibid. § 3.

any master from employing whomever he pleased.[14] Finally, a workman once hired could not refuse to work with any other workman.[15] Attending a meeting held for illegal purposes or encouraging others directly or indirectly to attend such a meeting was criminal, as was the payment or collection of money for illegal purposes.[16] In a penal section comparable in severity to those in earlier acts, each of the above offences was made punishable by up to three months in the common gaol or up to two months' hard labour in a house of correction.[17]

In a further penal section it was declared illegal for anyone to pay expenses incurred in acting contrary to the act or to support any workman for the purpose of inducing him to refuse to work. The master millwrights had detailed the uses of the general fund raised by their journeymen, and the act made such uses criminal as to all workmen. To contribute money was made punishable by a fine of up to £10; to collect or receive it, by a fine of up to £5. In case a fine was not paid, it could be levied by distress and sale; should that fail, the offender was subject to not more than three nor less than two months' imprisonment either in the common gaol or at hard labour in a house of correction.[18] Forms for recording both fines and imprisonment were provided in a schedule attached to the act. Money collected for illegal purposes before the passing of the act had to be divided up within three months; otherwise, it was forfeit. Money collected for such purposes after the passing of the act was forfeit at once. In case of forfeiture half the money went to the common informer using the *qui tam* action.[19]

To provide 'more speedy and exemplary justice' the act authorized examination by a single justice of the peace as in the papermakers' act (1796), although the limitation period was extended to within three months of the alleged offence, rather than one month as in the earlier act.[20] Process began with complaint and information on oath; the justice of the peace then issued a summons, which was to be served personally or left at the accused's usual place of abode. In the event the alleged offender failed to appear as summoned, the justice of the peace was authorized to issue a warrant for his arrest.[21] In their petition to parliament the master millwrights had laid particular stress on the possibility that journeymen might abscond before trial. To close that loophole a provision in the papermakers' act was made general in 1799: if the justice of the peace saw fit, he could dispense with the initial summons and proceed immediately to issue the warrant.[22] Once the defendant was before the justice of the peace, whether in response to a summons or by compulsion of a warrant, trial proper began. In case of conviction, the decision had to be supported by the confession of the accused or by the sworn testimony of at least one witness.[23] The statute provided compulsory process for securing the requisite witness: the justice

---

[14] 39 Geo. 3, c. 81, § 3.   [15] Ibid.   [16] Ibid. § 4.   [17] Ibid. §§ 2–4.
[18] Ibid. § 5 and schedule.   [19] Ibid. § 6.   [20] Ibid. §§ 2–4, 10.
[21] Ibid. § 10.   [22] Ibid.   [23] Ibid.; also §§ 2–5.

of the peace was required at the request in writing of any party to summon witnesses.[24] The details of summonsing were spelled out as in the papermakers' act: either the witness had to be served personally or the summons could be left at his usual place of abode. If a witness refused to appear, he could be committed to prison; the same fate awaited a witness who appeared but refused to testify.[25] The 'form of commitment of a person summoned as a witness' was given in a schedule attached to the act.[26] An offender too could be compelled to appear and testify, the odium of the ex-officio oath being dispelled by a grant of immunity from prosecution.[27]

If the accused was convicted, the justice of the peace had to make a record. The 'form of conviction and commitment' was provided by the act; the justice filled in the date, the name of the offender, the justice's own name and county, the offence committed, and the punishment assigned.[28] This form (or another to the same effect) engrossed on parchment was to be filed at the next quarter sessions.[29] The person convicted was permitted to appeal to quarter sessions; the judgment appealed from was suspended on his entering into a recognizance with two sureties in the penalty of £20.[30] The decision of the sessions was final, and 'no *certiorari* shall be granted'.[31] Appellant was required to pay such costs as to the justices appeared just and reasonable; if he did not promptly pay, he was to be imprisoned until he did.[32] By a cruel irony, restraints on appeal that had been added to prevent abuse by masters became formidable barriers to appeals by workmen.

In addition to providing 'more speedy and exemplary justice' the act also struck at the economic underpinnings of successful combinations. As we have seen, the master millwrights had complained particularly about the general fund raised by journeymen, and the act provided 'for the better discovery of all sums of money which have been or shall be paid or given for any purpose prohibited by this act'.[33] To this end, a person suspected of holding money for an unlawful combination could be compelled by a court of equity to answer under oath to any information[34] preferred against him by the Attorney-General or at the relation of any informer.[35] The person against whom the information was preferred could not refuse to answer on the ground that he might thereby become liable to a penalty or forfeiture; the only way he could save himself was by paying the money into court.[36] This also discharged him from all lawsuits respecting the surrendered money[37]—as by contributors for misapplication of the funds.

[24] Ibid. § 11.   [25] Ibid.   [26] Ibid. § 12 and schedule.   [27] Ibid. § 9.
[28] Ibid. § 12 and schedule.   [29] Ibid. § 13.   [30] Ibid. § 14.
[31] Ibid. § 13 (italics in original).   [32] Ibid. § 14.   [33] Ibid. § 7.
[34] In addition to the informations used to initiate criminal proceedings before justices of the peace, informations were also used in equity courts to initiate proceedings on behalf of the Crown.
[35] 39 Geo. 3, c. 81, § 7. On equitable proceedings 'at the relation of' (*ex rel.*) an informer see William Blackstone, *Commentaries on the Laws of England* (1765–69), iii. 427–8.
[36] 39 Geo. 3, c. 81, § 8.   [37] Ibid.

Such proceedings could be entertained only by courts of equity, a distinctive branch of the English legal system that handled a limited number of issues. In this case the restriction was presumably made because the money in question was viewed as a trust, the special preserve of equity. The practical effect was severely to limit the availability of this type of suit. Unlike the justices of the peace 'in every particular county', courts of equity were few and far between. The principal equity court, the High Court of Chancery, sat at Westminster. Until 1813 when a Vice-Chancellor was added,[38] it had only two judges: the Master of the Rolls[39] and the Lord High Chancellor himself. In addition, there were four equity courts for the counties palatine:[40] the Chancery of Durham, the Duchy Chamber of Lancaster,[41] the Chancery of the County Palatine of Lancaster, and the Exchequer of Chester. Summary procedure, elsewhere provided by the act, was compromised by this provision. Although the celebrated equity case of *Jarndyce* v. *Jarndyce*[42] lay still in the future, equity in the age of Lord Eldon, Chancellor for all but one year between 1801 and 1827, was not noted for summariness.[43]

After expressly continuing in force all other regulatory legislation,[44] the act added a further procedural novelty. One justice could grant a licence permitting masters to use otherwise illegal labour

[w]henever the qualified journeymen or workmen usually employed in any manufacture, trade, or business, shall refuse to work therein for reasonable wages, or to work for any particular person or persons, or to work with any particular persons, or shall by refusing to work for any cause whatsoever, or by misconducting themselves when employed to work, in any manner impede or obstruct the ordinary course of manufacture, trade, or business, or endeavour to injure the person or persons carrying on the same.[45]

This was, as earlier legal historians of trade unionism have observed, 'a severe blow at the apprenticeship provisions of the Statute of Artificers':[46] men who had not completed their apprenticeships, or who had served no

---

[38] 53 Geo. 3, c. 24 (1813).

[39] See 3 Geo. 2, c. 30 (1730) (declaring orders of Master of the Rolls valid, subject to appeal to Lord Chancellor).

[40] The counties of Durham, Lancaster, and Chester—on the frontiers of English power in the middle ages—were endowed with some royal prerogatives. They were distinguished by the addition 'palatine', from Latin *palatinus*, 'of the palace'. They were gradually stripped of their special powers by legislation beginning in 1830.

[41] See 43 Eliz. 1, c. 4 (1601) (authorizing chancellor of Duchy of Lancaster, who presided over the Duchy Chamber, to inquire into abuses of charitable donations in the Duchy).

[42] Charles Dickens, *Bleak House* (1853), *passim*. See William S. Holdsworth, *Charles Dickens as a Legal Historian* (New Haven, Conn., 1928), 79–115.

[43] See Holdsworth, *A History of English Law*, xiii., ed. A. L. Goodhart and H. G. Hanbury (London, 1952), 287–94 (agitation for reform of Chancery, 1811–24).

[44] 39 Geo. 3, c. 81, § 15.

[45] Ibid. § 16.

[46] R. Y. Hedges and Allan Winterbottom, *The Legal History of Trade Unionism* (London, 1930), 23.

apprenticeships at all, could fill places reserved by law for journeymen. It was also a well-calculated blow at the effectiveness of workmen's combinations. Apprenticeship limited legal access to skilled trades; the licensing provision permitted increased access in cases in which workmen were using their limited numbers to enhance their bargaining power. Such a licence had to be in writing and include the reason why it was granted.[47] As we have seen, the first Spitalfields Act (1773) and the hatters' combination act (1777) had earlier relaxed apprenticeship in those trades, but parliament was now moving towards total abolition of the legal requirement. In 1814 it was to end the system altogether by repealing the relevant clauses of the Elizabethan statute.[48]

Finally, actions against persons enforcing the act had to be commenced within three months after the conduct complained of. If for any reason plaintiffs in such an action were unsuccessful, defendants were entitled to treble costs,[49] a harsher penalty than the double costs allowed under the papermakers' act (1796).

The Combination Act of 1799 remained in force for one year only. After its passage parliament received petitions from workmen all over the country—London and Westminster, Liverpool, Manchester, Bristol, Plymouth, Bath, Lancaster, Leeds, Derby, Nottingham, and Newcastle—all complaining that 'the law is materially changed to the great injury of all journeymen and workmen'.[50] Similar if not identical in wording, the petitions bespeak a well-organized campaign. The wave of petitioning itself confirms the supposition based on the first Spitalfields Act (1773) that 'combinations to present petitions to the King or to parliament were regarded as legal'.[51] The Combination Act was criticized for vagueness; the specific offences of endeavouring to prevail on a workman to leave and of refusing to work with a particular workman were singled out. These, of course, struck at the source of workmen's power, control over the supply of labour. But none of the petitions made extensive criticism of the substantive sections, and none protested at the absence of wage regulation. It was the procedures that attracted most attention. Every petition lamented the loss of trial by jury, which the workmen of Newcastle insisted upon as 'the grand paladium [*sic*] of English liberty'[52]—notwithstanding the exclusion of the

[47] 39 Geo. 3, c. 81, § 16.
[48] 54 Geo. 3, c. 96 (1814). See T. K. Derry, 'Repeal of the Apprenticeship Clauses of the Statute of Apprentices', *Economic History Review*, 1st ser., 3 (1931–2), 67–87 (the Statute of Apprentices is another name for the Statute of Artificers).
[49] 39 Geo. 3, c. 81, § 17.
[50] *Commons Journal*, 55 (1799–1800), 645–6, 665, 672, 706, 712. On the petition from Manchester, see John Bohstedt, *Riots and Community Politics in England and Wales, 1790–1810* (Cambridge, Mass., 1983), 139–41.
[51] Holdsworth, 'Industrial Combinations and the Law in the Eighteenth Century', 18 *Minnesota Law Review* n. 85 (1934) (repr. in *History of English Law*, xi. (1938), 489 n. 14). See Chap. 2, n. 122.
[52] *Commons Journal*, 55 (1799–1800), 712.

propertyless. Every petition objected to the denial of *certiorari*. Two petitions, one from Liverpool and the other from Manchester, drew attention to the absence in the 1799 Act of a provision comparable to that in the hatters' act (1777) disqualifying justices of the peace engaged in trade. Even making allowance for the politics of petitioning, the workmen's reaction to the Combination Act reveals how widespread was the preoccupation with proper legal form. Men, no less than masters, laid claim to due process of law and knew from a century's experience a good deal about the specifics. Despite years of war with revolutionary France a certain consensus still prevailed in England about the right way of doing things.

Perhaps stung by the workmen's criticism, the House of Commons reacted promptly to the petitions. On 30 June 1800 the subject was referred to a committee of six, who were to bring in a bill to explain and amend the earlier act. Two of the six, the playwright Richard Brinsley Sheridan and General Banastre Tarleton,[53] were Whigs opposed in principle to the 1799 legislation. The other four favoured moderate change, and some attempt was made to meet petitioners' objections. The committee's bill passed rapidly through both houses of parliament and became law on 29 July 1800, one year and seventeen days after the first general Combination Act. For the next quarter century, until its repeal in 1824, the Combination Act of 1800 was the primary statute against trade unions.

The 1799 Act was repealed and replaced,[54] but the changes were mainly in detail.[55] The definition of an illegal agreement was clarified. By the addition of parenthetical matter it was made clear that a contract between a master and his workman concerning the work of that workman was not voided by the act: '(save and except any contract made or to be made between any master and his journeyman, for or on account of the work or service of such journeyman or manufacturer with whom such contract may be made)'.[56] Some such exception was necessary, since on a literal reading the 1799 Act had outlawed all employment contracts. (A question might perhaps have been raised concerning the weaving trade as to which a 1757 act had validated, as we have seen, wage agreements between masters and journeymen.[57]) Also a series of minor amendments seemed aimed at meeting the petitioners' complaints about vagueness. The words 'wilfully and maliciously' supplanted 'directly or indirectly' in the definition of the

---

[53] Tarleton (1754–1833) represented Liverpool, the source of one of the petitions, from 1790–1806 and again from 1807–12. He had served with distinction in the British Army battling the American revolutionaries. His *History of the Campaigns of 1780 and 1781 in the Southern Provinces of North America* (1787) remains a valuable source; see Robert Middlekauff, *The Glorious Cause: The American Revolution, 1763–1789* (New York, 1982), 474–5 nn. 27–8.

[54] 39 & 40 Geo. 3, c. 106, § 1. Despite repeal, any proceedings under the 1799 Act were valid (ibid. § 24).

[55] For a section-by-section comparison of the 1800 Act with the 1799 Act, see Appendix I.

[56] 39 & 40 Geo. 3, c. 106, § 1.

[57] 30 Geo. 2, c. 12, § 2 (1757). See Chap. 2, n. 104.

crimes of endeavouring to prevent a workman from agreeing to work and of endeavouring to prevail on a workman already hired to leave work; the same substitution was made in the definition of the offence of attempting to prevent any master from employing whomever he thought proper.[58] The phrase 'without any just or reasonable cause' was inserted in the offence of refusing to work with any other workman.[59] 'Directly or indirectly' was deleted from the crimes of endeavouring to induce attendance at an illegal meeting and of paying or collecting money for illegal purposes,[60] and the word 'wilfully' was added to the offence of paying the expenses of anyone violating the act.[61]

Finally, a new crime was created: combination by masters—thus belatedly falsifying Adam Smith's observation a quarter century earlier: 'We have no acts of parliament against combining to lower the price of work.'[62] As we saw in the last chapter, there had been an indication less than two years earlier that the common law was moving to cover this ground: in *Hammond and Webb* (1799), the shoemakers' case, Lord Kenyon had warned the masters that 'they were as liable to an indictment for a conspiracy as the journeymen',[63] although he had instanced raising rather than lowering wages. As with workmen's combinations the strategy was to void illegal contracts, in this case defined as those made

[1.] for reducing the wages of workmen, or
[2.] for adding to or altering the usual hours or time of working, or
[3.] for increasing the quantity of work.[64]

Formal contracts to this effect were well known: according to Adam Smith, 'When masters combine together in order to reduce the wages of their workmen, they commonly enter into a private bond or agreement, not to give more than a certain wage under a certain penalty.'[65] In a later chapter, we shall see a suit, brought after the repeal of the combination laws, to enforce just such a private bond.[66] In the mean time, however, masters who made such agreements were to be punished. Unlike workmen who combined, guilty masters were not immediately liable to imprisonment; instead, their punishment was set at £20, of which half went to the Crown, a quarter to the informer, and a quarter to the poor of the parish. Only in case the fine was not paid and could not be levied by distress and sale, were masters liable to two to three months' imprisonment either in the common

---

[58] 39 & 40 Geo. 3, c. 106, § 3.
[59] Ibid.   [60] Ibid. § 4.   [61] Ibid. § 5.
[62] Adam Smith, *An Inquiry into the Nature and Causes of the Wealth of Nations*, ed. Edwin Cannan (New York, 1937), 66.
[63] 2 Esp. 720, 170 Eng. Rep. 508. See Chap. 3, n. 49.
[64] 39 & 40 Geo. 3, c. 106, § 17.
[65] Smith, *Wealth of Nations*, 142.
[66] *Hilton v. Eckersley*, 6 El. & Bl. 47, 119 Eng. Rep. 781 (Exch. Ch. 1855). See Chap. 6, n. 13.

gaol or at hard labour in the house of correction[67]—reminding one of Fielding's tart observation about the unequal use of 'that house'.[68]

With regard to procedures some changes were also made. First, two justices instead of one were now necessary for the examination of offences.[69] This was a concession to Whig sensibilities, as well as a reversion to the norm for combination acts prior to that for papermakers. Second, a new section disqualified justices of the peace who were also masters 'in the particular trade or manufacture in or concerning which any offence is charged to have been committed'.[70] This responded to the complaint heard from Liverpool and Manchester. Other changes made in 1800 amended in more or less significant ways the proceedings prescribed in 1799. The typical prosecution still began with complaint and information on oath before one justice of the peace who summoned the person charged to appear for trial.[71] Now, however, the procedure for summonsing was improved: if service was effected by leaving the summons at the person's usual place of abode, 'the same shall be so left twenty-four hours at the least before the time which shall be appointed to attend the said justices upon such summons'.[72] With this provision the logic of natural justice, which had prompted the requirement of a summons to offenders in the papermakers' act (1796), was carried one step further: not only did there have to be a summons, but it had to be served in time to permit appearance. If the alleged offender failed to appear as summoned, then the justices issued a warrant for his arrest. If the even speedier alternative of immediate arrest, dispensing with the initial summons, was adopted, then two justices of the peace had to act.[73] Compulsory process could also be used to summon a witness. Once more, however, the provision for service of process by leaving the summons at the witness's usual place of abode was tightened: to be effective the summons had to have been left at least twenty-four hours before the time appointed for appearance.[74] Thus far, such amendments as the 1799 Act underwent before its reincarnation in 1800 may be characterized as in favour of workmen, relatively speaking.

One change going directly contrary to their interests, however, was introduced: the 1800 Act permitted trials in the absence of the accused. The justices of the peace were to proceed to judgment either upon the appearance of the accused or 'upon proof on oath of such person or persons absconding'.[75] Seen against the history of the combination laws, such a

---

[67] 39 & 40 Geo. 3, c. 106, § 17.

[68] Henry Fielding, *Tom Jones* (1749) (London, 1959), 112–13. See Chap. 2, n. 20.

[69] 39 & 40 Geo. 3, c. 106, §§ 2–5, 10, 17.

[70] Ibid. § 16. J. Steven Watson overlooked this section when he wrote concerning the Combination Acts that the 'provision for the trial of industrial offences before two magistrates simply made the masters judges of their own men in many cases' (*The Reign of George III, 1760–1815* (Oxford, 1960), 362).

[71] 39 & 40 Geo. 3, c. 106, § 10.

[72] Ibid.   [73] Ibid.   [74] Ibid. § 11.   [75] Ibid. § 10.

provision is surprising. Not only was it unprecedented, it also was contrary to the long established trend towards greater procedural safeguards in the summary courts. Ever since the common-law courts had, as Blackstone expressed it, 'thrown in one check upon them, by making it necessary to *summon* the party accused before he is condemned',[76] parliament had shown increasing sensitivity to due process. Ordinarily, no common-law indictment could be tried without the personal appearance of the accused.[77] That trial by two justices of the peace was possible *in absentia* is good evidence that the rule of law was buckling under the strain of social tension and military fear.[78] The millwrights' complaint had indeed borne poisonous fruit.

In case of conviction—with or without the accused—the justices of the peace had to file a record with the next quarter sessions. As in 1799 forms were provided in the act. In fact, the draftsman in 1800 simply carried over the earlier forms, replacing the one justice of the peace required in 1799 by the two required in 1800.[79] With this change the forms were re-enacted. But in his haste the draftsman had failed to make two other necessary changes. First, the 'form of conviction and commitment' and the 'form of commitment of a person summoned as a witness' still referred to 'the statute made in the thirty-ninth year of the reign of His present Majesty' (King George III), that is, to the repealed 1799 Act. Second, the 'form of conviction in a pecuniary penalty' stated, as in 1799, that fines were 'for the use of His Majesty' despite the fact that under the 1800 Act a quarter of the fine was reserved for the informer and a quarter for the poor of the parish. These failures required new legislation, and the next year a short act amended the forms of conviction.[80] Until 1824, when the combination laws were repealed, convictions under the 1800 Act were recorded on the forms as corrected in 1801 (see Fig. 1).

As in 1799 the person convicted had a right of appeal. Judgments appealed from were suspended on the appellant's entering into a recognizance. As in 1799 the total sum put in penalty was £20, but under the 1800 Act the distribution was different: instead of two sureties for £20, the appellant himself had to enter into a recognizance for £10 with two sureties for £5 each.[81] No longer were quarter sessions the court of last resort. Unlike the 1799 Act which had expressly declared that 'no *certiorari* shall

[76] Blackstone, *Commentaries*, iv. 279 (italics in original). See Chap. 2, n. 171.

[77] Blackstone, *Commentaries*, iv. 313. Blackstone attributes this to 'the rules of equity in all, and the express provision of statute 28 Edw. III. c. 3 [1353] in capital, cases'. (The equity referred to is abstract justice, not the Court of Chancery.)

[78] Cf. *R. v. Paine*, 22 ST 358 (KB 1792) (Tom Paine convicted of seditious libel *in absentia*) (Erskine for defence). See E. P. Thompson, *Whigs and Hunters: The Origin of the Black Act* (New York, 1975), 269.

[79] 39 & 40 Geo. 3, c. 106, § 12 and 1st schedule.

[80] 41 Geo. 3, c. 38 (1801). The 'form of commitment of a person summoned as a witness' was not corrected.

[81] 39 & 40 Geo. 3, c. 106, § 23.

FIG. 1. Form of Conviction and Commitment (1801)

Be it remembered, that on the ____ day of ____ in the ____ year
of His Majesty's reign, and in the year of our Lord ____ A.B. is
convicted before us, [*naming the justices*], two of His Majesty's
justices of the peace for the county, [*or* riding, division, city,
liberty, town, *or* place], of ____ of having [*stating the offence*],
contrary to the statute made in the thirty-ninth and fortieth years
of the reign of His present Majesty, intituled *An Act to repeal an
Act, passed in the last Session of Parliament, intituled, 'An Act to
prevent unlawful Combinations of Workmen', and to substitute
other Provisions in lieu thereof*; and we the said justices do
hereby order and adjudge the said *A.B.* for the said offence, to be
committed to and confined in the common Gaol for the said
county, [*or* riding, division, city, liberty, town, *or* place], for the
space of ____ [*or* to be committed to the house of correction at
____ within the said county, [*or* riding, division, city, liberty,
town, *or* place], there to be kept to hard labour for the space
of ____ ____.

Given under our hands, the day and year above written.

Source: 41 Geo. 3, c. 38 (1801).

be granted', the 1800 Act omitted all mention of it, thus *sub silentio*
conceding one of the petitioners' demands and restoring to the Court of
King's Bench the power of review.

In proceedings for forfeiture of funds, a change was made that
strengthened the safeguards against self-incrimination: the person holding
funds collected for an illegal purpose could, as in 1799, be compelled by an
equity court to answer under oath, and paying the money into court was
still the only way he could save himself from suit by private plaintiffs, but
the 1800 Act stipulated in addition that his payment rendered him immune
from criminal prosecution.[82] In the third major proceeding contemplated
under the prior Combination Act, an application for a licence to use illegal
labour, the 1800 Act made no changes. One justice of the peace remained
competent to grant the licence.[83] Whether this was an oversight in an act
that required two justices of the peace to exercise every other significant
power is unclear. Finally, in an action brought against a person for anything
done in pursuance of the act the limitation on actions remained three
months. The penal clause of 1799 awarding treble costs against an
unsuccessful plaintiff was, however, eliminated; after 1800 full costs only
were permitted to be taxed[84]—a lesser penalty than the double costs
allowed under the papermakers' act (1796).

[82] 39 & 40 Geo. 3, c. 106, § 8.   [83] Ibid. § 15.   [84] Ibid. § 25.

In 1799 and 1800 parliament outlawed collective action and voided collective agreements. The paradigmatic employment contract was to be between individuals: one master contracting for the service of one workman. The Tudor–Stuart policy of wage regulation by the justices of the peace was defunct: suspended as to woollen manufacture in 1803, the legislation was finally repealed as to all workmen ten years later.[85] Mark Twain's Connecticut Yankee had exaggerated when he predicted that 'the magistrate will tranquilly arrange the wages . . . into the nineteenth century', but he spoke the simple truth when he said that the wage earner would finally 'take a hand in fixing his wages himself'.[86] Within the new legislative scheme the role of the justices of the peace was to prevent group action and to enforce the individual contract, eked out by the law of master and servant. In place of their historic role as regulators they received a limited role as arbitrators.[87]

Arbitration was not new in the industrial context, but before 1800 it had been limited to specific industries. By the Combination Act (1800) it was for the first time extended to 'all disputes' respecting

[1.] the price or prices to be paid for work actually done in any manufacture, or
[2.] any injury or damage done or alleged to have been done by the workmen to the work, or respecting
[3.] any delay or supposed delay on the part of the workmen in finishing the work, or
[4.] the not finishing such work in a good and workman-like manner, or according to any contract.[88]

The extension of arbitration is comparable to the extension of the ban on combination. Just as parliament had come to think of workmen generally in place of tailors, papermakers, and millwrights, so it had begun to think in terms of all industrial disputes rather than of stoppages in particular trades. Now that contract was in the centre of things, it was only natural to make provision for arbitration of disputes concerning its terms. That leaving work unfinished was within the terms of reference trenched on the law of master and servant, demonstrating the slow migration of the employment relationship from criminal to civil law.

The parliamentary history of the arbitration sections reveals just how conscious was the turn from the old policy of regulation towards the new policy of arbitration. The committee that proposed amendments to the 1799 Act had incorporated provisions based on the then-pending cotton arbitration bill.[89] These had applied to 'all cases . . . respecting the price or

---

[85] 43 Geo. 3, c. 136 (1803); 53 Geo. 3, c. 40 (1813).
[86] Mark Twain, *A Connecticut Yankee in King Arthur's Court* (1889) (New York, 1963), 239 ('Sixth-Century Political Economy') (general epigraph of this book).
[87] On the 'magistrate as mediator' in the eighteenth century, see C. R. Dobson, *Masters and Journeymen: A Prehistory of Industrial Relations, 1717–1800* (London, 1980), 74, 92.
[88] 39 & 40 Geo. 3, c. 106, § 18.
[89] Enacted as 39 & 40 Geo. 3, c. 90 (1800).

prices to be had for work done or to be done in any manufacture'.[90] They provided, in other words, arbitration concerning wages for future as well as for past work. Such arbitration would, as alert contemporaries quickly perceived, have meant the revitalization of wage regulation. When the motion was made for the third reading of the combination bill, the Attorney General, Sir John Mitford, opposed the arbitration clauses for that very reason: 'The obvious tendency of the clauses was to fix the wages'.[91] On the motion of Prime Minister William Pitt debate was adjourned until the next day. When the matter was again brought forward, an amendment was offered deleting the language giving arbitration prospective effect.[92] What was left was a system by which to settle disputes respecting the performance of existing contracts ('work actually done') not the terms of future contracts. Either party could demand arbitration within three days by two arbitrators, one appointed by each side. If the arbitrators could not agree, the matter was to be settled within three more days by a justice of the peace, who was given power to summon witnesses and compel them to testify.[93] If either party failed to perform as directed, he was to be imprisoned until he complied. If an arbitration was demanded by one side and the other failed to appoint an arbitrator, the defaulting party was liable to be fined £10.[94]

The general Combination Acts of 1799 and 1800 have long occupied a capital place in the history of English trade unionism. Looking backward a century later, Fabian historians regarded them as literally opening a new chapter: Sidney and Beatrice Webb called it the 'Struggle for Existence',[95] while J. L. and Barbara Hammond, writing during World War I, substituted a military metaphor for the Darwinian one and called it the 'War on Trade Unions'.[96] The former stressed their novelty: a 'far-reaching change of policy', 'a new and momentous departure';[97] the latter their unfairness: 'the most unqualified surrender of the State to the discretion of a class in the history of England'.[98] After the General Strike of 1926, irritated by Fabian rhetoric and loose talk about the 'monstrous' Combination Acts,[99]

---

[90] See Lord Amulree, *Industrial Arbitration in Great Britain* (Oxford, 1929), 27 n. 1 (citing source in House of Commons Library).

[91] *Parliamentary Register*, 12 (1800), 459.

[92] *Commons Journal*, 55 (1799–1800), 776.

[93] 39 & 40 Geo. 3, c. 106, § 18. By agreement the parties could extend the time permitted the arbitrators (ibid. § 19). Forms were provided (ibid. § 20 and 2nd schedule); each party was entitled to a copy of the 'form of submission' (ibid. § 21).   [94] Ibid. § 22.

[95] Sidney Webb and Beatrice Webb, *The History of Trade Unionism* (1st edn., 1894; rev. edn., London, 1920), title to chap. 2.

[96] J. L. Hammond and Barbara Hammond, *The Town Labourer, 1760–1832: The New Civilization* (London, 1917), title to chap. 7.

[97] Webb and Webb, *History of Trade Unionism*, 64, 72.

[98] Hammond and Hammond, *Town Labourer*, 113.

[99] E.g., L. A. Atherley-Jones, 'Labour Disputes', *Fortnightly Review*, NS 720 (1926), 761 (Combination Acts [1799–1800] described as 'the first legislative enactments against the right of working men to combine' and a 'monstrous act of injustice').

M. Dorothy George entered an early and influential rejoinder: in light of the earlier legislation and the common law of conspiracy, she dismissed both Acts as 'no change in policy'[100] and the 1800 Act, the only one to endure, as 'in practice a very negligible instrument of oppression'.[101]

For more than half a century the battle lines have held. Sir William Holdsworth, the pre-eminent historian of English law, has judged the 1799 and 1800 Acts 'very different in their character from the earlier combination acts',[102] while J. H. Plumb has asserted: 'Time and time again these Acts were invoked to suppress savagely and indiscriminately the movement towards trade unionism.'[103] With more attention to the sources, E. P. Thompson admitted that they were 'not as widely employed as might have been expected'—he never identified whose expectations he had in mind— although he insisted that 'no one familiar with these years can doubt that their general prohibitive influence was ever-present'.[104] Of even more moment, Thompson went on to denounce them as fateful steps by England's élite away from the rule of law.[105] (He seems to have been referring to the substance of the two acts, not their procedural niceties.) In reply A. E. Musson crudely restated George's argument: 'the cruelly oppressive Combination Laws' were 'myths' based on 'confusion of the Combination Laws of 1799–1800 with other, older legal controls, which were actually more severe and more frequently enforced'.[106] On behalf of a self-proclaimed 'conservative interpretation of labour history',[107] C. R. Dobson has also emphasized continuity: the 1799 Act 'codified and generalized existing legislation';[108] together the two acts 'carried into the nineteenth century the eighteenth-century experience of mediation by the magistrates'.[109] In 1986 John Batt called for further exploration of the insights of George and Musson.[110]

The extent to which the general Combination Acts represented a change of policy can now be looked at anew. To be sure, they created no new crime; they never pretended to. The 1799 Act was officially entitled 'An Act to

---

[100] M. Dorothy George, 'The Combination Laws Reconsidered', *Economic Journal* (Supp.), Economic History Ser., 2 (May 1927), 226–7.

[101] Ead., 'The Combination Laws', 172 (a 'revision in economic history') (epigraph of the present chapter of this book).

[102] Holdsworth, 18 *Minnesota Law Review* 387 (1934) (repr. in *History of English Law*, xi. (1938), 498).

[103] J. H. Plumb, *England in the Eighteenth Century* (Harmondsworth, 1950), 158. In a curious confusion, Professor Plumb continued: 'in 1799, with the harsh laws against Combination, the government ... made the combination of workmen in clubs and societies, for the sake of improved working conditions and wages, conspiracy.'

[104] E. P. Thompson, *The Making of the English Working Class* (New York, 1963), 505.

[105] Id., *Whigs and Hunters*, 269.

[106] A. E. Musson, *British Trade Unions, 1800–1875* (1972), 22.

[107] Dobson, *Masters and Journeymen*, 151.   [108] Ibid. 141.   [109] Ibid. 122.

[110] John Batt, ' "United to Support but not Combined to Injure": Public Order, Trade Unions and the Repeal of the Combination Acts of 1799–1800', *International Review of Social History*, 31 (1986), 187 and n. 7.

prevent *unlawful* Combinations of Workmen', and the 1800 Act was passed to explain and amend it. Workmen in various sectors of the economy, including the all-important cotton industry, were already covered by combination acts; those not covered by legislation (as well as those covered) were also liable, in appropriate cases, to prosecution for common-law conspiracy. Sentences under the earlier acts never exceeded three months, while those for conspiracy ranged up to two years. Yet neither the statutory nor the common-law regime had proved satisfactory. 'Many subtil devices' had rendered earlier acts ineffectual, and (as the master millwrights complained) the cumbersome procedures of the common law could be thwarted even less subtly: by simply walking out of the jurisdiction. The 1799 Act, on which that of 1800 was based, had promised only 'more speedy and exemplary justice'. With that end in view the legislative draftsman could profit from trial and error spread over eight decades. Even at that, it took two tries to adjust the combination law to the existing social and political balance. As we saw in the last chapter, common-law conspiracy was not abolished: it was paralleled by the speedier, cheaper, more foolproof alternative of prosecution for combination.

Not only were the procedures improved, but the crime itself was described more comprehensively. The simple contract to raise wages or shorten hours outlawed in the first tailors' act (1721) had been elaborated in successive acts until it reached final form in the papermakers' act (1796), from which it was transferred to the general acts. The procedural sections, too, collected the lessons learned over the years. From the papermakers' act came provisions, improved upon in 1800, for summoning offenders, as well as provisions for arrest without prior summons. From the second tailors' act (1768) came provisions to compel witnesses to appear and testify, while the papermakers' act contributed protection against self-incrimination. From the second tailors' act, too, came sections regulating counteractions against those enforcing the act. From the second weavers' act (1756)—not strictly a combination act since it did not amend the sections concerning combined action—and from the hatters' act (1777) came detailed provisions concerning recognizances required for appeal. Forms to simplify the work of the justices of the peace were taken from the second Spitalfields Act (1792).

Even the concessions to workmen granted in 1800 were not new under the sun. Two justices of the peace had been required in all but one of the earlier combination acts; only the papermakers' act (1796) had allowed one to decide guilt or innocence. Likewise the disqualification of justices of the peace engaged in a trade in which a dispute had arisen had a precedent in the hatters' act (1777). *Certiorari* had been expressly prohibited in only three earlier acts: the second weavers' act (1756), the second Spitalfields Act (1792), and the papermakers' act (1796). Masters had also not been immune from prosecution. Although 1800 saw the creation of the first statutory crime of combination by masters, they had earlier been liable to prosecution for, among other things, paying more than the rates set by the first tailors' act (1721) or paying more or less than the rates set by the first Spitalfields Act (1773). Masters who paid in truck contrary to the first weavers' act (1726), as well presumably as those who violated the hours provisions in the papermakers' act (1796), could also have been prosecuted. Finally, as we have seen, the common law may have anticipated parliament's 'general proposition' by including masters' combinations in the law of conspiracy.

Not every provision of the 1800 Act was traceable, however, to prior legislation. Trial *in absentia* and forfeiture of funds were specific responses to the master millwrights' complaints about practices in that trade generalized to apply to all trades, while licensing of illegal labour was a step on the road to abolishing legal apprenticeship. Above all, general arbitration procedures were new in 1800. In this regard the Combination Act did represent a change of policy, although not exactly in the direction of oppression. As the Webbs observed long ago, in prior acts 'the prohibition of combination was in all cases incidental to the regulation of the industry',[111] although the regulation had been progressively attenuated. The *quid pro quo* of anti-combination provisions had been, in other words, provisions setting wages and hours or outlawing the truck system. In 1800, as Attorney-General Mitford made clear, wage regulation was consciously abandoned; in its place was offered arbitration concerning existing contracts. The withdrawal of the state from the field of wage regulation would seem to be a triumph of Smithian economics: *Laissez-faire, laissez-passer.* But it was also a confession of failure: the recent and minimal parliamentary regulation of the hours of 'vat men' and 'dry workers' in the paper industry was almost immediately obsolete. Particular acts regulating every trade, many just emerging and some changing rapidly, throughout the length and breadth of England, were simply unthinkable—even without the distractions provided by the Emperor Napoleon. Nor were the justices of the peace in every particular county any more competent to manage the changing economy than their social superiors in parliament. Despite the advice of 'discreet and grave persons', authorized by the Statute of Artificers,[112] the gentlemen justices were simply incapable of providing consistent and comprehensive regulation of every trade and manufacture. On the other hand, justices of the peace who were also masters in the particular trade or manufacture, while certainly knowledgeable, were disabled by constitutional proprieties from being judges in their own cases.

None the less, even before the machinery of wage regulation had been fully dismantled—the wages clauses of the Statute of Artificers were not finally repealed until 1813—humanitarians had already launched the

---

[111] Webb and Webb, *History of Trade Unionism*, 65.
[112] 5 Eliz. 1, c. 4, § 15. See Chap. 1, n. 12.

movement for factory acts to regulate working conditions.[113] The ban on payment in truck, which had grown up with the combination acts, was eventually perfected,[114] and legal limits on hours, also a regular part of combination legislation, were eventually imposed.[115] Although such regulation affected overall compensation, it constituted a less obvious breach in *laissez-faire* than wage regulation; even Adam Smith gave his personal blessing to the truck acts.[116] The new system, too, faltered in practice until a corps of professional inspectors later in the century attended to the details.

The combination acts of the eighteenth century represent a search for a policy of industrial relations; the general Combination Act (1800) represents the policy finally arrived at. After decades of dealing with the problem piecemeal, in response to a crisis here or there or at the instigation of an interested party, parliament at last faced the general issue. The lawmakers hesitated long before abandoning the age-old policy of wage regulation; their ambivalence was demonstrated when authority for wage regulation in weaving was granted in 1756 and revoked in 1757. At the end of the century their decision was irrevocable. Wages would no longer be state business; capital and labour would fight it out for themselves. For better and worse, that decision held for years to come; it has not been finally rejected yet. Ample room for controversy, of course, remained. Rules for the economic struggle—in particular, the law of strikes—had yet to be drafted; the degree of state involvement, short of wage regulation, had yet to be determined. But the primacy of the employment contract had been established once and for all, if only by default. Once the state ceased to regulate wages, no other legal device remained except contract. When the draftsman of the 1800 Act realized that the language adopted a year earlier to suppress combinations had included all employment contracts in its sweep, he hastily inserted the parenthetical: '(save and except any contract made or to be made between any master and his journeyman, for or on account of the work or service of such journeyman or manufacturer with whom such contract may be made)'.[117] Because combination had been defined in terms of contract, the employment contract appeared as an exception to a general rule of criminal law. By a clumsy saving clause, status finally yielded to contract.

[113] 42 Geo. 3, c. 73 (1802) (Peel's Act I); 59 Geo. 3, c. 66 (1819) (Peel's Act II); 3 & 4 Will. 4, c. 103 (1833). On this legislation, see B. L. Hutchins and A. Harrison, *A History of Factory Legislation* (London, 1903), chaps. 2–3.

[114] 1 & 2 Will. 4, cc. 36–7 (1831).

[115] 10 & 11 Vict., c. 29 (1847) (Ten Hours Act—for women and children under 18). See Maurice Walton Thomas, *The Early Factory Legislation: A Study in Legislative and Administrative Evolution* (Leigh-on-Sea, 1948), chap. 18.

[116] Smith, *Wealth of Nations*, 142 (truck acts 'quite just and equitable'). The Chicago School of Economics, intellectual heir to Adam Smith, has differed with the master on this point. See George W. Hilton, *The Truck System: Including a History of the British Truck Acts, 1465–1960* (Cambridge, 1960), 59–60; Hilton's book is a 'slightly revised version' of his Ph.D. thesis in economics at the Univ. of Chicago.   [117] 39 & 40 Geo. 3, c. 106, § 1.

With regard to the 1800 Act, in effect until 1824, M. Dorothy George argued that it was 'negligible' because infrequently enforced. Although she suggested at one point that this had been due to 'compromise and toleration, good sense and moderation',[118] her principal argument was that statutes conferring summary jurisdiction like the combination acts tended to become inoperative. 'They were defeated', she said, 'by the difficulties of drafting an information, by appeals to the [Quarter] Sessions (often at a distance), and by the frequent quashing of convictions on technical points.'[119] We have seen that parliament had been moved to legislate in the eighteenth century because 'many subtil devices' had been practised (mostly by masters) to evade regulations. In addition, we have seen that eighteenth-century combination acts had become more complex procedurally because of the common-law courts' concern for principles of natural justice. Summons to offenders and perhaps safeguards against self-incrimination had been added to eliminate potential grounds for review and orders to quash. The writ of *certiorari* had itself been originally denied, in the second weavers' act (1756), because the expense it entailed had frustrated 'several prosecutions' of masters.

To support her argument that informations were so easily defeated on technicalities, George quoted L. B. Allen, a London justice of the peace, who wrote in 1821:

it is not, I believe, generally known, that informations before magistrates must be drawn with exactly the same care and nicety as indictments in courts of law; with this extra inconvenience, that in nineteen out of twenty cases, appeal from the conviction of the magistrate is permitted to the Quarter Sessions, and that, without the appellant being obliged to allege any reason whatever: the consequence is, that a vast number of informations, substantially founded in justice, fail before the magistrate; and of those which do not, a great many more are quashed on the appeal at the Quarter Sessions . . .[120]

We have seen that the Combination Act (1800) did not in fact require an appellant to allege any reason for appeal, but it did require the execution of

[118] George, *Economic Journal* (Supp.), Economic History Ser., 2, 227.

[119] Ead., *Economic History Review*, 1st ser., 6, 174.

[120] Ead., *Economic Journal* (Supp.), 217–18 (quoting—with a few errors—L. B. Allen, *Brief Considerations on the Present State of the Police of the Metropolis* (1821), 45–6). This pamphlet is, incidentally, attributed in the British Museum catalogue and many others to Lucas Benjamin Allen. But the text includes a copy of 'an information . . . laid before me', in which the author identifies himself as Lancelot Baugh Allen (pp. 58–60). I assume this is the same 'Mr. L. Baugh Allen' who was a six clerk in Chancery and a clerk of enrolments when those offices were abolished in 1842 and who received the enormous compensation for the loss of his posts of £44,647. See L. H. Razzall, 'The Golden Handshake of All Times', *The Times* (30 Jan. 1963). 'Magistrates' here means justices of the peace, although the word was often used to refer specifically to justices of the peace who were paid a salary (or stipend). 'Stipendiary magistrates' of which Allen may have been one, were appointed in Middlesex from 1792. After 1835 any municipal borough could petition for a stipendiary. The Metropolitan Police Courts Act (1839)· created the office of Chief Metropolitan Stipendiary Magistrate in London and provided that the stipendiaries' courts should be known as police courts.

a recognizance for £20, £10 from the appellant and £5 each from two sureties, to ensure that the appeal was prosecuted in good faith. In case of loss on appeal, the appellant was liable for costs. It seems likely that in the case of workmen, especially those whose earnings were interrupted by a dispute with their masters, these pecuniary barriers would be effective in preventing the obstructionist appeals that Allen had in mind.

In context it is clear that George's source was not thinking about the Combination Act at all but about the Coal Acts,[121] the Coach Acts,[122] and the Bread Acts[123] which authorized London magistrates to regulate the various trades in the interests of consumers. This appears from the conclusion of the quoted sentence (which George deleted):

while all the richer class of offenders, such as the coal merchants, coach masters, and bakers, seem to have come to a resolution, in all cases of conviction, to take the chance of the appeal: this is known and felt, and must deter the informers considerably, as it is meant to do.[124]

The victories won for due process of law in the Civil War and the Glorious Revolution had their dark side as well: proper procedures are technical, slow, and expensive. In a society of economic inequality they strengthened the hands of the 'richer class of offenders', who are usually well counselled and better able to endure—even to profit by—the law's delay.

With respect to the Combination Act itself George asserted:

many convictions which survived the Sessions perished in the King's Bench. There was a remarkably interesting case in 1805 on the Combination Act, whose importance appears from the fact that Erskine, Garrow, and three other counsel had been briefed for some cotton spinners who were appealing against a conviction. The conviction was quashed and the decision, which shows how difficult it must have been to draft an information under the Act, may well have discouraged prosecutions.[125]

The case relied on is *Rex* v. *Nield*,[126] which *pace* George is the only conviction under the act known to have 'perished' in the King's Bench. On

---

[121] 45 Geo. 3, c. ii (1805) (renewed annually); 47 Geo. 3, c. lxviii (1807). Private acts concerning one locality, in this case London, came to be cited with their chapter numbers in lower-case Roman numerals. See Courtenay Ilbert, *Legislative Methods and Forms* (Oxford, 1901), 27.

[122] 39 & 40 Geo. 3, c. 47 (1800); 48 Geo. 3, c. 87 (1808); 50 Geo. 3, c. 48 (1810).

[123] The medieval Assize of Bread was a statute of uncertain date, traditionally ascribed to 51 Hen. 3 (1267–8). It was brought up to date for London by 45 Geo. 3, c. xxiii (1805); 55 Geo. 3, c. xcix (1815); 59 Geo. 3, c. cxxvii (1819); 60 Geo. 3, c. i (1820); 1 Geo. 4, c. iv (1820). The Assize of Bread and other regulations concerning bread were abolished for London in 1822, the year after Allen wrote (3 Geo. 4, c. cvi (1822)). For the special form of citation used for private local acts, see n. 121, above.

[124] Allen, *Brief Considerations*, 46.

[125] George, *Economic History Review*, 174. Cf. her earlier more exact discussion in *Economic Journal* (Supp.), 218–19.

[126] 6 East 417, 102 Eng. Rep. 1346 (KB 1805).

28 November 1804 Nield and seven others had been convicted before two Lancashire justices of the peace of having on 1 November entered into

a certain agreement for the purpose of then and there controlling W. Borradaile, etc. then and there carrying on the management and trade of cotton spinning, as masters and partners, in the conduct and management of their said trade and manufacture; the said agreement not being a contract made between any master and journeyman, or manufacturer, for or on account of the work or service of such journeyman or manufacturer; contrary to the form of the Stat. 39 & 40 Geo. 3, intitled, etc.[127]

For this offence they were to be confined in the common gaol for three months. The defendants promptly exercised their right of appeal, presumably giving the necessary recognizances. Quarter sessions affirmed the conviction, and the defendants were presumably taxed with full costs. As permitted by the 1800 Act, the defendants then petitioned for a writ of *certiorari*, which was granted. Subsequently, the case came before the Court of King's Bench, Chief Justice Lord Ellenborough presiding, on 22 May 1805. On behalf of the defendants, Thomas Erskine[128] alleged two defects in the form of conviction. First, the agreement for which the defendants had been convicted was not quoted but was summarily stated to be an 'agreement for the purpose of . . . controlling' their masters. Such conclusory language deprived the defendants of effective review. There was 'a wholesome rule of law', insisted Erskine,

which is even more necessary to be observed on convictions before inferior magistrates than in indictments before the higher tribunals, namely, that every indictment or conviction should contain a charge of the offence with such certainty as that the Court may see that the offender is plainly brought within the law which he is alleged to have broken; so that an innocent person may not be condemned upon a misconstruction of the law by an inferior tribunal, without any means of redress.[129]

(As we shall see in a later chapter, Jervis's Act in 1848 effectively ended review by writ of *certiorari* by severely limiting the record of what went on before the inferior tribunal.) Erskine's second argument, an old-fashioned pleading point on which he wasted little time, drew attention to the fact that although the act outlawed agreements entered into 'for controlling' a master, the conviction was for an agreement entered into 'for *the purpose of*

---

[127] Ibid. 1346–7. Note the English rendering of the Latin phrase *contra formam statuti* at issue in the Cambridge Tailors' Case (1721). A statute in 1730 (4 Geo. 2, c. 26) had directed the use of English in all legal records.

[128] Thomas Erskine (1750–1832) has been described as 'the greatest advocate who has ever practised at the English bar' (Holdsworth, *History of English Law*, xiii. 580). Noted for devotion to liberal causes, he defended many unpopular clients. With Garrow he had earlier been briefed for the shoemakers in *Hammond and Webb* (1799). Created Lord Erskine in 1806, he was briefly Lord Chancellor in the 'Ministry of All the Talents', interrupting Lord Eldon's long tenure.

[129] 6 East 417, 422, 102 Eng. Rep. 1348–9.

... controlling' a master. 'Though the difference may seem to be small', he insisted, 'yet in a case of this sort even a literal variance is important'.[130]

The judges, who quashed the conviction, were persuaded. Lord Ellenborough, speaking to the first point, paraphrased the workmen's advocate in an unremarkable statement of the law:

In all instances where jurisdiction is given to inferior magistrates in certain cases, it is necessary that the Court should see that they do not exceed that jurisdiction. The statute in question gives the magistrates a summary jurisdiction to repress agreements by journeymen for controlling their masters in their trade, they should therefore have stated what the agreement was, in order that the Court might see whether it were an agreement for controlling the masters in their trade within the meaning of the statute.[131]

On the second point, he also agreed with Erskine, although he raised it from a mere pleading point to the level of substantive law:

It is necessary to shew a criminal object, as well as a criminal intent . . . It is not enough that the agreement should be for the purpose of controlling, that is, with intent to control; but it must be entered into for controlling, that is, for effecting that object.[132]

Here his lordship may have been misled into gobbledegook by his well-known pride in his own subtlety. James Scarlett, a distinguished barrister who went on to a political and judicial career, later recalled the turn of Lord Ellenborough's mind: 'his sagacity in discovering what had escaped the counsel achieved a triumph which . . . flattered his vanity'.[133] Improving on the brilliant Erskine would have been a triumph indeed.

Nield is what George called it, 'a remarkably interesting case', but it does not support her conclusion as stated. The case has nothing whatsoever to do with the difficulty of drafting informations. The conviction, to be sure, was quashed and one of the grounds might fairly be described as a technicality, but the fault lay not in the prosecutor's information but in the justices' form of conviction. No formality was required for informations under the Combination Act. The only record that was certified to the higher court in response to the writ of *certiorari* was embodied in the form of conviction, filled in by the justices of the peace. Frequent reversals might certainly discourage prosecutions, but the judges' ire in this case was directed not at the complainants' information but at the record made by 'inferior magistrates'. Throughout the eighteenth century, as George rightly observed, the Court of King's Bench had insisted that statutes conferring summary

---

[130] 6 East 417, 424, 102 Eng. Rep. 1349.
[131] 6 East 417, 425, 102 Eng. Rep. 1350.
[132] 6 East 417, 426, 102 Eng. Rep. 1350.
[133] James Scarlett (Lord Abinger), 'Autobiography', quoted in his son's biography: Peter Campbell Scarlett, *A Memoir of . . . James, First Lord Abinger* (1877), 83. Although Scarlett appeared for the prosecution, the losing side in *Nield*, there is no reason to think that his remarks on Lord Ellenborough, written many years later, refer specifically to that case.

jurisdiction be strictly construed; particular zeal had been shown that justices of the peace not exceed their jurisdiction.[134] Yet by the early nineteenth century concern about summary procedure was waning. The eighteenth-century obsession with due process had been a reaction to the earlier centralism and absolutism of the Stuarts. As the Civil War and the Glorious Revolution receded into the past, and as time familiarized lawyers with the enhanced powers of the justices of the peace, supervision had begun to relax. The French Revolution and the Napoleonic wars brought other concerns to the fore. Fear of subversion among the 'lower ranks' increased respect for the local justices as bulwarks of social order. The hypertechnicality of *Nield* and its condescension towards inferior magistrates was already an anachronism in 1805.

This conclusion is supported by another interesting case on the Combination Act, one not mentioned by George: *Rex v. Ridgway*[135] in 1822. In that case, also from Lancashire, the offence was more amply described:

Be it remembered, that on the 19th day of March, 1821, T. H. etc. are convicted before us, R. P. and S. W. Esquires, two of His Majesty's justices of the peace for the county of Lancaster, of having, on the 10th of March in the year aforesaid, and within the space of three calendar months next before this present 19th day of March, in the year aforesaid, at Great Bolton, in the county of Lancaster, attended a meeting of journeymen and workmen, then and there had and held, for the purpose of maintaining, supporting, continuing, and carrying on a combination, for a purpose, by the statute in such case made and provided, and hereinafter next mentioned, declared to be illegal, to wit, a combination of journeymen and workmen in the business of bleaching, for the purpose of obtaining an advance of wages in that business, contrary to the statute made in the 39th and 40th years of the reign of His late Majesty, King George the Third, intituled etc.[136]

On appeal to quarter sessions the conviction was quashed because of objections to the form of conviction, subject, however, to review by the Court of King's Bench by writ of *certiorari*. At the hearing on 11 February 1822 counsel for the journeymen bleachers were in the unusual situation of arguing in support of an order of sessions. Their argument involved two contentions. First, King's Bench should not intervene after quarter sessions had quashed a conviction: 'This is like moving for a new trial after an acquittal for a misdemeanour, owing to a misdirection on the part of the Judge, which is never allowed.'[137] In America this propriety had constitutional protection: the Fifth Amendment prohibited putting a person twice in

---

[134] See e.g. *R. v. Chandler*, 1 Ld. Raym. 581, 91 Eng. Rep. 1288 (KB 1702).
[135] 5 B. & A. 527, 106 Eng. Rep. 1283 (KB 1822).
[136] 5 B. & A. 527–8, 106 Eng. Rep. 1284.
[137] 5 B. & A. 528, 106 Eng. Rep. 1284. Seventy years earlier Blackstone (citing Hawkins) had been more cautious: 'there hath yet been no instance of granting a new trial, where the prisoner was *acquitted* upon the first' (*Commentaries*, iv. 355 (italics in original)).

jeopardy for the same offence.[138] Also, the act limited actions to three months after the crime. If the court were to find quarter sessions in error on a matter of form and send the case back for an appeal on the merits, then a period much longer than that contemplated by the statute—in this case almost a year—would have elapsed. But if the first argument should not prevail, there was a second for supporting the order of sessions. Put simply, it was that quarter sessions had been right in finding the form of conviction defective: it did not follow the words of the act. The combination was alleged to be 'for *the purpose of* obtaining an advance of wages' not 'for obtaining an advance of wages'. Here, of course, the oracular utterance of Lord Ellenborough in *Nield* (1805) on the difference between 'criminal object' and 'criminal intent' was relevant.

The judges were not convinced. Without waiting for argument against the order of sessions, they quashed it and sent the case back with directions to hear the appeal on the merits. The argument that the court should not interfere when quarter sessions quash a conviction they ignored; there was no question of a second trial, only whether to enter the judgment arrived at in the first place. In addition, the judges held the form of conviction unexceptionable. Lord Ellenborough's reasoning was deliberately and expressly rejected. In the words of Sir Charles Abbott, Ellenborough's successor as chief justice:

No man entertains greater respect for the opinion of Lord Ellenborough than I do, but I own that the observation quoted from *Rex v. Nield and Others* is not satisfactory to my mind. He seems to have considered the word purpose as synonymous with the word intent, and to have thought that an agreement with intent to control might not be an agreement to control.[139]

What was the law after this decision? First, in cases like *Ridgway* involving illegal actions it was sufficient to state the offence in general terms without including the evidence to support it. This, as we have seen, had been the rule with regard to common-law conspiracy ever since *Eccles* in 1783. Second, in cases like *Nield* involving illegal agreements it remained necessary to set out the agreement and not simply to describe it as illegal. This was true because only the second ground for decision in *Nield* was overruled in *Ridgway*. It is, of course, also true that *Nield* was decided in 1805, that *Ridgway* was decided in 1822, and that the Combination Act (1800) was repealed in 1824–5. It is one of the mysteries of legal history whether the second ground in *Nield* would have been rejected before 1822 had an appropriate case been presented.[140] Hypertechnicality in dealing with summary convictions was definitely falling into disfavour. Within

---

[138] US Const., amend. V (1791) ('nor shall any person be subject for the same offence to be twice put in jeopardy of life or limb').

[139] 5 B. & A. 530, 106 Eng. Rep. 1284–5.

[140] For reflections on such problems in legal historiography, see John V. Orth, 'Doing Legal History', 14, NS *Irish Jurist* 114–23 (1979).

months of the decision in *Ridgway* parliament passed an act to facilitate summary proceedings that prohibited setting aside a conviction in consequence of any defect of form and that called for 'such a fair and liberal construction as will be agreeable to the justice of the case'.[141] Suspicion of the justices of the peace was definitely on the wane. As we shall see in a later chapter, law reform associated with the name of Sir John Jervis, Attorney-General in a Whig government at mid-century, quietly ended effective judicial review of local government by writ of *certiorari*.

By the end of the first quarter of the nineteenth century, parliament and the courts between them had finally formulated a general proposition concerning the groups soon to be known as trade unions: they were illegal. They were illegal at common law as conspiracies because any agreement their members made to gain their ends would prejudice either masters or other workmen. By statute they were illegal because they were constituted by 'contracts, covenants or agreements' to raise wages, lessen hours or work, or affect the way business was carried on. At the same time, parliament finally abandoned the Tudor–Stuart policy of decentralized control over the economy: wage regulation by particular orders of the justices of the peace in every particular county, and skills training by legally required apprenticeships in various workshops. Wages were to be set by contract between master and man; training was to be catch as catch can. The only remaining question was whether workmen would ever be permitted to bargain in combination as to any or all of the terms of that all-important contract. Influence in parliament would be necessary if the scope of contract was to be extended, or if, to put it in the language soon to become fashionable, freedom of contract was to be perfected.

---

[141] 3 Geo. 4, c. 23, § 3 (1822) (15 May).

5

Combination: 1824–1859

The barbarous laws against Trades' Unions fell in 1825 before the threatening bearing of the proletariat. Despite this, they fell only in part. Certain beautiful fragments of the old statute vanished only in 1859.

Karl Marx (1867)

The barbarous combination laws are part of popular history. Yet if every schoolboy knows of them, he also knows they fell in 1825. Of course, like so much schoolboy knowledge, this is less than half the truth. The 1799 Combination Act had been repealed by the 1800 Combination Act; the latter was, along with all the other eighteenth-century acts, repealed in 1824. Thereafter, the 1800 Act and all the earlier statutes were without effect. But the 1824 Act was itself repealed in 1825 by an act that then re-repealed the 1800 Combination Act as well as all the others. The reason for this double repeal lay in an old rule of English law; as Blackstone put it: 'If a statute, that repeals another, is itself repealed afterwards, the first statute is thereby revived, without any formal words for that purpose.'[1] It is, therefore, correct to say that the combination laws, whether barbarous or not, fell in 1824–5. By which is meant that after 1824 and for all future time they were without effect but that the ultimate authority for that fall, what gave it its final effect, was the 1825 Act.

The parliamentary campaign that ultimately overthrew the settlement of 1800 began in 1822. In that year Joseph Hume, a firm believer in *laissez-faire*—the only member of parliament Jeremy Bentham thought 'thoroughly deserves that name'[2]—announced his intention of bringing in a bill to repeal all the laws against combination.[3] No action was taken until the next session when Hume made preliminary preparations for the appointment of a parliamentary select committee. Before he was ready to act, however, the initiative had been seized by another member, Peter Moore, who secured leave to bring in his own bill.[4] Presented on 22 April 1823, this bill had been

---

[1] William Blackstone, *Commentaries on the Laws of England* (1765–9), i. 90.
[2] Quoted in J. H. Burns, 'Jeremy Bentham and University College' (London, 1962), 3 (citing Bentham MSS at University College, box VIII, fo. 130ʳ) (Bentham's comment dated 1822).
[3] Graham Wallas, *The Life of Francis Place, 1771–1854* (3rd edn., New York, 1919), 206.
[4] *Parliamentary Papers* (1823), 2, 261–311.

drafted by George White, a clerk of committees at the House of Commons, and Gravener Henson, a leader of the Nottingham framework knitters.[5] In aspiration a nineteenth-century Statute of Artificers, Moore's bill would have replaced existing legislation with a comprehensive system for regulating industrial relations. (It is revealing that this large bill would not have repealed the Spitalfields Acts, which banned combination in the silk trade but only incident to a scheme of regulation.) According to Francis Place, 'Mr. Moore's bill produced considerable alarm to many members, and especially to ministers, at whose request Mr. Moore at length consented 'that the discussion on its merits should be postponed to the next session.'[6] In the mean time parliament passed a comprehensive Master and Servant Act,[7] designed, as its title spelled out, 'to enlarge the powers of justices [of the peace] in determining complaints between masters and servants'.[8] Thereafter the government looked more favourably on Hume's proposal.

Just at this moment, economic orthodoxy in the person of J. R. McCulloch, a disciple of David Ricardo, denounced Moore's bill. In an article in the influential *Edinburgh Review* for January 1824, artfully timed for maximum parliamentary effect, the economist announced that 'wages, like everything else, ought always to be left to be regulated by the fair and free competition of the parties in the market, and ought never to be controlled by the interference of the Legislator.'[9] Assuming that the meeting of supply and demand in the market-place produced the '*natural* and *proper* rate of wages',[10] as it produced the price of everything else, McCulloch distinguished three cases: wages below the natural rate, at the natural rate,

---

[5] With copies of his bill Moore distributed a pamphlet containing the drafters' clause-by-clause analysis: [George White and Gravener Henson], *A Few Remarks on the State of the Laws, at Present in Existence, for Regulating Masters and Work-People* (1823), 111–37. The copy in the Kress Collection, Graduate School of Business Administration, Harvard Univ., is inscribed—apparently in Moore's own hand—to Lord Holland, the peer who a quarter-century earlier had opposed the 1799 Combination Act. On Henson, see Roy A. Church and S. D. Chapman, 'Gravener Henson and the Making of the English Working Class', in E. L. Jones and G. E. Mingay (eds.), *Land, Labour and Population in the Industrial Revolution: Essays Presented to J. D. Chambers* (London, 1967), 131–61, and Malcolm I. Thomis, 'Gravener Henson: The Man and the Myth', *Transactions of the Thoroton Society of Nottinghamshire*, 75 (1971), 91–7.

[6] Quoted in Wallas, *Life of Place*, 208 (citing British Library, Add. MS 27798, fos. 15–24).

[7] The law of master and servant is the subject of Chap. 7.

[8] 4 Geo. 4, c. 34 (1823) (17 June).

[9] [J. R. McCulloch], 'Combination Laws—Restraints on Emigration, etc.', *Edinburgh Review*, 39 (1824), 318 (attribution in Walter E. Houghton (ed.), *The Wellesley Index to Victorian Periodicals, 1824–1900* (Toronto, 1966–72), i. 465). Cf. David Ricardo: 'Like all contracts, wages should be left to the fair and free competition of the market, and should never be controlled by the interference of the legislature' (*On the Principles of Political Economy and Taxation* (1817), ed. R. M. Hartwell (Harmondsworth, 1971), 126).

[10] McCulloch, *Edinburgh Review*, 39 (1824), 319 (italics in original). Ricardo had defined the 'natural price of labour', as 'that price which is necessary to enable the labourers, one with another, to subsist and to perpetuate their race, without either increase or diminution' (*Principles*, 115).

and above the natural rate. In the first case, voluntary combination to raise wages was just, even commendable. In the second it was 'improper and unreasonable'.[11] Finally, in case wages were already above the natural rate, combination could gain nothing. Legislation was unnecessary in any case. After stressing the difficulty of common action when the labour market was overstocked, McCulloch continued: 'Assuming, however, that the mass of workmen occasionally combine together, it appears absurd in the last degree to suppose that their combinations should ever enable them to obtain from their masters more than a due share of the produce of their labour.'[12] 'The laws to prevent combinations are', he concluded, 'either unnecessary, or unjust and injurious'.[13] Antinomianism only permitted the real (economic) laws to take effect: 'It is impossible that anyone who will calmly consider the subject can resist coming to the conclusion, that a combination for an improper object, or to raise wages above their proper level, must *cure itself*—that it must necessarily bring its own chastisement along with it.'[14] This was, of course, the perennial dream of *laissez-faire* ideologues: that a 'general disease' did not require a general remedy because it would— indeed, 'must'—'*cure itself*'. The calm of the practical man might, however, have been ruffled by McCulloch's subsequent concession that '*the result of the combination* is, in fact, the only test by which we can discover whether the advance of wages claimed by the workmen has been fair and reasonable or the reverse'.[15] Cost-conscious masters might not relish risking their fortunes on the outcome of that test.

Hume, who was already working on the reform of commercial legislation with William Huskisson, newly appointed president of the Board of Trade and himself a believer in Smithian economics, now persuaded the minister to add the combination laws to the terms of a select committee that was to investigate two delicate subjects: laws against the emigration of skilled artisans and, more momentous still, laws against the exportation of advanced machinery.[16] For critics the issue was whether England would export the Industrial Revolution, its new-found source of wealth and power. On 12 February 1824 Hume moved the appointment of the committee in a speech that began with an invocation of the spirit of David Ricardo, who had died the previous year. Commenting on each of the subjects of inquiry in turn, Hume revealed the unity he saw in their diversity. Concerning the emigration of artisans, he announced the principle, applicable to the combination laws as well, that 'every law ought

---

[11] McCulloch, *Edinburgh Review*, 39 (1824), 320.   [12] Ibid. 321.
[13] Ibid. 323.   [14] Ibid 322 (italics in original).
[15] Ibid 323 (italics in original).
[16] See e.g. 5 Geo. 1, c. 27 (1719) (emigration of artisans); 23 Geo. 2, c. 13 (1750) (emigration of artisans and exportation of machinery used in woollen or silk-manufactures); 22 Geo. 3, c. 60 (1782) (emigration of artisans and exportation of machinery used in printing calicoes, muslins, and linen); 25 Geo. 3, c. 67 (1785) (emigration of artisans and exportation of machinery used in making iron and steel); 39 Geo. 3, c. 56 (1799) (emigration of artisans).

to be repealed which shackled any man in the free disposition of his labour, provided that free disposition did not interfere with any vital interest, and thereby endanger the political existence of the state'.[17] (It was the proviso that troubled the doubters.) Concerning the exportation of machinery, Hume predicted that the old, protectionist objection would 'give way before the sounder, more liberal, and more enlightened principles of late years adopted'.[18] These principles, the gospel of Ricardo, formed the keynote of his address.

Regarding the combination laws, Hume implied that he was concerned only with out-of-date legislation and the 1800 Combination Act. He declared roundly that 'if all the penal laws against combinations by workmen for increase of wages were struck out of the Statute-book, the common law of the land would still be amply sufficient to prevent the mischievous effects of such combinations.'[19] For authority Hume appealed to James Scarlett, eminent barrister and member of parliament.[20] Scarlett was familiar with labour law, having been briefed in some of the leading cases on the subject: in *Nield* (1805) and *Ferguson and Edge* (1819) for the prosecution, and in *Connell* (1819) for some of the defendants. Concluding his address, Hume sought the support of Huskisson, 'who had taken such an effective part in removing the restrictions by which the commerce of the country had been long fettered'.[21] This support was readily offered: the president of the Board of Trade spoke warmly on behalf of Hume's motion, which was carried without further ado.

Hume promptly nominated the twenty-one members of the select committee. He himself would serve as chairman. Huskisson, Charles Grant, the vice-president of the Board of Trade, and the Attorney-General Sir John Singleton Copley (son of the famous American portraitist) represented the government. Peter Moore was included, probably because of his endeavours in 1823, but, if Place can be believed, never attended a single session.[22] Finally, Hume extended an open invitation to members to join the committee. The very next day ten volunteers accepted; by early May, two weeks before the conclusion of business, a total of twenty-eight[23] had joined the original group, more than doubling its size.

[17] *Hansard*, 2nd ser., vol. 10, col. 143 (12 Feb. 1824).   [18] Ibid. 144.   [19] Ibid. 146.

[20] James Scarlett (1769–1844) became Attorney-General in 1827 and was knighted; in 1834 he became Chief Baron of the Exchequer and was subsequently created Lord Abinger. As a judge he was responsible for the fellow-servant rule, which prevented workmen from recovering damages from their masters for work-related injuries due to the fault of other workmen (see *Priestley* v. *Fowler*, 3 M. & W. 1, 150 Eng. Rep. 1030 (Exch. 1837)). In addition, he was responsible for deciding the case used to prevent purchasers who bought goods at retail from suing the producer for injuries caused by any defect (see *Winterbottom* v. *Wright*, 10 M. & W. 109, 152 Eng. Rep. 402 (Exch. 1842)).

[21] Hansard, 2nd ser., vol. 10, col. 143 (12 Feb. 1824), 147.

[22] Wallas, *Life of Place*, 213.

[23] *Commons Journal*, 79 (1824) (see index under 'Artizans and Machinery; Select Committee'). The *Journal* lists twenty-nine members added, but one, George Phillips, was also among the original twenty-one.

Between 17 February and 20 May 1824 the committee examined 122 witnesses, including sixty employers, forty-four workmen, and several officials and experts, most notable among the latter, perhaps, the Revd T. R. Malthus. The system by which these witnesses were recruited was described by Francis Place:

Mr. Hume wrote a circular letter announcing the appointment of the Committee, and inviting persons to come and give evidence; copies of this were sent to the mayors and other officers of corporate towns, and to many of the principal manufacturers. Some one country paper having obtained a copy, printed it, and it was presently reprinted in all the newspapers, and thus due notice was given to everybody. Meetings were held in many places; and both masters and men sent up deputations to give evidence.[24]

Very quickly, the combination laws overshadowed the two other items on the agenda, although in parliamentary documents it was still referred to as the select committee on 'artizans and machinery'. While a few witnesses continued to address themselves exclusively to those subjects, no master escaped questions about the combination laws. At this time questioners were not identified in the *Parliamentary Papers*, and although discordant voices are occasionally noticeable, the chairman seemed to dominate the interrogation, frequently asking leading or argumentative questions. Such cross-questioning may explain the reluctance of opponents of repeal to come forward, particularly if, as Lord Stanley claimed in parliament during the course of the inquiry, masters feared violence at the hands of their workmen if they spoke up on behalf of the status quo.[25] Whatever the reason, few witnesses gave the combination laws even grudging support.

If witnesses were led by the chairman, some came well prepared to follow. The story of Francis Place's coaching is by now notorious:

The delegates from the working people had reference to me, and I opened my house to them . . . I heard the story which every one of these men had to tell. I examined and cross-examined them; took down the leading particulars of each case, and then arranged the matter as briefs for Mr. Hume; and, as a rule, for the guidance of the witnesses, a copy was given to each.[26]

In addition, each received a brief discourse on classical economics. In all this, Place was seconded by George White, veteran of 1823 and clerk to the committee. Reconciled to the loss of Moore's bill, White became Place's active collaborator.

In addition to hearing testimony from masters and men, the committee was flooded with petitions urging repeal of the combination laws. These petitions had been precipitated by an organized campaign in the popular

[24] Quoted in Wallas, *Life of Place*, 212 (citing British Library, Add. MS 27798, fos. 15–24).
[25] *Hansard*, 2nd ser., vol. 11, col. 409 (14 Apr. 1824).
[26] Quoted in Wallas, *Life of Place*, 212–13 (citing British Library, Add. MS 27798, fos. 15–24).

press.[27] Originally a response to Moore's bill, they were referred to Hume's committee. In all, 115 petitions against the combination laws were funnelled through parliament to the select committee.[28] On the other hand, only one petition opposing repeal was received, from the cotton-manufacturers of Preston, who urged the committee to recommend no change in any of the three areas under review.

Breaking with customary practice, the select committee made no report to parliament, in the sense of a summary statement of findings and a reasoned recommendation for action. Instead, on 21 May it presented six transcripts of evidence, filling a quarto volume of six hundred pages. The last of these was prefaced by a set of resolutions, single-sentence propositions stating facts or directing action. The emigration of artisans proved easiest: the committee resolved that all restrictions be repealed so that 'artisans may be at liberty to go abroad, and to return home, whenever they may be so disposed, in the same manner as other classes of the community now go and return'.[29] Rejection of mercantilism and the growing appeal of equality before the law, combined with undoubted difficulties in enforcing restrictions, produced quick consensus. A bill to implement this resolution was promptly introduced.[30] The exportation of machinery proved hardest: more than ideological consistency was involved here. In the end, the committee formed no resolution except that perennial favourite of deadlocked politicians: 'further inquiry, and a more complete investigation, should take place'.[31]

It is indicative of the preoccupation with the combination laws that this subject, though it had been added to the terms of reference almost as an afterthought, received the most extended treatment, no fewer than eleven resolutions:

[1.] That it appears, by the evidence before the committee, that combinations of workmen have taken place in England, Scotland and Ireland, often to a great extent,

---

[27] See e.g. *Cobbett's Weekly Register*, 47 (30 Aug. 1823), 553. E. P. Thompson cites later appeals in the *Black Dwarf* (17 Jan. 1824) and in the *Mechanics Magazine* (24 Jan. and 7 Feb. 1824) (*The Making of the English Working Class* (New York, 1963), 520 n. 2).

[28] Calculated from *Commons Journal*, 79 (1824).

[29] Artisan Resolution, 4, *Parliamentary Papers* (1824), 5, 589. For some observers this was the most important question before the committee. A writer—probably Charles Ross—in the *Quarterly Review* devoted only one of twenty-eight pages to the combination laws; the rest focused on the emigration of artisans. 'Artizans and Machinery', *Quarterly Review*, 31 (1825), 391–419 (attribution in *Wellesley Index*, i. 704).

[30] Enacted as 5 Geo. 4, c. 97 (1824).

[31] Machinery Resolution, *Parliamentary Papers* (1824), 5, 589. For others there was more than enough evidence to recommend repeal. See [William Ellis], 'Art. 5', *Westminster Review*, 3 (1825), 386–94 (attribution in Frank W. Fetter, 'Economic Articles in the *Westminster Review* and their Authors, 1824–1851', *Journal of Political Economy*, 70 (1962), 584). None the less, although some restrictions were repealed in 1825, 6 Geo. 4, c. 105, § 163 (repealing 22 Geo. 3, c. 60) and § 174 (repealing 25 Geo. 3, c. 67), the remaining restrictions were not lifted until 1843 (6 & 7 Vict., c. 84, § 24 (1843)).

to raise and keep up their wages, to regulate their hours of working, and to impose restrictions on the masters, respecting apprentices or others whom they might think proper to employ; and that, at the time the evidence was taken, combinations were in existence, attended with strikes or suspension of work; and that the laws have not hitherto been effectual to prevent such combinations.

[2.] That serious breaches of the peace and acts of violence, with strikes of the workmen, often for very long periods, have taken place, in consequence of, and arising out of the combinations of workmen, and been attended with loss to both the masters and the workmen, and with considerable inconvenience and injury to the community.

[3.] That the masters have often united and combined to lower the rates of their workmen's wages, as well as to resist a demand for an increase, and to regulate their hours of working; and sometimes to discharge their workmen who would not consent to the conditions offered to them; which have been followed by suspension of work, riotous proceedings, and acts of violence.

[4.] That prosecutions have frequently been carried on, under the statute and the common law, against the workmen, and many of them have suffered different periods of imprisonment for combining and conspiring to raise their wages, or to resist their reduction, and to regulate their hours of working.

[5.] That several instances have been stated to the committee, of prosecutions against masters for combining to lower wages, and to regulate the hours of working; but no instance has been adduced of any master having been punished for that offence.

[6.] That the laws have not only been inefficient to prevent combinations, either of masters or workmen; but, on the contrary, have, in the opinion of many of both parties, had a tendency, to produce mutual irritation and distrust, and to give a violent character to the combinations, and to render them highly dangerous to the peace of the community.

[7.] That it is the opinion of this committee, that masters and workmen should be freed from such restrictions, as regard the rate of wages and the hours of working, and be left at perfect liberty to make such agreements as they may mutually think proper.

[8.] That, therefore, the statute laws that interfere in these particulars between masters and workmen, should be repealed; and also, that the common law, under which a peaceable meeting of masters or workmen may be prosecuted as a conspiracy, should be altered.

[9.] That the committee regret to find from the evidence, that societies, legally enrolled as benefit societies, have been frequently made the cloak, under which funds have been raised for the support of combinations and strikes, attended with acts of violence and intimidation; and without recommending any specific course, they wish to call the attention of the House to the frequent perversion of these institutions from their avowed and legitimate objects.

[10.] That the practice of settling disputes by arbitration between masters and workmen, has been attended with good effects; and it is desirable that the laws which direct and regulate arbitration, should be consolidated, amended, and made applicable to all trades.

[11.] That it is absolutely necessary, when repealing the combination laws, to enact such a law as may efficiently, and by summary process, punish either workmen or masters, who by threats, intimidation, or acts of violence, should interfere with that perfect freedom which ought to be allowed to each party, of employing his labour or capital in the manner he may deem most advantageous.[32]

Having presented its resolutions on 21 May, the committee acted promptly to implement them. At the session of 24–5 May leave was given to bring in a bill for the repeal of the combination laws. Hume, W. Sturges Bourne, and Peter Moore were deputed to prepare it. (The inclusion of Moore's name on the list may cast doubt on Place's assertion of his indifference.) The initial drafting was committed to Anthony Hammond,[33] a barrister chosen by the Attorney-General, but Place and White made significant alterations before the finished product was presented to the House on 27 May.[34] At the session of 31 May–1 June the bill was considered by a committee of the whole. Several amendments, apparently minor, were made at this time and also on 4 June when the House again resolved itself into a committee of the whole. On 5 June, not ten days after its first presentation, the bill was passed without recorded division. Its passage through the Lords was equally swift; only one, essentially trivial, amendment was made. To this the Commons readily assented at its session of 18–19 June, and on 21 June the bill received the royal assent and entered the statute book as 5 George 4, c. 95. A new arbitration act followed as c. 96, and the act permitting free emigration of artisans as c. 97.

The celerity of passage was due to the absence of debate. Adjournment was drawing near, and interested members had followed the matter in committee. Also, there was a calculated silence on the part of supporters. 'I had still one fear, namely, of speech-making', wrote Francis Place. 'I was quite certain that if the bills came under discussion in the House they would be lost.'[35] In the end, the barbarous laws against combination fell, not as Marx fantasized 'before the threatening bearing of the proletariat',[36] but because of the machinations of clever intriguers who manipulated the select committee, indoctrinated the readers of Reviews, and exploited the workmen's peaceful petitions in favour of a different bill. The process has been labelled, in the curious jargon of the sociologists, 'suscitation'—one of several techniques by which Benthamite ideas were translated into practice.[37]

[32] *Parliamentary Papers* (1824), 5, 589–91. Note the early official use of the word 'strike' (in resolution 2). For the law of strikes in the third quarter of the nineteenth century see Chap. 8. Note also that the committee did not recommend permitting restrictions concerning apprentices.

[33] Anthony Hammond (1758–1838), an authority on criminal law, was particularly busy at this time: in 1824 he testified to a select committee on law reform and prepared a draft criminal code; in 1825 he was consulted by New York State on the reform of its criminal law.

[34] Wallas, *Life of Place*, 215.

[35] Quoted in ibid. 214 (citing British Library, Add. MS 27798, fos. 15–24).

[36] Karl Marx, *Capital: A Critique of Political Economy*, trans. Samuel Moore and Edward Aveling, ed. Friedrich Engels (1887), i. 740 (1st German edn., 1867) (epigraph of the present chapter of this book).

[37] S. E. Finer, 'The Transmission of Benthamite Ideas, 1820–50', in Gillian Sutherland (ed.), *Studies in the Growth of Nineteenth-Century Government* (Totowa, NJ, 1972), 13, 19–26.

What Place and Company had effected was a revolution in the legal status of workmen's organizations. In fulfilment of the resolution 'that . . . the statute laws . . . should be repealed', all the combination acts were erased.[38] The 1800 Combination Act was repealed, although that part of it that repealed the 1799 Act was spared; as already explained, had the repealer been repealed, the earlier act would have revived. The arbitration clauses were repealed and replaced by the companion statute.[39] The relevant parts of the eighteenth-century combination acts described in Chapter 2 were also swept away. Involved were eight acts providing regulations and prohibiting combinations, as well as one, the second weavers' act (1756), that authorized wage regulation by the justices of the peace. Absentmindedly the legislators ignored the fact that only a few days earlier they had repealed both Spitalfields Acts.[40] In a further fit of absence of mind they also overlooked the fact that the wage regulation sections of the second weavers' act had been repealed so long ago as 1757.[41]

In addition, four earlier English acts were repealed. The oldest dated from the reign of Edward I, the statute in Law French, quoted at the beginning of Chapter 3, that defined 'Who be Conspirators'.[42] In actual fact, as we have seen, that statute said nothing whatever about combination but was the foundation of common-law conspiracy which had in time been extended to cover this area—thus lending support to Professor Plucknett's claim that 'a thorough commentary upon the statutes of Edward I would be in effect a history of the common law from the thirteenth century down to the close of the eighteenth'.[43] In 1824 it was repealed in so far as it related to 'combinations or conspiracies of workmen or other persons to obtain an advance or to fix the rate of wages, or to lessen or alter the hours or duration of the time of working, or to decrease the quantity of work, or to regulate or controul the mode of carrying on any manufacture, trade, or business, or the management thereof'.[44] Three other pre-eighteenth-century statutes were ancillary to earlier wage regulation. Within a century of the Black Death and the legislation to which it had given rise, parliament outlawed 'confederacies' of masons that were subverting the 'good course and effect of the statutes of labourers'.[45] In the days of the Tudors concern about inflation led to a crackdown on 'conspiracies' of victuallers and craftsmen.[46] Soon after the Stuart Restoration regulation of silk-manufacture was tightened.[47] The only part of the last-mentioned statute to fall before Place's

[38] See Appendix II, Statutes Repealed by Name in 1824 and 1825.

[39] 5 Geo. 4, c. 96, § 1 (1824) (repealing 39 & 40 Geo. 3, c. 106, §§ 18–22).

[40] 5 Geo. 4, c. 66 (1824) (17 June) (repealing 13 Geo. 3, c. 68 (1773) and 32 Geo. 3, c. 44 (1792)).

[41] 30 Geo. 2, c. 12, § 1 (1757) (repealing 29 Geo. 2, c. 33, §§ 1–2 (1756)). See Chap. 2, n. 103.

[42] 33 Edw. 1, st. 2 (1304).

[43] T. F. T. Plucknett, *The Legislation of Edward I* (Oxford, 1949), 157.

[44] 5 Geo. 4, c. 95, § 1.   [45] 3 Hen. 6, c. 1 (1424).

[46] 2 & 3 Edw. 6, c. 15 (1548).   [47] 13 & 14 Car. 2, c. 15 (1662).

onslaught was the section prohibiting wage-setting by the Corporation of Silk Throwers, in other words, a combination of masters. In all, counting the 1800 Combination Act, fourteen statutes applying to England were repealed, of which twelve outlawed combination by workmen.

Loose writing has led historians (and the public) to believe the number much higher. M. Dorothy George referred in her 1927 article to 'some thirty or forty [combination laws], including Scottish and Irish Acts'.[48] The numbers have a way of growing. A British labour historian in 1981 wrote of 'over forty earlier acts against combination',[49] while in 1987 a popular historian, ignoring George's mention of Scottish and Irish Acts, talked airily of 'nearly fifty' English statutes.[50] Mention of the other component parts of the United Kingdom is, however, key to the discrepancy. Scotland had its own parliament until 1707 and even thereafter retained a distinctive legal system.[51] Unless acts of the Westminster parliament were accommodated to Scottish institutions, they were held not to apply there. The 1800 Combination Act, for instance, was of no effect north of the Tweed.[52] Ireland retained its own parliament until 1800, although its legislation was conditioned during most of its history upon approval from Westminster.[53] Since the union with Great Britain did not become effective until 1 January 1801,[54] the 1800 Combination Act did not apply across the Irish Sea. In consequence, no fewer than twenty-one combination acts existed in 1824 that applied outside England. Three had been passed by the union parliament after 1800: two for Ireland,[55] one for both Ireland and Scotland.[56] Of the remaining eighteen, seven applied to Scotland[57] and eleven to Ireland.[58] The Irish statutes, all but one of which were passed in the eighteenth century, were generally limited, like their English counterparts, to particular trades and places; indeed, a few were modelled directly

---

[48] M. Dorothy George, 'The Combination Laws Reconsidered', *Economic Journal* (Supp.), Economic History Ser., 2 (May 1927), 214.

[49] E. H. Hunt, *British Labour History, 1815–1914* (Atlantic Highlands, NJ, 1981), 198.

[50] Christopher Hibbert, *The English: A Social History, 1066–1945* (New York, 1987), 480.

[51] See 5 Anne, c. 8 (1706) (union of England and Scotland).

[52] *Parliamentary Papers* (1824), 5, 486 (testimony of Sir William Rae, Lord Advocate of Scotland). On the Lord Advocate of Scotland, see Chap. 3, n. 79. On 'The Law of Combination in Scotland', see an article by J. L. Gray in *Economica*, os 8 (1928), 332–50.

[53] 10 Hen. 7 (1495) (Ireland) (Poynings's Law) (repealed by 23 Geo. 3, c. 28 (1783)).

[54] 39 & 40 Geo. 3, c. 67 (1800) (union of Great Britain and Ireland).

[55] 43 Geo. 3, c. 86 (1803); 47 Geo. 3, st. 1, c. 43 (1807).

[56] 57 Geo. 3, c. 122 (1817).

[57] 5 Parl. Jac. 1, c. 78 (1426); 5 Parl. Jac. 1, c. 79 (1426); 5 Parl. Jac. 1, c. 80 (1426); 7 Parl. Jac. 1, c. 102 (1427); 5 Parl. Mar., c. 23 (1551); 7 Parl. Jac. 6, c. 121 (1581); 39 Geo. 3, c. 56 (1799). The last act was applicable only to Scotland.

[58] 33 Hen. 8, st. 1, c. 9 (1542); 3 Geo. 2, c. 14 (1729); 17 Geo. 2, c. 8 (1743); 3 Geo. 3, c. 17 (1763); 3 Geo. 3, c. 34 (1763); 11 & 12 Geo. 3, c. 18 (1771); 11 & 12 Geo. 3, c. 33 (1772); 19 & 20 Geo. 3, c. 19 (1780); 19 & 20 Geo. 3, c. 24 (1780); 19 & 20 Geo. 3, c. 36 (1780); 25 Geo. 3, c. 48 (1785). See Patrick Park, 'The Combination Acts in Ireland, 1727–1825', 14, ns *Irish Jurist* 340–59 (1979).

on English precursors. A 1780 Irish statute regulating the silk trade,[59] for example, was patterned on the first Spitalfields Act (1773). In sum, thirty-five statutes were repealed by name in 1824, of which fourteen applied to England, seven to Scotland, thirteen to Ireland, and one to both Ireland and Scotland. Furthermore, to ensure that no mischief would be caused by any ancient act that happened to have been overlooked, general language was added repealing

all other laws, statutes, and enactments now in force throughout or in any part of the United Kingdom of *Great Britain* and *Ireland*, relative to combinations to obtain an advance of wages, or to lessen or alter the hours or duration of the time of working, or to decrease the quantity of work, or to regulate or controul the mode of carrying on any manufacture, trade, or business, or the management thereof.[60]

The combination acts had always been in Hume's sights: he had specifically inveighed against them in his address to parliament. Less foreseeable, particularly in light of his ostentatious deference to Scarlett's opinion, was that conspiracy would also be touched. Yet the committee had resolved 'that the common law . . . should be altered'. Now, altering the common law was not so simple as repealing assorted statutes. Custom, it was still asserted, made the common law, not parliament; even the judges, the law's oracles, only declared it. The best the legislature could do under the circumstances, it seemed, was to grant an exemption from prosecution:

journeymen, workmen, or other persons who shall enter into any combination to obtain an advance or to fix the rate of wages, or to lessen or alter the hours or duration of the time of working, or to decrease the quantity of work, or to induce another to depart from his service before the end of the time or term for which he is hired, or to quit or return his work before the same shall be finished . . . or to regulate the mode of carrying on any manufacture, trade, or business, or the management thereof, shall not therefore be subject or liable to any indictment or prosecution for conspiracy, or to any other criminal information or punishment whatever, under the common or the statute law.[61]

This was sweeping language indeed. Its principal object of freeing combinations from prosecution for conspiracy was plainly achieved, but two other restrictions—one savouring of the past, the other of the future— were also affected. The hoary crime of leaving work unfinished, the centre-piece of the law of master and servant, was modified: no prosecution 'under the common or the statute law' could be brought for inducing a workman to quit or return work 'before the same shall be finished'. Nor could a prosecution be mounted for inducing a workman to depart 'before the end of the time or term for which he is hired'. In more recognizable terminology this would be inducing a breach of contract, a still inchoate offence that

[59] 19 & 20 Geo. 3, c. 24 (1780). [60] 5 Geo. 4, c. 95, § 1.
[61] Ibid. § 2. Penal proceedings presently under way under any repealed statute or for conspiracy to commit an act exempted from punishment were declared null and void (ibid. § 4).

would later become a major issue in the law of strikes. Both had been included only the year before in the Master and Servant Act (1823).

In pursuit of the new ideal of legal equality, combinations of masters were also exempted from punishment. These combinations were conceived of as mirror images of combinations of workmen. Now that wage regulation was a thing of the past, it was no longer possible to speculate, as Lord Kenyon had in *Hammond and Webb* (1799), about masters combining to pay *more* than the approved wages. Under the tutelage of the new political economy masters were assumed to seek only to lower the rate of wages or to increase the hours or quantity of work. All statutes relative to such combinations were repealed.[62] In addition, the act declared that 'masters, employers, or other persons' who combined for such purposes 'shall not therefore be subject or liable to any indictment or prosecution for conspiracy, or to any other criminal information or punishment whatever, under the common or the statute law.[63]

Thus far, the 1824 Act was negative only: it swept away all the laws (common as well as statute) on combination and conspiracy. The positive part of the act defined the only remaining legal limit on industrial action, implementing the committee's resolution 'to enact such a law as may efficiently, and by summary process, punish either workmen or masters, who by threats, intimidation, or acts of violence, should interfere with that perfect freedom which ought to be allowed to each party . . .'. Punishment of up to two months' imprisonment with or without hard labour was provided. The distinction between the common gaol and the house of correction where hard labour was exacted was no longer so sharp as it had once been. Prison reformers in the early nineteenth century had begun to emphasize the corrective discipline of the gaol as well, and in 1865 gaols and bridewells were amalgamated to form local prisons.[64] In the 1824 Act the distinction had already been pushed out of the text and lingered only in the 'form of conviction and commitment' in the attached schedule. This punishment would be meted out

[1.] if any person, by violence to the person or property, by threats or by intimidation, shall wilfully or maliciously force another to depart from his hiring or work before the end of the time or term for which he is hired, or return his work before the same shall be finished, or damnify, spoil, or destroy any machinery, tools, goods, wares, or work, or prevent any person not hired from accepting any work or employment; or
[2.] if any person shall wilfully or maliciously use or employ violence to the person or property, threats or intimidation towards another, on account of his not complying with or conforming to any rules, orders, resolutions, or regulations made

---

[62] Ibid. § 1.   [63] Ibid. § 3.
[64] See Joanna Innes, 'Prisons for the Poor: English Bridewells, 1555–1800', in Francis Snyder and Douglas Hay (eds.), *Labour, Law and Crime: An Historical Perspective* (London, 1987), 107–9.

to obtain an advance of wages, or to lessen or alter the hours of working, to decrease the quantity of work, or to regulate the mode of carrying on any manufacture, trade or business, or the management thereof; or

[3.] if any person, by violence to the person or property, by threats or by intimidation, shall wilfully or maliciously force any master or mistress manufacturer, his or her foreman or agent, to make any alteration in their mode of regulating, managing, conducting, or carrying on their manufacture, trade, or business.[65]

The offence was the same whether committed singly or in combination, and the same punishment was provided for both.[66] As radical individualists, Hume and Place may have perceived no greater danger in combined action than that caused by the sum of its parts.

The remainder of the act concerned the procedure for punishing offences, as called for in the resolution, 'efficiently, and by summary process'. As under the 1800 Combination Act, prosecution under the 1824 Act began with complaint and information on oath before at least one justice of the peace.[67] Such justice then summoned the accused to appear before two justices at a time and place to be named, although this time it was specified: 'such place to be as near to the place where cause of such complaint shall have arisen as may be'.[68] If the person summoned failed to appear and if it was proved on oath that the summons had been served personally or left at the person's usual place of abode at least twenty-four hours before the time set for the hearing, then the justices of the peace issued a warrant for his arrest.[69] This was the normal procedure. As in 1800, however, a speedier alternative was also provided: at the justices' discretion, they could dispense with the summons and proceed immediately to order the arrest of the accused.[70]

Once the person charged was before the justices of the peace, whether by summons or by warrant, the examination began. Predictably no provision was made for proceeding *in absentia*. To be convicted the accused had to confess or two witnesses had to testify to his offence. The requirement of two witnesses more than doubled the difficulty of obtaining a conviction under the act. We have traced the elaboration of provisions in earlier statutes to secure the needed witness, probably a fellow-workman: summonses had been provided, then compulsion to testify, finally immunity from prosecution. Requiring two witnesses was an innovation in the history of combination laws.[71] All previous statutes had required but one; the common law asked no more for a conviction for conspiracy—or for any other

---

[65] 5 Geo. 4, c. 95, § 5 (numbers in brackets added).   [66] Ibid. § 6.
[67] For a key for comparing the 1824 and 1800 Acts, see Appendix III.
[68] 5 Geo. 4, c. 95, § 7.   [69] Ibid.   [70] Ibid.
[71] Other statutes conferring summary jurisdiction may have required more than one witness: in an ambiguous passage Blackstone said that 'the magistrate, in summary proceedings, may go on to examine one or more witnesses, as the statute may require, upon oath' (*Commentaries*, iv. 280).

offence except perjury.[72] Occasionally delicate consciences were troubled by the fact that Jewish law had demanded at least two witnesses[73] and that this rule had been affirmed in the New Testament, not just by St Paul[74] but by Jesus Christ himself.[75] Canon law required two witnesses,[76] and so incidentally did Roman law[77] and the Western European legal systems based on it,[78] but in England statutes required two witnesses only for treason.[79] America's Founding Fathers followed English practice, writing the extra requirement into the United States Constitution itself: 'No person shall be convicted of treason unless on the testimony of two witnesses to the same overt act, or on confession in open court.'[80]

Provisions to secure the necessary evidence recapitulated earlier developments. The original justice of the peace was required at the request in writing of any party to summon witnesses to appear for examination. If a witness did not appear or offer some reasonable excuse and if it was proved on oath that the summons had been served personally or left at the person's usual place of abode at least twenty-four hours before the time set for appearance, then two justices of the peace could issue a warrant for his arrest. A witness who refused to testify could be committed to gaol for up to two months, or until he was prepared to answer.[81] Finally, it was provided that no witness could refuse to testify on the ground that he had himself offended against the act; in such cases, however, he was granted immunity from prosecution.[82] To ensure impartiality in the justices, the provision against masters sitting as judges in their own cases received an extraordinary extension: 'No justice of the peace, being also a master, or the father or son of any master in any trade or manufacture, shall act as such justice under this Act.'[83] Presumably the only qualified magistrates were landowners or parsons of old families, all of whose sons (even the youngest!) had eschewed trade.

As opposed to the 1800 Act, the 1824 Act lengthened the period of limitation of actions: in place of the earlier three months, six months was now provided.[84] Also unlike the settlement of 1800, the 1824 Act provided

---

[72] See John H. Wigmore, 'Required Number of Witnesses: A Brief History of the Numerical System in England', 15 *Harvard Law Review* 83–108 (1901–2) (repr. in id., *Wigmore on Evidence*, rev. James H. Chadbourne (Boston, 1978), § 2032).

[73] Deut. 19: 15.

[74] 2 Cor. 13: 1; 1 Tim. 5: 19–20.   [75] Matt. 18: 16.

[76] *Corpus Juris Canonici*, Decret. Greg., lib. ii, tit. xx *de testibus*, c. 23; see also ibid., c. 28, c. 4 (quoting Bible).

[77] *Code of Justinian* 4.20.9.

[78] See e.g. Robert Joseph Pothier, *Œuvres*, ed. M. Siffrein (1821), xiv. 81 (*Traité de la Procédure Civile*, pt. 1, chap. 3; composed prior to 1777).

[79] 7 & 8 Will. 3, c. 3 (1696); 1 & 2 Ph. & Mar., c. 10 (1554); 5 & 6 Edw. 6, c. 11 (1552); 1 Edw. 6, c. 12 (1547). See L. M. Hill, 'The Two-Witness Rule in English Treason Trials: Some Comments on the Emergence of Procedural Law', *American Journal of Legal History*, 12 (1968), 95–111.

[80] US Const. art. III, § 3, cl. 1.   [81] 5 Geo. 4, c. 95, § 9.

[82] Ibid. § 10.   [83] Ibid. § 8.   [84] Ibid. § 13.

for no appeal from the decision of the justices of the peace.[85] Whatever it was worth—and *Ridgway* (1822) showed that it was not worthless—appeal to quarter sessions was denied. Perhaps in consequence of this exclusion, the act neglected even to require the transmission of records of conviction, although forms were provided in a schedule attached to the act.[86] Since there was no mention of *certiorari*, however, that means of review presumably remained available. In case of an unsuccessful counter-action against a person enforcing the act, plaintiff was liable for full costs.[87]

The repeal of the combination laws coincided with one of the periodic upturns in the business cycle,[88] giving workmen increased bargaining power. Strikes, or 'suspension of work' as the 1824 resolutions called them, blossomed all over the British Isles. Inevitably there was violence in Dublin, and in Glasgow the refusal of journeymen weavers to deal with an unpopular master attracted national attention. The alacrity with which workmen seized their new-found freedom implied an efficient and well-informed organization. To some extent friendly or benefit societies had substituted for trade combinations as such during the dark years of repression; the select committee in 1824 had called the attention of the House to this 'perversion'. Francis Place knew whereof it spoke: years earlier he had reorganized the breeches-makers' union under the guise of a tontine sick club.[89] Though the laws against combination and conspiracy had proved unable to destroy this organization, they had at least restrained its capacity to strike. Freed from this restraint, workmen sought to try their strength with masters, and successful strikes brought pleas for renewed repression. Put to the test, workmen's claims for higher wages seemed unanswerable by ordinary means. The shipping interest, long familiar with labour militancy, was the loudest in its complaint. Union treasuries were again the target. A proposed bill drafted by the shipowners would have prohibited workmen from subscribing funds for any purpose without the consent of a justice of the peace; even approved funds could have been raised only if a justice served as treasurer.[90]

The architects of repeal, still committed to *laissez-faire*, opposed the forces of reaction. Joseph Hume, on the urging of Francis Place, wrote to many provincial newspapers and to many strike-leaders.[91] In an open letter to the Glasgow weavers he warned that their 'imprudent conduct' would lead the masters 'to apply for and to obtain a renewal of the power they formerly had to oppress'.[92] George White issued his own 'Address to the

[85] 5 Geo. 4, c. 95, § 12.
[86] Ibid. § 11 and schedule.   [87] Ibid. § 14.
[88] See W. W. Rostow, 'Trade Cycles, Harvests, and Politics, 1790–1850', in *The British Economy of the Nineteenth Century* (Oxford, 1948), 116.
[89] Wallas, *Life of Place*, 19.   [90] Ibid. 223.   [91] Ibid. 218.
[92] Repr. in [George White (comp.)], *Combination and Arbitration Laws, Artizans and Machinery* (1824), 3 (attribution in Judith Blow Williams, *A Guide to the Printed Materials for English Social and Economic History* (New York, 1926), ii. 313).

Working People', in which he counselled caution.[93] Place himself wrote numerous letters, including one to the Glasgow weavers.[94]

The government's response was to seek a new select committee. In a major speech on 29 March 1825 Huskisson himself moved its appointment and announced its terms of reference: 'to inquire into the effects of the act of the 5th Geo. IV, c. 95, in respect to the conduct of workmen and others in different parts of the United Kingdom: and to report their opinion how far it may be necessary to repeal or amend the said act'.[95] Such an investigation was needed because of what he called 'the hurried and inconsiderate manner'[96] in which the combination laws had been repealed the year before. Huskisson belaboured the 1824 committee for issuing resolutions rather than a report. He also observed that the 1824 Act had passed without discussion.[97]

The occasion was an awkward one. Hudson Gurney, who had served on the 1824 committee, reminded Huskisson that he 'or the vice president of the Board of Trade [Charles Grant] and another right honourable gentleman connected with administration [Attorney-General Sir John Singleton Copley] attended all its sittings' and that it 'had come unanimously to the resolutions which closed their inquiries, with the full approbation, as he then understood, of all those right honourable gentlemen'.[98] Huskisson had no alternative but to shuffle. Admitting his own membership, he claimed the distraction of other business. The very size of the previous committee was an embarrassment. Sir Robert Peel, then Home Secretary, claimed 'he was not aware before that evening, that the committee which sat upon the combination laws last year, had consisted of so many as fifty members',[99] and Charles Grant was quick to add that 'not more than half that number attended it'[100]—not a bad showing for parliament at any time, let alone during the Age of Liverpool. However uncomfortable, the government was determined on change. This determination sprang not from disinterested zeal to protect individual workmen against the claims of combination, as Dicey later claimed,[101] but rather from the feeling that the 1824 legislation had gone too far in the direction of labour. The gravamen of Huskisson's appeal was not for the rights of men but for the rights of masters:

As a general principle, he admitted that every man had an inherent right to carry his own labour to whatever market he liked; and so to make the best of it: and, accordingly, he had always maintained that labour was the poor man's capital. But,

---

[93] Ibid. 1–3.
[94] Wallas, *Life of Place*, 218–20.
[95] *Hansard*, 2nd ser., vol. 12, col. 1301 (29 Mar. 1825).
[96] *Annual Register*, 67 (1825), 91.
[97] *Hansard*, 2nd ser., vol. 12, col. 1290.   [98] Ibid. 1310.   [99] Ibid. 1305.
[100] Ibid. 1311.
[101] A. V. Dicey, *Lectures on the Relation between Law and Public Opinion in England during the Nineteenth Century* (2nd edn., London, 1914), 197. Dicey admitted that the 'true' motives were 'unperceived' at the time.

then, on the other hand, he must as strenuously contend for the perfect freedom of those who were to give employment to that labour.[102]

This time Huskisson named the committee. Indicative, perhaps, of the government's intention to seek moderate rather than drastic change, he sought no revolution in personnel. Nine names on Hume's original list, including Hume himself, were carried over. In addition, Huskisson nominated five of the self-appointed additions to the earlier committee. But government control was to be tighter: Peel was among the seven new members, and the all-important chairmanship was confided to Thomas Wallace, Master of the Mint in Ireland. If Place stage-managed the first committee, the government directed the second. A new discipline is evident in the proceedings. Rather than attempt to canvass the whole economy, the committee selected seven sectors for study: (1) the coopers of London, (2) the seamen in the North, (3) the weavers in Yorkshire, (4) the shipwrights of Bristol, (5) the shipwrights on the Thames, (6) Ireland, and (7) Scotland. Concentration on shipping reflects the initiative taken by the shipowners in agitating against the 1824 Act. The committee moved promptly in investigating these sectors and completed its hearings in less than two months. Government control is evident in more than matters of procedure: in addition, the committee was fed a diet of communications from the Home Office and the Board of Trade.[103] This regimen, perhaps, explains the lessened interest among members outside the committee, as shown by the smaller number of volunteers. Unlike the stampede by twenty-eight members in 1824, a more modest (but still substantial) corps of ten added their names to the list in 1825.

Not surprisingly, the committee eschewed newfangled resolutions and embodied its findings and recommendations in an orthodox report, presented to the House on 6 June 1825. Equally unsurprising was the emphasis in the report, foreshadowed in Huskisson's speech, on the rights of capital. This issue was clearly perceived by the committee: what it reprobated was 'that assumption of control on the part of the workmen in the conduct of any business or manufacture which is utterly incompatible with the necessary authority of the master at whose risk, and by whose capital, it is to be carried on'.[104] The remedy, however, was not to be reaction. The committee was emphatic that the old legislation should not be revived. Indeed, it sought to clothe itself in the 1824 resolutions; what it recommended, it claimed, was 'in strict conformity to the principle' of those resolutions.[105] However that may be, it proposed to restore the common law of conspiracy, albeit with an exemption for peaceful consultation on wages or hours. Why exactly this course was chosen rather than more

---

[102] *Hansard*, 2nd ser., vol. 12, col. 1292. Francis Place responded to this speech in a pamphlet, 'Observations on Mr. Huskisson's Speech' (1825).
[103] *Parliamentary Papers* (1825), 4, 501.   [104] Ibid. 508.   [105] Ibid. 506.

straightforward legislation was not explained. Or rather, if there was an explanation, it was a preference for the evolutionism of common law: combinations outside the exception should be 'open as heretofore, to the animadversion of the common law, and be dealt with according to the circumstances of each case'.[106] In other words, the programme implied in Hume's reference to Scarlett a year earlier was now in fact to be implemented. Violence or near-violence would, however, remain a statutory crime, punishable as before 'efficiently, and by summary process'.

Why did the committee determine to avoid a restoration of the status quo ante 1824? Certainly, the hotchpotch of ancient statutes offered no allure to the practical men gathered around Sir Robert Peel. Also, the workmen's response to restoration was bound to be powerful, perhaps violent. Expectations had been raised. Reflection on the French Revolution as well as on England's own revolutionary experience in the seventeenth century had deepened perceptions concerning the use of power and the management of change, even among Tories. In the words of an anonymous contributor to the *Monthly Review*, no enthusiast for classical economics:

Yet we do not mean to insinuate that we are prepared to wish for the re-enactment, in their original shape, of those laws which have been recently repealed. All counter-revolutions are injurious when they attempt to restore things exactly to their former state. Allowance must be made for the feelings which have been generated, and the ideas which have grown up in the minds of the workmen during this period of Saturnalian liberty which they have enjoyed.[107]

None the less it was the rights of capital, not the rights of labour, that claimed the attention of parliament. Huskisson was particularly adamant that there was to be no going back on the repeal of the apprenticeship clauses of the Statute of Artificers. Hume and Place had agreed with that the year earlier. Although workmen could participate with masters in setting wages and hours, they were not to attempt to regulate the supply of skilled labour.[108] One government supporter even went so far as to claim that such regulation had 'nothing to do with the rate of wages, but was a dictation to the master, as to the way in which he was to conduct his business'. Expressed in such apparently libertarian terms, the rights of capital became the right of an individual workman 'to make his own agreement with his employer'.[109] As one master had informed the 1824 committee, nothing struck more effectually at the root of all combination.[110] Another parliamentarian openly avowed the economic consequences of such

[106] Ibid. 508.
[107] Anon., 'Critique of a Speech by Francis Jeffrey in Praise of Joseph Hume, 18 November 1825, Edinburgh', *Monthly Review*, 3rd ser., 1 (1826), 9. Jeffrey's speech was published as 'Combinations of Workmen' (1825).
[108] *Hansard*, 2nd ser., vol. 13, col. 354.   [109] Ibid. 357 (Maberly).
[110] *Parliamentary Papers* (1824), 5, 27 (testimony of Alexander Galloway, the leading engineering employer in London). According to E. P. Thompson, Galloway had once believed in the communism of Thomas Spence (*English Working Class*, 156, 161).

rhetoric: 'He was a friend to the workmen: and he now spoke in behalf of that large body of individuals, who had taken, or who were ready to take, less wages than the associators thought they should'; it was parliament's duty to protect their 'right . . . of appreciating what their labour was worth'[111]—how little, in other words. Such sentiments were an ironic echo of Adam Smith's critique of wage regulation: while the sage had objected to levelling down 'the ablest and most industrious',[112] government spokesmen in 1825 denounced the attempt to level up. This solicitude for capital was well understood out-of-doors. It prompted Thomas Hodgskin to compose the early socialist tract, *Labour Defended against the Claims of Capital*: 'In all the debates on the law passed during the late session of Parliament, on account of the combinations of workmen, much stress is laid on the necessity of protecting capital. What capital performs is therefore a question of considerable importance, which the author was, on this account, induced to examine.'[113] Unlike the government supporters, Hodgskin found capital's contribution to be minimal and labour to be the original source of value.

Despite Huskisson's complaint about the hurry in 1824, the new bill's passage was even more meteoric. Introduced at the session of 17–18 June, it passed without recorded division on 30 June. The only real threat to its original purity was an amendment, reminiscent of Whig sentiment a quarter-century earlier, that would have substituted trial by jury for summary proceedings. This was defeated by a vote of seventy-eight to fifty-three.[114] A successful amendment, restoring appeal to quarter sessions, was moved by the Attorney-General; the government was notably more willing than Hume or Place to check the discretion of the local justices of the peace. So rapid was the bill's progress through the Commons that it was left to the upper chamber to fill up a couple of blanks.[115] Even this did not delay their lordships above a week. The Commons accepted the Lords' amendments on 5 July. The next day came the royal assent, and the new act was enrolled as 6 George 4, c. 129.

First, the 1824 Act was repealed,[116] its provisions not having been found 'effectual'.[117] New legislation was said to be needed 'as well for the security and personal freedom of individual workmen in the disposal of their skill and labour, as for the security of the property and persons of masters and employers'.[118] So all the old legislation was repealed once more: the same thirty-five statutes enumerated in 1824 were again repealed by name, and a

[111] *Hansard*, 2nd ser., vol. 13, col. 360 (Lord A. Hamilton).

[112] Adam Smith, *An Inquiry into the Nature and Causes of the Wealth of Nations*, 142. See Chap. 2, n. 68.

[113] [Thomas Hodgskin], *Labour Defended against the Claims of Capital* (1825), 2 (3rd edn., with introd. by G. D. H. Cole, 1922).

[114] *Hansard*, 2nd ser., vol. 13, col. 1407 (amendment moved by Thomas Denman).

[115] *Lords Journal*, 62 (1825), 1277.

[116] For a section-by-section comparison of the 1825 Act with the 1824 Act, see Appendix IV.

[117] 6 Geo. 4, c. 129, § 1.   [118] Ibid.

general repealer was also included.[119] The general prohibition of prosecution for common-law conspiracy was not, however, carried over; instead, two limited exemptions were provided for workmen

[1.] who shall meet together for the sole purpose of consulting upon and determining the rate of wages or prices, which the persons present at such meeting or any of them, shall require or demand for his or their work, or the hours or time for which he or they shall work in any manufacture, trade, or business, or
[2.] who shall enter into any agreement, verbal or written, among themselves, for the purpose of fixing the rate of wages or prices which the parties entering into such agreement, or any of them, shall require or demand for his or their work, or for the hours or time for which he or they will work, in any manufacture, trade, or business.[120]

Wages and hours were to be the only legitimate objects of combination. Masters were granted a complementary right to meet and agree on the wages they would pay and the hours their shops and factories would be open.[121]

The sole substantive section outlawed anew the use of 'violence . . . threats, or intimidation'. Punishment of up to three months in gaol with or without hard labour—compared to the two-month maximum under the 1824 Act—was provided

[1.] if any person shall by violence to the person or property, or by threats or intimidation, or by molesting or in any way obstructing another, force or endeavour to force any journeyman, manufacturer, workman, or other person hired or employed in any manufacture, trade, or business, to depart from his hiring, employment, or work, or to return his work before the same shall be finished, or prevent or endeavour to prevent any journeyman, manufacturer, workman, or other person not being hired or employed from hiring himself to, or from accepting work or employment from any person or persons.[122]

Compared with the corresponding section of the 1824 Act, this section effected several changes. First, the interdicted means were expanded to include 'molesting or . . . obstructing'. By adding words of such vague and legally indeterminate meaning the new statute invited judicial interpretation. Second, the words 'wilfully or maliciously' were dropped from the description of the offence. It may be recalled that these words had not been included in the 1799 Combination Act but had been added in 1800. In the legislation of 1824–5 that process was reversed. It is difficult to imagine that they made much difference either way. Third, the words 'endeavour to force' and 'endeavour to prevent' were added as alternative offences to successfully forcing or preventing. The mere attempt would be criminal. Fourth, in the crime of forcing or endeavouring to force a workman to

[119] Ibid. § 2.   [120] Ibid. § 4.   [121] Ibid. § 5.
[122] Ibid. § 3. Note that here 'manufacturer' is synonymous with journeyman and means a 'person hired or employed'.

depart from his hiring, the words 'before the end of the time or term for which he is hired' were omitted. This made it risky to approach a workman even at the end of his service. As we shall see, inducing breach of contract was to prove a thorny issue in the developing law of strikes at mid-century. Finally, the offence of damnifying, spoiling, or destroying any machinery, tools, goods, wares, or work—included in 1824—was dropped in 1825. This offence was certainly covered by other statutes, most providing Draconian punishments.[123]

Up to three months in gaol with or without hard labour was also provided

[2.] if any person shall use or employ violence to the person or property of another, or threats or intimidation, or shall molest or in any way obstruct another for the purpose of forcing or inducing such person to belong to any club or association, or to contribute to any common fund, or to pay any fine or penalty, or on account of his not belonging to any particular club or association, or not having contributed or having refused to contribute to any common fund, or to pay any fine or penalty, or on account of his not having complied or of his refusing to comply with any rules, orders, resolutions, or regulations made to obtain an advance or to reduce the rate of wages, or to lessen or alter the hours of working, or to decrease or alter the quantity of work, or to regulate the mode of carrying on any manufacture, trade, or business, or the management thereof.[124]

This clause differed in three respects from the 1824 version: the illegal means were again expanded by the inclusion of words referring to molestation and obstruction; the words 'wilfully or maliciously' were again dropped from the description of the offence; and the illegal purposes were increased by the addition of words referring to coerced support for any 'club or association' or obedience to its rules. The name 'trade union' had still not appeared—the Webbs found no instance of its use in the first third of the nineteenth century[125]—but some substitute for the bad names 'combination' and 'conspiracy' was necessary in light of the limited exemption from prosecution.

Finally, up to three months in gaol with or without hard labour was provided

[3.] if any person shall by violence to the person or property of another, or by threats or intimidation, or by molesting or in any way obstructing another, force or

---

[123] In 1827 the statutes concerning malicious injury to property were consolidated (7 & 8 Geo. 4, c. 30). See § 3 (destroying silk, wool, linen, or cotton in the loom or machinery used in their manufacture punishable by transportation for not less than 7 years or imprisonment for not more than 4 years and—for male offenders—up to 3 whippings); § 4 (destroying machinery not covered by § 3 punishable by transportation for 7 years or imprisonment for not more than 2 years and—for male offenders—up to 3 whippings); § 8 (rioters destroying factories or machinery punishable by death).

[124] 6 Geo. 4, 129, § 3.

[125] Sidney Webb and Beatrice Webb, *The History of Trade Unionism* (rev. edn., London, 1920), 113.

endeavour to force any manufacturer or person carrying on any trade or business, to make any alteration in his mode of regulating, managing, conducting, or carrying on such manufacture, trade, or business, or to limit the number of his apprentices, or the number or description of his journeymen, workmen, or servants.[126]

In this clause, too, changes were made that enlarged the scope of the offence or contracted the number of defences. The words 'molesting or . . . obstructing' were again added, the words 'wilfully or maliciously' again dropped. Endeavouring to force as well as forcing any manufacturer was outlawed. Finally, the explicit reference to apprentices was added.

The procedure for enforcing the statute was as summary as before, although some of the excesses of the earlier act were pruned. A prosecution began with complaint and information on oath before at least one justice of the peace. Such justice then summoned the person charged to appear before two justices of the peace 'at a certain time and place to be specified';[127] unlike in 1824, it was not required that the place specified be 'as near to the place where cause of such complaint shall have arisen as may be'. If the person summoned failed to appear and if it was proved on oath that the summons had been served personally or left at the person's usual place of abode at least twenty-four hours before the time set for the hearing, then the justices issued a warrant for his arrest. This was the normal procedure. As in 1824, a speedier alternative was also provided: the justices could omit the initial summons and proceed directly from complaint and information to warrant, if they saw fit. The examination began once the person charged was before the justices or—under a clause not included in 1824—'upon proof on oath of such person or persons absconding'.[128] This section, copied from the 1800 Act, revived the trial *in absentia*, originally designed to satisfy the complaint of the master millwrights. It remained on the books until 1871. For a conviction the accused had to confess or one witness had to testify to his offence. The extraordinary requirement of two witnesses was predictably dropped.

In order to secure the necessary evidence two justices of the peace were empowered to summon a witness at the request in writing of any party.[129] If the witness failed to appear or offer some reasonable excuse and if it was proved on oath that the summons had been served personally or left at the person's usual place of abode at least twenty-four hours before the time set for the hearing, then the justices could issue a warrant for his arrest. A

---

[126] 6 Geo. 4, c. 129, § 3. Note that here 'manufacturer' means a 'person carrying on any trade or business', that is, a master.

[127] Ibid. § 7.   [128] Ibid.

[129] Ibid. § 8. Unlike the 1824 Act which clearly permitted one justice of the peace to summon witnesses, the 1825 Act seemed to require two: 'the justices of the peace before whom any such complaint and information shall be made as aforesaid . . . are hereby authorized and required' to summon witnesses as requested. The same section went on, however, to refer to '*his* or their summons'. And it was plain that the complaint and information could be made 'before any *one or more* justice or justices of the peace' (ibid. § 7 (emphasis added)).

recalcitrant witness was to be committed to gaol for three months or until he saw fit to answer.[130] Finally, it was provided that no one could refuse to testify on the ground of self-incrimination; a witness could be compelled to give evidence but was granted immunity from prosecution.[131]

To no one's surprise, perhaps, the sweeping disqualification of justices of the peace who were also masters or the fathers or sons of masters in any trade, included in 1824, was relaxed: 'No justice of the peace also a master in the particular trade or manufacture, in or concerning which any offence is charged to have been committed under this Act, shall act as such justice under this Act.'[132] Like the 1824 Act, that of 1825 imposed a six months' limitation on actions.[133] Unlike the earlier Act, it provided a regular system for record-keeping. Convictions, engrossed on parchment, had to be drawn up 'in the form or to the effect set forth in the schedule'[134] (see Fig. 2). Such convictions had then to be transmitted to quarter sessions and filed with its records.[135] In another departure from 1824—added, as we have seen, on the motion of the Attorney-General—the 1825 Act permitted an appeal to quarter sessions. Pending decision, execution of the sentence was suspended if the appellant entered into a recognizance for £10 with two sureties, also for £10.[136] The sessions heard and determined the appeal and awarded costs to either party. Again, in the absence of express prohibition, the writ of *certiorari* presumably remained available.

FIG. 2.   Form of Conviction and Commitment (1825)

Be it remembered, that on the ____ day of ____ in the ____ year of His Majesty's reign, and in the year of our Lord ____ A.B. is convicted before us [*naming the justices*] two of His Majesty's justices of the peace for the county, [*or* riding, division, city, liberty, town, or place] of ____ of having [*stating the offence*] contrary to the Act made in the sixth year of the reign of King *George* the Fourth, intituled An Act [*here set forth the Title of this Act*]; and we the said justices do hereby order and adjudge the said A.B. for the said offence to be committed to and confined in the common gaol for the said county, [*or* riding, division, city, liberty, town, or place] for the space of ____ *or* to be committed to the house of correction at ____ within the said county, [*or* riding, division, city, liberty, town, or place], there to be kept to hard labour for the space of ____.

Given under our hands, the day and year above written.

Source: 6 Geo. 4, c. 129 (1825).

[130] 6 Geo. 4, c. 129, § 8.
[131] Ibid. § 6.
[132] Ibid. § 13.
[133] Ibid. § 7.
[134] Ibid. § 9.
[135] Ibid. § 10.
[136] Ibid. § 12.

Unlike earlier combination acts, the 1825 Act made specific reference to Scotland and accommodated to procedures north of the Tweed. A Scottish sheriff could take the place of two justices of the peace in the trial of offences, and, more notably, all prosecutions under the act had to be initiated by the Scottish Public Prosecutor.[137] England, as we have seen, still lacked a comparable legal officer and most prosecutions were begun by private complainants.

In 1825 the economic changes entailed by the Industrial Revolution were still far from complete, and the social changes consequent on the economic ones had only just begun. Belated by the French wars, these developments occurred in a society still greatly influenced by eighteenth-century values. Fifty years later, England was a fully fledged industrial nation, the world's first. Capital was organized in companies, labour in trade unions. The leap into the democratic dark had been managed successfully, and the political élite was learning to live with its new masters. While confronting these challenges during this long half-century, England changed in every significant respect: economically, socially, politically. But labour law changed little. Until 1871 when it was repealed and replaced, the 1825 Act remained labour's Magna Carta, such as it was. The eighteenth century had, as we have seen, exalted legal procedure and dealt with issues piecemeal. The legal ideal of the nineteenth century was equality; only a 'savage race', as Tennyson put it, deserved 'unequal laws'.[138] The 1825 Act was equal in the sense that it applied to masters as well as to men, to all trades in all places, to every year in a half-century of fundamental change. It set the ground rules, so to speak, for an economic contest that was fought over changing terrain.

The 1825 Act permitted common action in pursuit of common claims for wages and hours; yet the sanctions available to labour could be effectively applied only by groups that were strategically placed economically or socially. Concerted leave-taking would be effective only when new recruits, trained or quickly trainable, were not standing by. Concert meant organization, discipline, and loyalty. Success usually depended on money, and a sizeable fund could be raised only by the well paid. The ground rules, in other words, favoured the skilled workmen who constituted the 'aristocracy of labour'.[139] Unskilled workmen, on the other hand, had little chance to organize effectively. Although the law fell equally on the skilled and the unskilled, the latter were normally unable to make use of their lawful rights. The chronic and crushing oversupply of unskilled labour throughout the period, except at the very peaks of booms, made permanent

---

[137] Ibid. § 11.

[138] Alfred Tennyson, 'Ulysses' (1842), l. 4.

[139] For a succinct survey of the current debate surrounding the significance of the aristocracy of labour, see Richard Price, *Labour in British Society: An Interpretative History* (London, 1986), 2–4.

and effective organization an impossibility. While skilled labourers were able in many cases to create an exception in their own behalf, the unskilled were relentlessly taught the uselessness of their attempts to control the supply of labour.

Between 1825 and 1871 labour law changed only in detail. Parliament acted once: in 1859 it passed a brief act concerning strikes to explain the meaning of the terms 'molesting' and 'obstructing', the 'beautiful fragments' Marx had caustically referred to. Otherwise it left to the courts the task of construing the vague immunities and vaguer offences laid down in 1825. By now the distinction should be clear between prosecutions on the act for combination, tried by summary procedure, and prosecutions off the act (and therefore at common law) for conspiracy, tried by standard procedure. In addition, it has been observed that prosecutions at common law could be for conspiracy as such, a common-law crime like any other, or for conspiracy to violate a statute, a sort of adjunct to the law of attempts. After 1825 the latter offence would, of course, be based on the penal section of that act. Whether on it or off it, however, all criminal prosecutions necessarily had to be squared with the act, because it exempted from prosecution or penalty, 'any law or statute to the contrary notwithstanding', all meetings or agreements for the purpose of fixing wages and hours.

The common law of conspiracy, out of which that exemption had been carved, was relied on in a prosecution of a miner named Bykerdike tried before Mr Justice Patteson at Lancaster on 13 March 1832, only a few months before the passage of the First Reform Act.[140] The indictment was in two counts. The first charged that he and others 'did conspire, combine, confederate, and agree unlawfully to intimidate, prejudice, and oppress one John Garforth in his trade and occupation, as agent for [the Fairbottom colliery] and to prevent the workmen of the said J. G. from continuing to work in the said colliery'. The second count charged them with conspiracy 'to oppress and injure Joseph Jones and others, partners in [the colliery] and to . . . compel the said J. J. and others, his partners, to discharge the said workmen in their employ'.[141] For some undisclosed reason the body of miners had refused to work with seven colliers. In an interesting manœuvre these seven engaged in collusive action with Garforth: they refused to work, and he summoned them before a justice of the peace, who obligingly ordered them back to work under the master and servant law. This appearance of compulsion did not deceive the others, however, who addressed a letter to Garforth threatening to leave in fourteen days unless the seven were discharged. At trial the defence led with a technicality: whereas the indictment charged a conspiracy 'to prevent the workmen of the said J. G. from continuing to work', the facts showed that only seven

---

[140] 2 & 3 Will. 4, c. 45 (1832).
[141] *R. v. Bykerdike*, 1 M. & Rob. 179, 174 Eng. Rep. 61 (Nisi Prius 1832).

men were objected to. Second, and more substantially, it claimed that the 1825 Act protected the men in combining not to work.[142]

The prosecution duly opposed both arguments. First, it relied on *Ferguson and Edge* (1819) for the proposition that an allegation as to 'the workmen' may be supported by proof. as to any of the workmen. The prosecution also cited *Rex* v. *Horne* (1777), a reference apparently to one of Lord Mansfield's characteristic dicta: 'It is the duty of the jury to construe plain words . . . according to their obvious meaning, and as everybody else who reads must understand them.'[143] Second, it pointed out the obvious fact that the 1825 Act (unlike its 1824 predecessor) did not protect a combination for preventing other workmen from continuing to work but only one for obtaining higher wages or shorter hours. On both points the prosecution prevailed. Had the case been brought under the statute, it would seemingly have been covered by the third branch of the offence, if threatening to leave was indeed a threat within the meaning of that section. Summing up for the jury, Mr Justice Patteson announced that a conspiracy to procure the discharge of any of the workmen would support the indictment. Further, he ruled that the statute did not exempt the conspiracy in this case: 'This compulsion was clearly illegal.'[144] Under such instructions the jury perforce found Bykerdike guilty as charged.

By 1851 England had arrived at economic maturity; that is, it had 'effectively applied the range of modern technology to the bulk of its resources'.[145] The first industrial nation had achieved its majority, and the occasion was fittingly observed by a grand party at the Crystal Palace, the Great Exhibition of the Works of Industry of All Nations. The representatives of land and capital who governed England at mid-century were united in their resolve that discontented labourers should not be permitted to disrupt the nation's economic progress. Their only disagreement concerned how far the law of strikes could be liberalized without jeopardizing that objective. In the year of the Great Exhibition, a strike caused by the application of the new technology to barrel-making resulted in a reaffirmation of the law as stated in Bykerdike's Case. Hewitt was president of the Philanthropic Society of Coopers, a friendly society. Charles Evans, a member of the society, worked for Turner. With his employer's permission, Evans spent four days working at another mill, where steam machinery was used in making casks. The society refused to allow any of its members to work with machinery, so Evans was fined £10, payable in instalments. When he refused to pay, the other coopers who worked for Turner left work and demanded that Evans be discharged; each was paid 9s. by the society

---

[142] In the report, 1 M. & Rob. 180, 174 Eng. Rep. 62, the act is cited as 6 Geo. 4, c. 120 (concerning legal procedure in Scotland), an obvious mistake for 6 Geo. 4, c. 129.

[143] 2 Cowp. 680, 98 Eng. Rep. 1304 (KB 1777)..

[144] 1 M. & Rob. 181, 174 Eng. Rep. 62.

[145] W. W. Rostow, *The Stages of Economic Growth: A Non-Communist Manifesto* (2nd edn., Cambridge, 1971), 59.

for his loss of time. The role of the Philanthropic Society in this dispute recalls the 1824 select committee resolution drawing attention to the use of funds of benefit societies to support strikes. However plain the distinction in law between friendly societies and trade unions, it was often ignored in practice, and remained a continuing source of conflict.

Evans apparently complained, and Hewitt and others were indicted 'for a combination . . . contrary to 6 Geo. 4, c. 129 [the 1825 Act], and for a conspiracy'.[146] The defence argued that although the charge was 'conspiring to do an unlawful act . . . it was not an unlawful act to impose a fine upon a member of the society for breach of one of the rules of the society, unless the rules were unlawful in themselves, or were made for an unlawful purpose'.[147] Furthermore, it claimed with some plausibility that 'the object of the act of Parliament was to protect the masters from the combinations of the men; but here the masters did not complain, and it was, therefore, difficult to imagine that the statute had been violated'.[148] Chief Justice Lord Campbell, before whom the case was tried on 7 February 1851, found no such difficulty: the facts fitted squarely within the third branch of the offence—again assuming that what the workmen did amounted to threatening, or to intimidation, molestation, or obstruction of their employer. Furthermore, the second branch was also implicated since the coercion was applied in consequence of a workman's refusal to pay a fine imposed by his club or association. With some exaggeration Campbell described the prosecution as 'one of the most important cases ever brought before a British jury'.[149] The Chief Justice stressed that the Philanthropic Society was legal as a friendly society, caring for the sick and burying the dead. 'But', he continued, 'it cannot be permitted that, under the guise of such laudable objects, the members shall enter into a combination or conspiracy to injure others . . . The men may take care not to enter into engagements of which they do not approve but they must not prevent another from doing so.'[150] Echoing the 1824 select committee, he denounced the payment from the funds of the society as 'a clear perversion of its objects'.[151] Campbell, as usual, worked his will with the jury[152] which returned a verdict of guilty. His lordship immediately passed judgment: 'The offence is a most serious one, and, if allowed to pass with impunity, would bring ruin upon the trade and manufactures of this country, and would involve in its ruin the workmen, upon whom the prosperity of this country mainly depends.'[153] Although he declared that defendants had to be 'severely punished', the report uninformatively concludes by saying that his lordship sentenced them to 'various terms of imprisonment'.[154]

[146] *R.* v. *Hewitt*, 5 Cox CC 162 (QB 1851).
[147] Ibid.
[148] Ibid. 163. [149] Ibid. [150] Ibid. [151] Ibid. 164.
[152] See James B. Atlay, *The Victorian Chancellors* (London, 1906–8), ii. 202–3.
[153] 5 Cox CC 164.
[154] Ibid.

Across the Atlantic, American lawyers too wrestled with the labour problem. Lacking legislation like that initiated by Joseph Hume and Francis Place, they were armed only with the common law of conspiracy, which as we have seen had been received by the states of the new republic.[155] Without the statutory exemption for agreements to fix wages or hours, all combinations of workmen were presumptively illegal, as appeared to have been established in the Philadelphia Cordwainers' Case (1806). In 1842, however, a prominent judge in Massachusetts, then a leading state in America's own Industrial Revolution, rewrote the law of conspiracy. In a case involving journeymen bootmakers who had agreed to refuse to work for any master who employed workmen not belonging to their club—a case involving what would today be called a demand for a closed shop—Chief Justice Lemuel Shaw found no conspiracy.[156] Surveying English cases up to and including Bykerdike's Case, Shaw restated the common law of his state more narrowly. Like Lord Denman, he defined conspiracy as the agreement of two or more persons to do an unlawful act or a lawful act by unlawful means.[157] Shaw then found neither the means (a strike) nor the end (a closed shop) unlawful. With dubious accuracy he described the agreement as 'perfectly justifiable under the recent English statute [i.e., the 1825 Act], by which this subject is regulated'.[158] With more candour he might have referred to the repealed Act of 1824. In time Shaw's ruling was adopted by courts in other American states, putting the erstwhile colonies ahead of the Mother Country in the development of labour law.[159]

Meanwhile in England a prosecution occurred in 1847 that was to lead, a dozen years later, to new legislation. The facts of the case as they were proved before Baron Rolfe at the South Lancashire Spring Assizes are easily stated.[160] The union of skilled workmen then known as mechanics and now

---

[155] See *Comm.* v. *Pulis* (Philadelphia, Pa., Mayor's Court, 1806) (Cordwainers' Case), pamphlet report repr. in *A Documentary History of American Industrial Society*, 10 vols. (New York, 1910–11), iii., ed. John R. Commons and Eugene A. Gilmore, 60–248. See Chap. 3, n. 93.

[156] *Comm.* v. *Hunt*, 35 Mass. (4 Metc.) 111 (1842) (Shaw, CJ). The case has attracted an extraordinary amount of scholarly interest. Among earlier writings see Walter Nelles, 'Commonwealth v. Hunt', 32 *Columbia Law Review* 1128–70 (1931–2) and Leonard W. Levy, *The Law of the Commonwealth and Chief Justice Shaw: The Evolution of American Law, 1830–1860* (New York, 1957), chap. 11. Among recent writings see Wythe Holt, 'Labour Conspiracy Cases in the United States, 1805–1842: Bias and Legitimation in Common Law Adjudication', 22 *Osgoode Hall Law Journal* 591–663 (1984) and Alfred S. Konefsky, ' "As Best to Subserve their own Interests": Lemuel Shaw, Labor Conspiracy, and Fellow Servants', *Law and History Review*, 7 (1989), 219–39.

[157] Cf. 35 Mass. (4 Metc.) 126 with *R.* v. *Jones*, 4 B. & Ad. 349, 110 Eng. Rep. 487 (KB 1832) (Lord Denman, CJ). See Chap. 3, n. 84.   [158] 35 Mass. (4 Metc.) 132.

[159] With somewhat more enthusiasm other courts also adopted Judge Shaw's holding the same term that the fellow-servant rule propounded by Lord Abinger (James Scarlett) was part of the common law. See *Farwell v. Boston and Worcester R.R.*, 35 Mass. (4 Metc.) 49 (1842).

[160] *R.* v. *Selsby*, 5 Cox CC 495 n. (Nisi Prius 1847); *The Trial of the Mechanics at Liverpool*, ed. W. P. Roberts (1847). See also James B. Jefferys, *The Story of the Engineers, 1800–1945* (London, 1946), 27.

known as engineers had gone on strike after their employer gave skilled work to men who had not served apprenticeships. The union sought to force the employer to discharge the nonconforming workmen. The strike was organized by Henry Selsby, secretary of the union, who posted four pickets outside the entrance to the foundry. The pickets were to persuade the men still at work to depart and other workmen not to take the strikers' places. The words the pickets used, words that were to become the centre of attention at trial, were: 'If you go to work there, you will repent it before the winter is over'; 'You had better not go there, for you will not stop long'; 'If you do, you shall be called a "knobstick" '.[161] Selsby and twenty-five strikers were indicted for conspiracy.

In Selsby's Case the prosecution attempted to prove that the defendants had conspired to commit the offence described in the first branch of the penal section of the 1825 Act: using threats to prevent workmen from accepting employment. The decisive legal issue in the case was whether the words used had, under all the circumstances, communicated any threats. In his summing up Baron Rolfe laid down the law that an attempt to persuade a workman that it was not in his interest to work under present conditions was not illegal; only an announcement that 'bodily harm' would be done to him if he did was an illegal threat.[162] In this ruling Rolfe was merely repeating the definition of threats in the common law of torts: 'menaces of bodily hurt, through fear of which a man's business is interrupted'.[163] He was, in other words, reading the *lex scripta* by reference to the *lex non scripta*. In Selsby's Case the jury found as a matter of fact that the menace was indeed one of bodily harm and convicted the accused. In due course the case was brought before the Court of Queen's Bench, but the defendants were, it appears, dismissed without judgment.[164] Regardless of the actual result, the law of strikes as it came from the mouth of Baron Rolfe in 1847 was not wholly unsatisfactory to the trade unionists of the day. Strikers could be called out and pickets could patrol, although their message could not go beyond persuasion or warnings of dire economic consequences.

In 1851, the year of the Great Exhibition, another strike caused by the application of new technology, this time to tin-working, resulted in prosecutions that provided the occasion for a provocative restatement of the law of strikes. This led, in turn, to political action by a trade union to induce

---

[161] 5 Cox CC 497. ('Knobstick', an opprobrious epithet of uncertain origin, means an employer who hires strike-breakers or, as here, a strike-breaker himself (also known as a 'blackleg', or in America, a 'scab').)

[162] Ibid. 497–8.

[163] Blackstone, *Commentaries*, iii. 120. See *Garret v. Taylor*, 2 Cro. [Jac.] 567, 79 Eng. Rep. 485 (KB 1620).

[164] [Ludwig Joseph Brentano], 'The Growth of a Trades-Union', *North British Review*, 53 (1870–1), 81 (attribution (probable) in *Wellesley Index*, i. 695). The author reported that the trial cost the union £1,800 and that in consequence a meeting of delegates ordered the secretary in future to stay out of local disputes. 'On the other hand', the report continued, the employers 'became bankrupt in 1851, in consequence of the losses inflicted by the strike'.

parliament to restore the law as laid down earlier. The success of this effort in 1859 was to be the first legislative victory that labour masterminded for itself. The repeal of the combination laws a quarter-century earlier had, after all, been arranged by the reforming element of the political élite; however much Francis Place had tried to trick out that campaign as a working-class movement, it had really been a concession in advance of a demand. The only evidence of the proletariat's 'threatening bearing' had been a campaign of peaceful petitioning. In the 1850s labour would be, if not demanding, at least actively asking for something, but again the method would be strictly parliamentary. It was the beginning of 'the struggle for acceptance', a struggle that turned out to be far longer and harder-fought than labour's leaders expected.[165] That labour eventually got what it wanted was due to competition between the Liberal and Conservative parties, prefiguring in that regard the more serious bidding for labour's support that followed the second Reform Act (1867).

The prosecutions that set off labour's lobby were tried before Mr Justice Erle at the Staffordshire Summer Assizes in 1851.[166] Two manufacturers had introduced machinery into their tin-works, and in consequence of the faster rate of production, paid lower piece rates than those paid by their competitors, although they claimed that overall compensation was comparable. The tin-workers[167] were members of a union that was affiliated with the National Association of United Trades, a London-based organization of labour's aristocracy, the skilled workmen.[168] When William Peel and Frederick Green, officers of the National Association, failed to persuade the two capitalists to raise wages, they called a strike. When it became clear that the strikers could indeed halt production, the employers prosecuted the local ringleaders, Henry Rowlands and George Duffield, together with the officers of the National Association, for conspiracy to violate the 1825 Act. While the prosecution in Selsby's Case (1847) had relied on the provision against threats, that in Rowlands's Case relied on the vaguer offences of molesting or in any way obstructing; and rather than regard the strikers' effect on other workmen, as in the earlier case, it now focused on their impact on the manufacturer. Attention turned, in other words, from the first

[165] See W. Hamish Fraser, *Trade Unions and Society: The Struggle for Acceptance, 1850–1880* (Totowa, NJ, 1974); Frances E. Gillespie, *Labor and Politics in England, 1850–1867* (Durham, NC, 1927).

[166] *R. v. Duffield*, 5 Cox CC 404 (Nisi Prius 1851); *R. v. Rowlands*, 5 Cox CC 436; 2 Den. 364, 169 Eng. Rep. 540 (Nisi Prius 1851). For the background to these cases, see T. J. Dunning, *Trades' Unions and Strikes: Their Philosophy and Intention* (1860), 31–5.

[167] This is the first appearance in this line of cases of the word 'workers' in place of the more common 'workmen'. The word was first used to refer to one who worked with a particular material, such as tin. In its article on 'worker' the *Oxford English Dictionary* (1st edn., 1884–1928) gives an example from 1765 of 'tin-plate-worker'. To mean a member of the class of wage-earners, worker was not yet standard. The original English translation of the famous last line of the *Communist Manifesto* (1848) was: 'Working men of all countries, unite!'

[168] See Webb and Webb, *History of Trade Unionism*, 192–5.

branch of the offence created in 1825 to the third: the labour leaders were charged with conspiring to molest and obstruct the employers in order to compel them to alter the way they paid wages. Unlike threats, the words molesting and obstructing had no established legal definitions. Summing up for the jury, Mr Justice Erle defined them in the broadest possible terms: 'if a manufacturer has got a manufactory, and his capital embarked in it for the purpose of producing articles in that manufactory, if persons conspire together to take away all his workmen, that would necessarily be an obstruction to him, that would necessarily be a molesting of him in his manufactory.'[169] Simply stated, calling a strike was illegal under the statute, and conspiring to call a strike was illegal at common law. Accordingly, the jury convicted the defendants, and in due course they were brought before the Court of Queen's Bench for sentencing. Mr Justice Patteson, who had presided at the trial in Bykerdike's Case twenty years earlier, first passed some strictures on the National Association of United Trades:

It must be an association, which, if they have, as they say, very large funds at their command, must be one, certainly, of a very dangerous character, and may be used for very bad and very oppressive purposes . . . there is nothing to be said in favour of persons who belong to an association of that kind, and who, of their own accord, no doubt, go down to different parts of the country, to assist workmen who have, or think they have, any grievance whatever as against their masters, and endeavour to regulate their wages. They are volunteers in that respect, and it is far better, it seems to me, for the workmen to be left to act as they themselves think proper.[170]

After these preliminaries, Peel and Green, the officers of the National Association, were sentenced to three months in Staffordshire gaol.[171] On their release, the two mounted a campaign to overturn Erle's summing up of the law of strikes. As we will see, these 'beautiful fragments' did not finally fall until 1859.

[169] 5 Cox CC 432.
[170] 5 Cox CC 492 (QB 1851).
[171] Ibid. 495. For Harriet Martineau's comment on this case, see 'Secret Organisation of Trades', *Edinburgh Review*, 110 (1859), 531–5 (attribution in *Wellesley Index*, i. 509).

6

Conspiracy: Restraint of Trade

Every contract, combination in the form of trust or otherwise, or conspiracy, in restraint of trade or commerce among the several States, or with foreign nations, is hereby declared to be illegal.

Sherman Antitrust Act (US 1890)

Conspiracy is an old crime; whatever it means exactly, it goes far back to the early days of the common law. 'Restraint of trade', on the other hand, is not so old.[1] Originally, it was used to describe certain illegal agreements: contracts (or covenants) in restraint of trade. At first, it had nothing to do with labour: it was an affair of masters rather than men. Nor was criminal law originally implicated. Usually a sale of property was involved; a master baker conveyed his bakehouse, for example, and covenanted not to compete with the buyer. The legal question was whether such an agreement in restraint of trade was lawful, in the sense of being enforceable by the buyer in court. Early in the eighteenth century the judges held that it was, if it was reasonable.[2] With the expansion of criminal conspiracy, the usage developed of summarizing the illegal purposes—originally, prejudice to masters or men, or, in time, to the public generally—as restraints of trade.[3] Later, in the abstract legal thought of the nineteenth century, trade (like contract) seemed almost a thing in itself, capable of sustaining legal rights: trade (like contract) ought to be free! By the end of the century 'conspiracy in restraint of trade' was a legal catchword, describing agreements to close markets, the deadly perversion of freedom of contract. By that time, restraint of trade had lost its freshness and seemed like one of those legal

---

[1] 'Restraint of trade' does not appear in the *Oxford English Dictionary* (1st edn., 1884–1928); it made its first appearance in the *Supplement* (1956), in which the earliest example given for its use is the Sherman Antitrust Act, Act of 2 July 1890, ch. 647, § 1, 26 Stat. 209, the epigraph for this chapter. In fact, as will appear, the phrase had occurred in English court decisions since the eighteenth century and was used in the Trades Union Funds Protection Act (1869) and the Trade Union Act (1871). See, generally, R. Y. Hedges, *The Law Relating to Restraint of Trade* (London, 1932).

[2] *Mitchell* v. *Reynolds*, 1 P. Wms. 181, 24 Eng. Rep. 347 (QB 1711) (case involving master baker).

[3] E.g., *R.* v. *Turner*, 13 East 231, 104 Eng. Rep. 358 (KB 1811) (Lord Ellenborough, CJ) (*Eccles* (1783) described as involving a 'conspiracy in restraint of trade, and so far a conspiracy to do an unlawful act affecting the public').

terms that had existed 'time out of mind', 'whereof the memory of man
runneth not to the contrary'.[4] Just as the undoubted antiquity of the crime
of conspiracy lent an air of authority to the labour cases beginning with the
Cambridge Tailors' Case (1721), so the relative antiquity of the law relating
to restraints of trade helped ground the notion that the common law had
always set its face against conspiracies to that end.

Restraint of trade ·proved to be a convenient label for an assortment of
legal doctrines originally quite distinct, such as the medieval crimes of
forestalling, regrating, and engrossing (which punished interferences with
the flow of food to market)[5] and the common-law policy against
monopolies, a product of the opposition to Stuart economic policy.[6] When
Blackstone attempted to reduce criminal law to a system in the mid-
eighteenth century, he used the chapter heading 'offences against public
trade' and included (along with the offences listed above): smuggling,
fraudulent bankruptcy, usury, cheating, violation of apprenticeship, and
encouraging the emigration of skilled artisans.[7] He had nothing to say
about combination and conspiracy in the labour market. In the nineteenth
century Blackstone's chapter was gradually emptied by the economic
reforms that enacted the programme of *laissez-faire*. Statutes against
forestalling, engrossing, and regrating were repealed, and (a separate
matter) their criminality at common law was extinguished.[8] Usury
eventually fell before the blast of Jeremy Bentham.[9] As we have seen, legal
apprenticeship was finally ended in 1814, while restraints on the emigration
of artisans were repealed in 1824, on the recommendation of the same select
committee that recommended repeal of the combination laws.

Restraint of trade did not long remain a mere label; it became in the
nineteenth century a generative source of law as well. Lawyers and judges,
having posited its existence, deduced from it the general principle that each
individual was free to work on whatever terms he chose—subject, of course,
to a few statutory restrictions, such as the law of master and servant, as well
as factory acts, truck acts, hours legislation, etc. A negative corollary of this
principle, applicable to the developing law of contract, was that any
agreement in restraint of trade was presumed to be unlawful and
unenforceable—unless, of course, it was found to be reasonable. By virtue
of this principle, trade unions were denounced as unlawful because in
contemplation of law they were constituted by contracts, covenants, or

---

[4] See e.g. William Blackstone, *Commentaries on the Laws of England* (1765–9), i. 67
(referring to customs that compose common law).

[5] 25 Edw. 3, st. 4, c. 3 (1350); 27 Edw. 3, st. 2, c. 11 (1354); 28 Edw. 3, c. 13, § 3 (1355); 5
& 6 Edw. 6, c. 14 (1552).

[6] See 21 Jac. 1, c. 3 (1624) (Statute of Monopolies).

[7] Blackstone, *Commentaries*, iv. chap. 12.

[8] 7 & 8 Vict., c. 24 (1844); see also 12 Geo. 3, c. 71 (1772).

[9] Jeremy Bentham, *Defence of Usury* (1787); 17 & 18 Vict., c. 90 (1854).

agreements that interfered with the 'perfect freedom' of each individual workman to make his own agreement.

Masters, of course, could restrain trade as well as men; indeed, as we have seen, agreements in restraint of trade had first been encountered at that level. In the nineteenth century manufacturers pioneered techniques for controlling markets, such as cartels and price-fixing. In America, trusts holding the shares of companies in the same industry were the favoured device, and 'antitrust' sentiment eventually resulted in the Sherman Act (1890), which voided such contracts and provided criminal penalties.[10] Agreements could also be used to control the cost of production, including the price of labour. In the eighteenth century Adam Smith had described such an arrangement: 'When masters combine together in order to reduce the wages of their workmen, they commonly enter into a private bond or agreement, not to give more than a certain wage under a certain penalty.'[11] In the mid-nineteenth century in *Hilton* v. *Eckersley* the legality of one such private bond was litigated at length. Eighteen cotton manufacturers had obligated themselves to abide by majority rule in the terms of wages and hours or forfeit £500. At last, the Exchequer Chamber[12] definitively held the agreement unenforceable because in restraint of trade.[13] Under the regnant political economy it could not be shown to be reasonable. No criminal prosecution was involved.

If agreements in restraint of trade were unenforceable, the question was bound to arise sooner or later whether bodies held together, as it were, by such unenforceable agreements were lawful for any purpose. Could they even bring suit against their own dishonest members or officers for misappropriation of common funds? The question became more acute with the growing affluence of trade unions of skilled workmen in the second half of the nineteenth century. In the first instance, the problem arose not from the law concerning restraint of trade but from the peculiar nature of the offence of larceny. We have seen in an earlier chapter how the common law failed to embody the developing concept of property in the work-place. As Blackstone flatly put it: 'no delivery of the goods from the owner to the

[10] Act of 2 July 1890, ch. 647, 26 Stat. 209. See Albert H. Walker, *History of the Sherman Law of the United States of America* (New York, 1910); William L. Letwin, *Law and Economic Policy in America: The Evolution of the American Antitrust Act* (New York, 1965). In *Loewe* v. *Lawlor*, 208 US 274 (1908), better known as the Danbury Hatters' Case, the US Supreme Court held the Sherman Act applicable to labour unions.

[11] Adam Smith, *An Inquiry into the Nature and Causes of the Wealth of Nations*, 142.

[12] The Court of Exchequer Chamber, not to be confused with the common-law Court of Exchequer, was created out of older precursors by statute in 1830, 11 Geo. 4 & 1 Will. 4, c. 70. It resolved disputes of law arising in any of the three common-law courts: King's (Queen's) Bench, Common Pleas, and Exchequer. Its judges were those of the two courts not involved in the case. The name of the court derived from the early practice of meeting in a room (or chamber) at the Exchequer.

[13] 6 El. & Bl. 47, 119 Eng. Rep. 781 (Exch. Ch. 1855).

offender, upon trust, can ground a larciny [*sic*].'[14] The principle had dangerous implications for any large enterprise. Since the property of a group was the joint property of all its members, the common law considered that the misappropriation of property by any member amounted merely to taking that which belonged to him jointly with the others. Trade unionists, as well as bankers and businessmen, found this one of the law's more serious asininities.

In order to protect their funds, trade unions had been granted special treatment in the Friendly Societies Act (1855), which provided summary proceedings before two justices of the peace in case of fraud by an officer or member of a society established 'for any of the purposes mentioned in . . . this Act, or for any purpose which is not illegal'.[15] Trade unionists relied, obviously, on the disjunctive: 'or for any purpose which is not illegal', although the developing law of restraint of trade made such reliance dubious. It was finally tested in the celebrated case of *Hornby* v. *Close*,[16] the Boilermakers' Case. The case began on 12 January 1866, when Hornby, president of the Bradford branch of the United Order of Boilermakers and Iron Ship Builders, filed an information with two justices of the peace charging Close, a local officer, with having unlawfully withheld money belonging to the union. At a hearing on 15 January the justices of the peace found the charge fully proved[17] but ruled that the union was not entitled to summary proceedings because, in addition to functioning as a friendly society, it had an illegal purpose, the restraint of trade. This appeared in the restrictive rules that prohibited members from working in a shop where a dispute between an employer and the union was in progress (a polite way of referring to strike-breaking), that provided relief to those on strike, and that prohibited members from facilitating the employment of non-members.

Counsel for Hornby took exception to this decision, using a new device for challenging summary convictions, a functional alternative to proceeding by the old writ of *certiorari*. In the nineteenth century, as we have seen, legal procedure was steadily separated from substantive law: no longer were codes of procedure included in every statute. Since 1857 it had been possible to apply to the justices of the peace (or magistrate) for a 'case stated' for the opinion of one of the superior courts of common law.[18] The Court of Queen's Bench, composed of Lord Chief Justice[19] Cockburn and Justices Blackburn, Mellor, and Lush, had no hesitation in affirming the decision of the justices of the peace in the Boilermakers' Case. All agreed that the union

---

[14] Blackstone, *Commentaries*, iv. 230. See Chap. 2, n. 109.
[15] 18 & 19 Vict., c. 63, § 44.
[16] 10 Cox CC 393 (QB 1867). See also *Farrer* v. *Close*, 4 LR–QB 602 (QB 1869).
[17] 10 Cox CC 394.   [18] 20 & 21 Vict., c. 43 (1857).
[19] Although in the past the Chief Justices of King's (Queen's) Bench had occasionally claimed the title of Lord Chief Justice, the office was not officially created until 1859 when Sir Alexander Cockburn, former Attorney-General (1851–2; 1852–6) and Chief Justice of Common Pleas (1856–9), was made Chief Justice of Queen's Bench.

had a significant purpose not analogous to that of a friendly society. In the words of Mr Justice Blackburn:

On the construction of such an Act as this, though the words are 'for any purpose which is not illegal', which may be in one sense taken to include every purpose which is not illegal, yet, in construing general statutes, and indeed in construing all documents, words cannot be taken to have that extensive meaning. For, if so, all they have previously said in enumerating various cases would in that case be quite superfluous; but when, in enumerating cases of a particular sort, the Act says 'or for any purpose', it means any *analogous* purpose.[20]

This was merely a questionable application of the *ejusdem generis* principle, by which general words following an enumeration of particulars are interpreted to refer to things of the same general kind as the particulars. As a second ground for affirming the decision, the court held that the rules singled out were illegal because in restraint of trade. In the view of the Lord Chief Justice, although the union had among its purposes the charitable ones of a friendly society, it had at the same time 'another purpose, namely, that of a trades union, and the controlling the whole body, and getting the dominion over their actions'.[21] Trade unions, in other words, were inherently in restraint of trade. Because the court held that the Boilermakers had been established for an illegal purpose, Hornby was barred from summary proceedings against Close, although he retained whatever right he had at common law. That this too was valueless was due to the peculiar jurisprudence on larceny.

After the decision in *Hornby*, the trade unions sought relief from parliament, which had just passed the Second Reform Act (1867).[22] To increase their influence, they convened the first Trades Union Congress which became in time a major institution in British politics.[23] Parliament responded to this democratic pressure with two statutes. The first, sponsored by Russell Gurney, the Recorder of London, was called after him Russell Gurney's Act or the Recorder's Act (1868).[24] It is a significant fact that many important statutes passed from the early eighteenth century until well into the nineteenth were known by the names of their sponsors.[25] (Jervis's Act (1848) in the next chapter is a further example.) Soon, the designation of official short titles, as well as the anonymity of party government, was to end the practice in England, although in America, as the Sherman Act suggests, it survived, and indeed still flourishes.

Russell Gurney's Act went to the underlying problem and altered the common law of larceny:

---

[20] 10 Cox CC 399 (italics in original).
[21] Ibid. 398.
[22] 30 & 31 Vict., c. 102 (1867).
[23] See B. C. Roberts, *The Trades Union Congress, 1868–1921* (London, 1958).
[24] 31 & 32 Vict., c. 116 (1868).
[25] See William S. Holdsworth, *A History of English Law* (London, 1903–72), xi. 371.

If any person, being a member of any copartnership, or being one of two or more beneficial owners of any money, goods, or effects, bills, notes, securities, or other property, shall steal or embezzle any such money, goods, or effects, bills, notes, securities, or other property of or belonging to any such copartnership or to such joint beneficial owners, every such person shall be liable to be dealt with, tried, convicted, and punished for the same as if such person had not been or was not a member of such copartnership or one of such beneficial owners.[26]

The first statute, in other words, gave a cause of action at common law, triable by standard procedure. The second, a stopgap measure known by its official short title as the Trades Unions Funds Protection Act (1869),[27] provided for summary process by glossing the Friendly Societies Act:

An association of persons having rules, agreements, or practices among themselves as to the terms on which they or any of them will or will not consent to employ or to be employed shall not, by reason only that any of such rules, agreements, or practices may operate in restraint of trade, or that such association is partly for objects other than the objects mentioned in the Friendly Societies Acts, be deemed, for the purposes of . . . the Friendly Societies Act, 1855 . . . to be a society established for a purpose which is illegal, or not to be a friendly society within the meaning of the . . . said Act.[28]

Unlike Russell Gurney's Act, the second statute was only temporary: by its own terms, it expired on 31 August 1870, although it was subsequently renewed for an additional year.[29]

It is worth pausing for a moment over the legal theory underlying both acts. There is a distinct air about it of unreality, of legal fiction. The first statute requires the courts to treat a member of a group as if he were not a member of a group, while the second requires them to ignore the consequences that would ordinarily follow from acting in restraint of trade. The problem stems from the nature of common law as it was seen in the nineteenth century. Parliament made statutes, the judges discovered the common law. Rather than try to alter discovered law, the legislators opted for the expedient of denying it effect as it bore on certain problems. Russell Gurney's Act was speedily accepted; it corrected an ancient misconception. But the Trades Unions Funds Protection Act continued to rankle; by creating an exception it marred the fine logic of the law. The strategy was not new, to be sure; the 1824–5 legislation had conferred greater and lesser exemptions from prosecution for common-law conspiracy. But the legal theory now showed a new explicitness: while the statutes repealing the combination acts conceded liability (in the absence of the statute) for conspiracy, presumably because of prejudice to masters or men, the latest act conceded liability (again, in the absence of the statute) for conspiracy in restraint of trade. Repeated in the far more momentous legislation in the years ahead, it was to prove a costly concession.

---

[26] 31 & 32 Vict., c. 116, § 1.   [27] 32 & 33 Vict., c. 61 (1869) (short title in § 3).
[28] Ibid. § 1.   [29] 33 & 34 Vict., c. 103 (1870).

Although the Trades Unions Funds Protection Act was short-lived, it had time to figure in *Regina* v. *Stainer*,[30] a case that epitomized the confusion at the close of the third quarter of the nineteenth century. James Stainer, secretary of the cumbersomely named Power Loom Carpet Weavers' Mutual Defence and Provident Association, had embezzled money from his trade union. Since the legislation of 1868–9, he could have been proceeded against by indictment at common law or summarily under the Friendly Societies Act (1855). The former course was chosen, and the trial took place at the Worcestershire quarter sessions on 3 January 1870. The prosecution proved Stainer's crime. The defence argued that the Carpet Weavers' Association was in restraint of trade: under its rules no member could apply for work 'at firms where there is no vacancy . . . thereby creating that spirit-crushing influence which all good men deplore'; no member could take a person into a shop to learn weaving 'where no vacant loom exists, and against the expressed wishes of his shopmates'; and no member could work overtime.[31] In *Hornby* it had been held that such societies were illegal, while earlier in *Regina* v. *Hunt* (1838)[32] it had been held that an indictment could not be maintained by any illegal society.[33] The chairman of the quarter sessions overruled the objection but reserved the point for appeal. The jury found Stainer guilty, and he was sentenced to one year in prison.

On appeal the defence renewed its argument: rules in restraint of trade made the society illegal under *Hornby* . . . Peremptorily Lord Chief Justice Cockburn interrupted: that case, he said, decided that 'the societies in question were only so far illegal that they could not enforce civil contracts'.[34] The defence pursued its argument: the Carpet Weavers' Association because of its rules was indictable for conspiracy . . . Again the Lord Chief Justice interrupted: 'What authority', he asked, 'is there for saying that where half a dozen men or more agree not to work at a factory where machinery is used, or where more than a certain number of apprentices are taken, that such a combination, although it may be in restraint of trade, is a criminal offence?'[35] Counsel was reduced to silence: if the court required authority for that proposition, then the old landmarks had been removed and the appeal was lost.

The judgment only elaborated on the Chief Justice's interventions in the argument. Rules in restraint of trade made a society illegal, but neither the word 'illegal' nor its synonym 'unlawful' necessarily meant 'criminal'; the rules were simply not enforceable in court. In the words of Mr Justice Byles: 'The object of the rules pointed out may be unlawful in the sense of being void, as in restraint of trade and contrary to public policy, but they are not

---

[30] 11 Cox CC 483 (QB 1870).   [31] Ibid. 485 n.
[32] 8 Car. & P. 642, 173 Eng. Rep. 654 (Nisi Prius 1838).
[33] The society in *Hunt* was illegal because it administered an unlawful oath. The law of unlawful oaths and its relationship to the emerging trade unions are described in the next chapter.
[34] 11 Cox CC 486.   [35] Ibid.

unlawful as being within the criminal law.'[36] The court found support for this distinction in the Trades Unions Funds Protection Act, although the statute itself applied only to summary proceedings. 'The late act', said Mr Justice Keating, 'contains a clear indication of the intention of the Legislature that the mere fact of societies having rules that are void as being in restraint of trade shall not cause such societies to be deemed illegal so as to deprive them of the protection of the law in respect of their property.'[37]

In *Stainer*, the judges may have been attempting to trim the common law in keeping with current legislative (and electoral) developments—just as, in reverse, their predecessors in the Cambridge Tailors' Case a century and a half earlier had discovered the common law to be as extensive as the statutory rule in the first tailors' combination act (1721). 'Half a dozen men', the Lord Chief Justice implied, could 'agree not to work at a factory . . . where more than a certain number of apprentices are taken'—a curious dictum in light of *Hewitt* (1851) and *Selsby* (1847). The pace of change in the late nineteenth century meant, however, that time was too short for such judicial sleight of hand. Besides, the bench was not united in the effort. Six workmen, as we shall see in a later chapter, could not threaten to strike in order to force the discharge of certain workmen. Nor, as we shall also see, could six pickets try to dissuade a workman who was willing to work. In fact, the confusion could not be cleared up by the evolutionary efforts of the common law: it required a statute, the Trade Union Act (1871).

[36] 11 Cox CC 488.
[37] Ibid. 489.

7

Master and Servant

[T]he combination Act is nothing; it is the law which regards the finishing of work, which masters employ to harass and keep down the wages of their work people; unless this is modified nothing is done, and by repealing the combination Acts, you leave the workman, in 99 cases out of 100, in the same state you found him,—at the mercy of his master.

George White and Gravener Henson (1823)

'Master and servant' came to be the shorthand by which the legal profession described the employment relationship. The label was not inevitable; originally it had applied only to domestic service. Blackstone, for whom master and servant was one of the 'three great relations in private life'—the other two being husband and wife and parent and child—lengthened the list to include (in addition to domestics): apprentices, agricultural labourers, and superior servants such as stewards, factors, and bailiffs.[1] The society implied by this catalogue was familiar to the Oxford students who heard Blackstone lecture in the mid-eighteenth century: it was the world as seen by the landed aristocracy and country gentry. The world as remade by the Industrial Revolution, the world of the mill and the factory, was peopled by masters, lately called employers, and workmen or journeymen, once also called (as we have seen) manufacturers. None the less the legal profession in the nineteenth century subsumed all the above into master and servant. Certainly it lent an air of antiquity, perhaps comforting in an age of upheaval; perhaps it was also meant to put—and in so far as possible to keep—the new industrial proletariat in its place.

The law of master and servant was a legacy of the days of the regulated economy. The Statute of Artificers (1563), principal authority for wage regulation and apprenticeship, contained a section on leaving work unfinished, what would later be thought of as breach of contract:

Every artificer and labourer that shall be lawfully retained in and for the building or repairing of any church, house, ship, mill or every other piece of work taken in great,

---

[1] William Blackstone, *Commentaries on the Laws of England* (1765–9), i. chap. 14. See Otto Kahn-Freund, 'Blackstone's Neglected Child: The Contract of Employment', 93 *Law Quarterly Review* 508–28 (1977).

in task or in gross, or that shall hereafter take upon him to make or finish any such thing or work, shall continue and not depart from the same, unless it be for not paying of his wages or hire agreed on . . . or for other lawful cause, or without licence of the master or owner of the work, or of him that hath charge thereof, before the finishing of the said work.[2]

Offenders were liable to a criminal penalty, one month in gaol, and masters could sue for the penal sum of £5 over and above ordinary costs and damages.[3]

The drafter of this sixteenth-century section obviously conceptualized production—and the concomitant employment relationship—in discrete units. A master builder was 'retained' to construct a church or a house, a master shipwright to repair a ship; on a smaller scale, a workman 'took upon him' to make or finish a piece of work. The idea seems to have been to require the proper discharge of the duties appropriate to one's rank in life, not to enforce the obligation of contract. Having once put his hand to the plough, the labourer was not to look back. There had always been exceptions, of course, but by the early nineteenth century the speeding up of production and the division of labour, hymned by Adam Smith in an unforgettable passage on pin-making, had increased them. Workmen in many trades literally never finished their work: before one piece was completed, they began another, so they were perpetually subject to the penalties of the Statute of Artificers.[4]

The eighteenth century, which seemed afraid to rise to the dignity of a general proposition, legislated piecemeal in the combination acts. The first tailors' act (1721) as well as the first weavers' act (1726) punished leaving work unfinished with the same severity as combination.[5] In the omnibus act (1749) workmen were prohibited from accepting any other work until they had finished that already delivered to them.[6] Finally, a 1777 statute, companion to the hatters' combination act, penalized any workmen who 'being hired, retained, or employed . . . shall wilfully neglect or refuse the performance thereof for eight days successively'.[7] Other statutes added to the hotchpotch. Under a 1747 statute, 'any misdemeanour, miscarriage or ill-behaviour' by a workman made him liable to hard labour in the house of correction for up to one month or, alternatively, to the abatement of part of his wages.[8] An act of 1766 imposed hard labour in the house of correction for one to three months 'if any artificer, callicoe printer, handicraftsman, miner, collier, keelman, pitman, glassman, potter, labourer, or other person,

---

[2] 5 Eliz. 1, c. 4, § 13 (1563).   [3] Ibid.
[4] [George White and Gravener Henson], *A Few Remarks on the State of the Laws, at Present in Existence, for Regulating Masters and Work-People* (1823), 51 (instancing wheelwrights and japanners) (attribution in catalogue of Kress Collection, Graduate School of Business Administration, Harvard Univ.).
[5] 7 Geo. 1, st. 1, c. 13, § 6 (1721); 12 Geo. 1, c. 34, § 2 (1726). See Chap. 2, nn. 21 and 72.
[6] 22 Geo. 2, c. 27, § 9 (1749).   [7] 17 Geo. 3, c. 56, § 8 (1777).
[8] 20 Geo. 2, c. 19, § 2 (1747) (extended by 31 Geo. 3, c. 11 (1791)).

shall contract with any person whomsoever for any time or term whatsoever, and shall absent himself from his service before the term of his contract shall be compleated, or be guilty of any other misdemeanour'.[9] As the phrasing of the last statute makes plain, status was gradually yielding to contract as the source of the obligation of service. What had begun as an offence against the established order of things was becoming a criminal punishment for breach of contract—as the established order itself was increasingly thought of in contractual terms. With the greater sophistication of legal thinking, the voluntary nature of contract was emphasized, and the remedy for breach was seen as compensatory, not punitive. Eventually this would make statutes like the above, bearing heavily on the contracting servant, seem anomalous and unjust.

Because of the scope of these statutes, the law of master and servant often loomed larger in workmen's minds than the combination laws themselves. George White and Gravener Henson, arguing in 1823 for the repeal of the Statute of Artificers, claimed: 'Very few prosecutions have been made to effect under the combination Acts, but hundreds have been made under this law, and the labourer or workman can never be free, unless this law is modified.'[10] Not only was the Statute of Artificers useful to masters in punishing workmen who stopped work (whether singly or in combination), it was also comparatively easy to use. In the words of White and Henson: 'the combination Act is difficult to convict upon; one of the workmen must turn traitor, to convict; but the neglecting the work it easy proved [*sic*]'.[11] His master's word would normally be sufficient. Whether or not it would leave the workman at the mercy of his master, White later joined actively in the campaign against the combination laws—once he was convinced that the objectionable part of the Statute of Artificers (unlike the wage and apprenticeship clauses) was not on the table.

Indeed, rather than repeal the old laws of master and servant, parliament added a new one in 1823.[12] This act, drafted with one eye on earlier

---

[9] 6 Geo. 3, c. 25, § 4 (1766).

[10] [White and Henson], *State of the Laws*, 51. Elsewhere the authors characterized the Combination Act (1800) as 'a tremendous millstone round the necks of the local artizan, which has depressed and debased him to the earth' (ibid. 86). For a further discussion of this observation, see John V. Orth, 'The English Combination Laws Reconsidered', in Francis Snyder and Douglas Hay (eds.), *Labour, Law, and Crime: An Historical Perspective* (London, 1987), 133–4.

[11] [White and Henson], *State of the Laws*, 53. Conviction may have been easy, but there is evidence that enforcement was sometimes hard. In 1758 Saunders Welch, one of Henry Fielding's successors as a justice of the peace in London, complained about the inadequacies of the constabulary: 'So low and so contemptible are peace officers become that it has been thought necessary to trouble the king's guards even to convey a poor journey-man taylor to gaol for quitting his master's service, and leaving work unfinished' (*Observations on the Office of Constable* (2nd edn., 1758), p. vii). Although the situation in London later improved, the eventual solution came in Sir Robert Peel's Metropolitan Police Act, 10 Geo. 4, c. 44 (1829), creating the London 'bobbies'. Comparable forces were provided elsewhere by later statutes.

[12] 4 Geo. 4, c. 34 (1823). The compendious language of the act was apparently not thought

legislation, provided up to three months at hard labour in the house of correction

if any servant in husbandry or any artificer, calico printer, handicraftsman, miner, collier, keelman, pitman, glassman, potter, labourer, or other person, shall contract with any person whomsoever, to serve him, her, or them for any time or times whatsoever, or in any other manner, and shall not enter into or commence his or her service according to his or her contract (such contract being in writing, and signed by the contracting parties), or having entered into such service shall absent himself or herself from his or her service before the term of his or her contract, whether such contract shall be in writing or not in writing, shall be completed, or neglect to fulfill the same, or be guilty of any other misconduct or misdemeanour in the execution thereof.[13]

Further thought had obviously gone into the contractual aspect of the relationship, although the draftsman had clearly had trouble incorporating all his insights. An action against a workman who had not yet entered into service had to be based on a writing signed by both parties, while an action against a workman who had already begun work could be based on an oral or, as the lawyers call it, a parol contract. This was in keeping with the longstanding practice, developed in equity, of enforcing parol contracts when one party had begun performance, even though the law generally required such contracts to be in writing. The problem was a matter of evidence, which as we have seen increasingly preoccupied English law-makers: in the former case the writing was the only proof of the employment relationship, while in the latter the servant's status was ascertained by a course of conduct. As alternatives to imprisonment, part of the wages could be abated or the workman discharged. To enforce this statute, summary proceedings were provided. The master initiated a prosecution by complaining on oath to one justice of the peace who was required immediately to issue a warrant for the arrest of the accused. Unlike the combination acts, no provision was made for proceeding first by summons, an omission that was to cause trouble later.

The Master and Servant Act (1823) preceded the repeal of the combination laws in 1824–5 and may have cleared the ground for it, but it did not sum up all the law (let alone all the prophets) on the subject. The 1825 Act also added to the law of master and servant: in the first branch of its criminal section, as we have seen, the act outlawed the use of violence, threats, intimidation, molestation, or obstruction 'to force or endeavour to force any journeyman, manufacturer, workman, or other person hired or employed in any manufacture, trade, or business, to . . . return his work before the same shall be finished'.[14] This apparent intrusion made perfect

to include all workmen. See 10 Geo. 4, c. 52 (1829) (extending 4 Geo. 4, c. 34 to trades enumerated in 17 Geo. 3, c. 56 (1777)).

[13] 4 Geo. 4, c. 34, § 3.

[14] 6 Geo. 4, c. 129, § 3 (1825). See Chap. 5, n. 122.

sense. The statute was designed to outlaw certain techniques used in strikes. Seeing that work (one's own or another's) went unfinished was a form of economic warfare that crossed legal boundaries. Just as trade unions and friendly societies overlapped, so did the law of combination and that of master and servant. A combination that did more than just consult or agree about wages and hours could easily run afoul of this law as well.

There were, in addition to the law of master and servant narrowly so-called, other laws that impinged to a greater or lesser extent on workmen. There were, first, the ordinary criminal laws. In 1838 after a long strike five Glasgow cotton-spinners were tried under Scottish law for conspiracy and murder.[15] The 'outrages', like those in Sheffield thirty years later (noticed in the next chapter), attracted national attention, and the House of Commons appointed a select committee with terms of reference to inquire specifically into the operation of the 1825 Act and 'generally into the constitution, proceedings, and extent of any trades' unions,[16] or combinations of workmen, or employers of workmen, in the United Kingdom'.[17] Despite the general terms of its assignment, the committee concerned itself almost exclusively with Ireland and Scotland, and even in those countries scarcely looked beyond Dublin, Belfast, and Glasgow. Although it published its evidence,[18] the committee never produced a report, and no legislative changes were recommended or made.

In addition to the ordinary criminal laws, which applied to everyone, some criminal statutes were specially directed at workmen. In 1828 parliament, in a burst of law reform under Sir Robert Peel, consolidated many of the statutory offences against the person. This enactment recognized a separate crime of 'assault committed in pursuance of any conspiracy to raise the rate of wages'.[19] The punishment for this offence, which was triable by ordinary common-law procedure, was up to two years' imprisonment with or without hard labour and, in the discretion of the court, a fine. Also in its discretion, the court could require the offender to find sureties for keeping the peace. In 1861 a further round of law reform produced several consolidation acts. The 1828 Act was repealed,[20] but its replacement made only minor changes in the law governing assaults in industrial disputes: two years' imprisonment with or without hard labour would still be imposed on a workman who 'in pursuance of any unlawful combination or conspiracy to raise the rate of wages, or of any unlawful

---

[15] *Report of the Trial of Thomas Hunter, Peter Hacket, Richard M'Niel, James Gibb, and William M'Lean, Cotton-Spinners in Glasgow* . . . by Archibald Swinton (1838); *Trial of Thomas Hunter, Peter Hacket, Richard M'Niel, James Gibb, and William M'Lean, the Glasgow Cotton Spinners* . . . reported by James Marshall (1838).

[16] Note this early official use of the phrase that later became standardized as 'trade union'.

[17] *Commons Journal*, 93 (1837–8), 271.

[18] *Parliamentary Papers* (1837–8), 8.

[19] 9 Geo. 4, c. 31, § 25 (1828). The new act was expressly declared not to affect the 1825 Act (ibid. § 37).

[20] 24 & 25 Vict., c. 95 (1861).

combination or conspiracy respecting any trade, business, or manufacture, or respecting any person concerned or employed therein, shall unlawfully assault any person.'[21]

In addition to these acts of special application there were others which, while not nominally applicable, were also capable of being pressed into service. Chief among them were the Unlawful Oaths Act (1797),[22] passed in response to naval mutinies at Spithead and the Nore, and the Unlawful Societies Act (1799),[23] which had received the royal assent on the same day as the Combination Act (1799). Products of the alarm produced by the spread of French Revolutionary ideas, these enactments could be turned from the world of politics to the world of industry.

Workmen's combinations often used oaths in a ritual celebrating and enforcing group solidarity, and the question soon arose whether the Unlawful Oaths Act covered an oath used in this way. In 1802 *Rex* v. *Marks*[24] returned an answer in the affirmative. The case arose in Wiltshire where the journeymen shearmen and the clothiers who employed them were engaged in a dispute, apparently over the payment of wages in truck. A journeyman who seems to have accepted payment in kind was called before a committee of the men which censured him and allegedly administered the following oath: 'You shall be true to every journeyman shearman, and not to hurt any of them, and you shall not divulge any of their secrets, so help you God.'[25] But the offending journeyman did not feel himself bound by this unlawful oath and later swore a lawful one before the justices of the peace. George Marks and four other shearmen were consequently committed to gaol to await trial. Contrary to accepted practice, the warrant of commitment failed to specify their offence, so their counsel promptly secured writs of habeas corpus, only recently restored, by which they were brought before the Court of King's Bench.

Two questions were raised at this proceeding: first, whether the warrant of commitment could be cured by subsequent depositions; second, whether the Unlawful Oaths Act covered the oath in question. In the end, the court did not decide the second question: it remanded the prisoners because it held that the depositions showed the charge against them. But the judges' opinion about the applicability of the act was clear. Chief Justice Lord Ellenborough observed: 'it certainly does appear from the preamble of the Act, as if it were mainly directed against combinations for purposes of

---

[21] 24 & 25 Vict., c. 100, § 41 (1861).

[22] 37 Geo. 3, c. 123 (1797) (strengthened by 52 Geo. 3, c. 104 (1812)).

[23] 39 Geo. 3, c. 79 (1799) (12 July) (strengthened by 57 Geo. 3, c. 19 (1817)).

[24] 3 East 157, 102 Eng. Rep. 557 (KB 1802).

[25] 3 East 158, 102 Eng. Rep. 557 (in a deposition). Defendants denied the oath; in their version the journeyman, 'having been censured by some of the shearmen' for accepting payment in truck, 'had voluntarily declared that he would not do so again, and by way of pretended sanction had kissed a book which happened to be there' (ibid. 158–9, 102 Eng. Rep. 558.

mutiny and sedition; but there are words sufficient in the enacting part to satisfy the preamble; and after dealing with offences of that description, the Act goes on in much more extensive terms, and embraces other more general objects'.[26] Mr Justice Lawrence admitted that 'the preamble and the first part of the enacting clause are confined in their objects to cases of mutiny and sedition', but he could not say that 'combinations like this, which strike at the root of the trade of the kingdom, may not be, though perhaps not so immediately, yet ultimately as mischievous in their consequences, and in the event beget a danger to the State itself to an extent beyond the power of the Government to repress'.[27] *Ejusdem generis* would not be used to limit the offence, despite the tradition that penal statutes were to be construed strictly, *in favorem libertatis*. The judges' opinions constitute a sort of retrospective confirmation of Lord Holland's suggestion three years earlier that the masters had availed themselves of the fear of revolution, 'to enforce their views, and render their workmen more dependent than they had hitherto been'.[28]

Three prosecutions in 1834, another stressful time in English history, when the First Reform Act (1832) had raised profound questions about the social order, reaffirmed the viability of these acts. The first, *Rex* v. *Loveless*,[29] was a prosecution of labourers for administering an unlawful oath. Known to history as the Tolpuddle Martyrs after their Dorset village, the defendants have been hailed as heroes of early trade unionism.[30] From a legal point of view Loveless's Case is less remarkable, except perhaps for the severity of the sentence. George Loveless and others had initiated two agricultural labourers into a trade society. The rules required that none of the members should divulge the secrets of the society and that all should refuse to work with any violator. At the trial at the Dorchester Assizes on 17 March 1834 Baron Williams followed *Marks* (1802) in ruling that the Unlawful Oaths Act (1797) extended to all illegal societies. The jury was left to decide if an oath was in fact taken and if it prohibited the taker from disclosing what was done. At the judge's direction the jury was also required to return a special verdict, that is, a finding on particular facts as opposed to a general verdict of guilty or not guilty, saying whether the defendants were members of a society that prohibited the revelation of its secrets. Answering

---

[26] 3 East 162, 102 Eng. Rep. 559.   [27] 3 East 165, 102 Eng. Rep. 560.

[28] *Parliamentary Register* 9 (1799), 563. See Chap. 4, n. 7.

[29] 1 M. & Rob. 349, 174 Eng. Rep. 119; 6 Car. & P. 596, 172 Eng. Rep. 1380 (Nisi Prius 1834).

[30] A bibliography of the Tolpuddle Martyrs would be long indeed. For a concise review of the legal issues, see Ralph Dickson, 'The Tolpuddle Martyrs: Guilty or Not Guilty?' *Journal of Legal History*, 7 (1986), 178–87; for an extended discussion of the social context see Joyce Marlow, *The Tolpuddle Martyrs* (London, 1971). Two hard-to-obtain articles are worth consulting: Barbara Kerr, 'The Dorset Agricultural Labourer, 1750–1850', *Proceedings of the Dorset Natural History and Archaeological Society*, 84 (1962), 158–77; W. H. Oliver, 'Tolpuddle Martyrs and Trade Union Oaths', *Labour History* (Journal of Australian Society for the Study of Labour History), 10 (May 1966), 5–12.

all questions in the affirmative, the jury found the defendants guilty as charged. The sentence of seven years' transportation (to Australia) was the maximum allowed under the act.

Baron Williams was not alone in his view of the law. Mr Justice Bosanquet announced similar views a few months later in *Rex* v. *Dixon*,[31] an abortive prosecution under the Seditious Meetings Act (1817)[32] that strengthened the earlier Unlawful Societies Act. In March 1834 a combination of Cambridge cordwainers (shoemakers) bound its members by oaths not to disclose any secrets. Because the group had dissolved before the case came on at the Cambridge Assizes on 23 July 1834, the prosecution presented no evidence. A verdict of not guilty was perforce returned, but not before Mr Justice Bosanquet had warned: 'It is for the sake of those who belong to associations like that of the late Cordwainers' Union of Cambridge, that I now declare, that all who engage in associations, the members of which, in consequence of being so, take any oaths not required by law, are guilty of an offence against the statute, which, if clearly proved, would, upon conviction, be in every case followed by exemplary punishment.'[33]

One ominous consequence of this line of cases soon became apparent. On 28 August 1838 the case of *Regina* v. *Hunt*[34] was tried at the Old Bailey before Common Serjeant Mirehouse. Hunt had been indicted for embezzling 9s. from a society he had served as clerk. In his defence it was objected that the society was illegal because it required an unlawful oath. After consulting Justices Bosanquet and Coleridge, the common serjeant ruled that the objection was good and the defendant in consequence not guilty. Of course, as we have seen in the last chapter, even had the society been legal the prosecution would not necessarily have succeeded. In the eye of the law, the misappropriation of joint property was merely taking that which belonged to each equally.

The Unlawful Oaths Act was not in its origin directed at trade unions; it was prompted by fears of mutiny and sedition during the wars with France. That it was turned against labour organizations shows how easily insubordination in the work-place could be analogized to mutiny in the armed services. Whatever the origin of the act against them, unlawful oaths came to occupy a special place in the middle class's imaginings about combinations. Charles Dickens, ever topical, included a dreadful oath in his early novel *Barnaby Rudge* (1841), a fictionalized account of the Gordon Riots that had convulsed London in 1780. Lit by candles set in human skulls and presided over by a bone-waving panjandrum, a novice seeking admission to the Secret Society of 'Prentice Knights took an oath binding him, at the bidding of his chief, 'to resist and obstruct the Lord Mayor, sword-bearer, and chaplain; to despise the authority of the sheriffs; and to

[31] 6 Car. & P. 601, 172 Eng. Rep. 1383 (Nisi Prius 1834).
[32] 57 Geo. 3, c. 19 (1817).   [33] 6 Car. & P. 602, 172 Eng. Rep. 1383.
[34] 8 Car. & P. 642, 173 Eng. Rep. 654 (Nisi Prius 1838).

hold the court of aldermen as nought; but not on any account, in case the fullness of time should bring a general rising of 'prentices, to damage or in any way disfigure Temple Bar, which was strictly constitutional and always to be approached with reverence'.[35] The gifted illustrator Phiz (Hablot K. Browne) provided an accompanying etching.[36] In his own incomparable way Dickens was drawing attention to the distinction noted earlier between workmen's rejection of certain laws and their acceptance of constitutional procedures in general. A few years later Benjamin Disraeli in *Sybil* (1845) described his vision of the initiation into a contemporary 'TRADES UNION'. Before a group wearing mystic robes and in the presence of a human skeleton, the candidate was made to take the following oath:

Do you voluntarily swear in the presence of Almighty God and before these witnesses, that you will execute with zeal and alacrity, so far as in you lies, every task and injunction that the majority of your brethren, testified by the mandate of this grand committee, shall impose upon you, in furtherance of our common welfare, of which they are the sole judges; such as the chastisement of Nobs, the assassination of oppressive and tyrannical masters, or the demolition of all mills, works and shops that shall be deemed by us incorrigible? Do you swear this in the presence of Almighty God, and before these witnesses?[37]

Legal memories are long and in 1912, after several rounds of trade union legislation, an attempt was made to demonstrate the criminality of a trade union by reliance on the Unlawful Societies Act (1799) and the Seditious Meetings Act (1817). Too much had changed by then to permit the attempt to succeed, and the acts although still unrepealed were ruled inapplicable.[38]

In the mean time, as the turbulent decade known in some quarters as the 'Hungry Forties' drew to a close, the law of master and servant, properly so-called, returned to centre stage. We have seen that under the 1823 Act a justice of the peace before whom a complaint was sworn had no alternative but to issue a warrant for the arrest of the accused. This procedure, a constant irritant to workmen, was altered in England in 1848 by general legislation. As remarked in the last chapter, legal procedure was being steadily separated in the nineteenth century from substantive law. Known as Jervis's Act,[39] after Sir John Jervis, Attorney-General in the Whig

---

[35] Charles Dickens, *Barnaby Rudge: A Tale of the Riots of 'Eighty* (1841) (Oxford, 1954), 66.

[36] Ibid. (New Oxford Illustrated Dickens, 1954), facing p. 64.

[37] Benjamin Disraeli, *Sybil, or the Two Nations* (1845) (Oxford, 1981), 221. For what is apparently the text of an actual initiation ceremony see [Edward Carleton Tufnell], *Character, Object, and Effects of Trades' Unions; with Some Remarks on the Law Concerning Them* (1834), 67–75. The 'Nobs' in question are probably not the social superiors also known as swells or toffs, but rather knobsticks or blacklegs.

[38] *Luby* v. *Warwickshire Miners' Association*, [1912] 2 Ch. 371.

[39] 11 & 12 Vict., c. 43 (1848) (Jervis's Act II). See John Frederick Archbold, *Jervis's Acts, 11 & 12 Victoria, cc. 42, 43 and 44; Relating to the Duties of Justices of the Peace* (3rd edn., 1851). See also David Freestone and J. C. Richardson, 'The Making of English Criminal Law, Part 7: Sir John Jervis and his Acts', 1980 *Criminal Law Review* 5–16.

government that adopted it, this act gave justices of the peace in all cases the alternative of first issuing a summons rather than immediately proceeding by warrant.[40] The gradual adoption of the former procedure removed the workmen's most immediate complaint. But Jervis's Act had another, less-well-known result: it ended as a practical matter judicial review of summary convictions by writ of *certiorari*. The appearance, to be sure, remained: the judges could still order the record to be certified and returned to them, but the form provided for use[41] contained so few details that the effect was to preclude a finding of illegality.[42] Judicial review of local government, a mainstay of the eighteenth-century constitution, thus received its obscure *quietus*.

Jervis's Act for good and bad did not, however, extend to Scotland. In that country a movement for the root-and-branch reform of the law began in 1863.[43] This movement achieved notable success soon after the passage of the Second Reform Act (1867)[44] with the enactment of a new Master and Servant Act (1867).[45] Under this statute the injured party could complain in writing

wherever the employer or employed shall neglect or refuse to fulfil any contract of service, or the employed shall neglect or refuse to enter or commence his service according to the contract, or shall absent himself from his service, or wherever any question, difference, or dispute shall arise as to the rights or liabilities of either of the parties, or touching any misusage, misdemeanour, misconduct, ill-treatment, or injury to the person or property of either of the parties under any contract of service . . .[46]

In Scotland the proceedings were before the sheriff; in England before two justices of the peace or one stipendiary magistrate.[47] A warrant was issued only if the accused failed to appear in response to a summons.[48] If the accused was convicted, the punishment was ordinarily a fine, not to exceed £20.[49] Only in aggravated cases was imprisonment with or without hard labour for up to three months provided,[50] and in such cases an offender was given a special right of appeal to quarter sessions.[51] Contractual thinking had made a further advance since 1823. As a matter of evidence, it was no longer significant whether or not the workman had yet entered into his status: parol contracts were as enforceable as written ones.[52] The contract of service was now all-important. As the further implications of this

---

[40] 11 & 12 Vict., c. 43, § 1.　　　　　　　　　　　　　　　　　[41] Ibid. § 17.

[42] See *R. v. Nat Bell Liquors*, [1922] 2 AC 159 (PC) (Lord Summer, J.) ('The effect [of Jervis's Act] was not to make that which had been error, error no longer, but to remove nearly all opportunity for its detection. The face of the record "spoke" no longer: it was the inscrutable face of a sphinx').

[43] See Daphne Simon, 'Master and Servant', in John Saville (ed.), *Democracy and the Labour Movement: Essays in Honor of Dona Torr* (London, 1954), 160–200.

[44] 30 & 31 Vict., c. 102 (1867) (15 Aug.).

[45] 30 & 31 Vict., c. 141 (short title in § 1) (1867) (20 Aug.).

[46] Ibid. § 4.　　　　　　　[47] Ibid. and § 2.　　　　　　　[48] Ibid. § 7.

[49] Ibid. § 9.　　　[50] Ibid. § 14.　　　[51] Ibid. § 15.　　　[52] Ibid. § 2.

viewpoint became clearer, the law of master and servant appeared ever more anomalous.

While not in so many words repealing all earlier statutes, the Master and Servant Act (1867) effectively superseded them. Like the Trades Unions Funds Protection Act (1869), however, the relief was only temporary; by its terms the act expired in one year.[53] The unsettled political climate that followed the Second Reform Act precluded for the present a long-term settlement. In fact, the 1867 Act was extended from year to year[54] until at last it and all previous acts were repealed and replaced by the Conspiracy and Protection of Property Act (1875).

[53] Ibid. § 26.
[54] 31 & 32 Vict., c. 111 (1868); 32 & 33 Vict., c. 85 (1869); 33 & 34 Vict., c. 103 (1870); 34 & 35 Vict., c. 95 (1871); 35 & 36 Vict., c. 88 (1872); 36 & 37 Vict., c. 75 (1873); 37 & 38 Vict., c. 76 (1874).

8

The Law of Strikes: 1859–1871

'What's a strike?' asked Gub-Gub. . . .
'A strike,' said the Doctor, 'is when people stop doing their own
particular work in order to get somebody else to give them what they
want.'

Dr Dolittle (1923)

The strike was a product of the Industrial Revolution as surely as were the miles of cotton cloth that rolled off the looms of Lancashire. The use of the word 'strike' to mean a concerted stoppage of work was a neologism in the late eighteenth century, apparently borrowed from the practice of protesting sailors to strike or lower the sails.[1] The 1824 select committee, as we have seen, introduced the word in its resolutions, explaining it as 'suspension of work'.[2] By the mid-nineteenth century it was established usage, although cautious writers continued to set it off in inverted commas in recognition of its recent origin.[3] In 1867 a barrister could take for granted that a jury knew what it meant, the term being, he said, 'now perfectly well understood'.[4] By 1923, a few years before the General Strike, only children and animals could have been in doubt, so Dr Dolittle obliged with his definition.[5]

As a social fact the strike was a withdrawal of labour. Strikers did not normally intend to terminate their employment, but rather (as the select committee recognized) to suspend it temporarily. On the theoretical level the strike was nothing but an attempt by labour to render capital unproductive until it met certain conditions. Under a strict regime of private property such an attempt, so long as it stopped short of violence to person or property, might have been regarded as a purely private matter. Many of

---

[1] *Oxford English Dictionary* (1st edn., 1884–1928), s.v. 'strike'. See also Marcus Rediker, *Between the Devil and the Deep Blue Sea: Merchant Seamen, Pirates, and the Anglo-American Maritime World, 1700–1750* (Cambridge, 1987), 110, 205. For a recent criticism of the traditional etymology, see C. R. Dobson, *Masters and Journeymen: A Prehistory of Industrial Relations, 1717–1800* (London, 1980), 19.

[2] *Parliamentary Papers* (1824), 5, 589 (Combination Resolution No. 1). See Chap. 5, n. 32.

[3] See e.g. H. Dunckley, *'Strikes' Viewed in Relation to the Interests of Capital and Labour* (1853); Francis D. Longe, *An Inquiry into the Law of 'Strikes'* (1860).

[4] *R. v. Druitt*, 10 Cox CC 594 (Cent. Crim. Ct. 1867) (Serjeant Ballantine).

[5] Quoted in Hugh Lofting, *Doctor Dolittle's Post Office* (Philadelphia, 1923), 168 (the epigraph of the present chapter of this book).

the competitive practices of contemporary business were regarded in just this light. But if in its primary aspects the strike was economic warfare against capital, it was patent to every observer that some strikes also involved civil war within the ranks of labour. Concerted action was of the essence of a strike: the departure of a mere handful of the work-force would be ineffectual in its object. Unanimity was therefore necessary, and there was an understandable temptation to coerce the will of reluctant strikers when it was lacking. Furthermore, the withdrawal of workmen would be fruitless if they were promptly replaced by others.

The standardization of labour occasioned by the new mechanical means of production made it simpler for capitalists in some industries to substitute one set of hands for another. So, sometime early in the nineteenth century, another social fact appeared, marked by another neologism, this one borrowed from military terminology.[6] The 'picket'—spelled 'picquet' as late as the last quarter of the nineteenth century[7]—was one or more strikers detailed to persuade workmen not to accept employment. In the 1867 case referred to earlier, the same barrister thought it necessary to explain to a jury what was meant by picketing. In a tailors' strike, it meant 'planting men . . . in the neighbourhood of a master tailor's shop, and, as a great deal of tailoring was done for the masters out of doors, watching who did that work . . . the object being to prevent any work being done'.[8] In sum, the modern strike involved three sets of oppositions: (1) strikers versus capitalists, (2) strikers versus waverers within their own ranks, and (3) strikers versus potential strike-breakers.

As we have seen, parliament had repealed and replaced the 'barbarous laws' against trade unions in 1825. Yet statutes mean no more than the judges say they mean, and the law of strikes at mid-century was, as we have also seen, a judicial gloss on that legislation. Once, in 1859, parliament attempted to correct the judges by explaining 'certain beautiful fragments of the old statute', but the oracles of the law quickly showed themselves proof against parliamentary meddling. During the dozen years from 1859 to 1871 the law of strikes had to be gathered from a collection of cases in which the judiciary revealed its skill at subtle reasoning and nice distinctions.

The history of the 1859 legislation can be traced to early 1852 when William Peel and Frederick Green, the officers of the National Association of United Trades who had been convicted in Rowlands's Case (1851), were released from Staffordshire gaol. They believed they had been unjustly imprisoned: the 1825 Act did not, they thought, support their conviction. On returning to London, the pair joined with other officers of the National Association in lobbying for change. Not until seven years had passed, did

---

[6] *Oxford English Dictionary*, s.v. 'picket'.

[7] *Judge* v. *Bennett*, 4 T. L. Rep. 75 (QB 1887). See also *The Trial of the Mechanics at Liverpool*, ed. W. P. Roberts (1847), p. iv (*R.* v. *Selsby*).

[8] *R.* v. *Druitt*, 10 Cox CC 594 (Serjeant Ballantine).

parliament amend the statute, thus altering the law as laid down by Mr Justice Erle. Entitled 'An Act to amend and explain an Act of the Sixth Year of the Reign of King George the Fourth [*i.e.*, the 1825 Act]',[9] the new statute was known to contemporaries as another combination act.[10] Later commentators, perhaps in an effort to avoid confusion with earlier legislation, have dubbed it the 'Molestation of Workmen Act'[11] in reference to its restrictions on the judicial definition of molestation, as well as obstruction.

The Molestation of Workmen Act resulted from a curious alliance between the National Association and the Conservative Party. When William Peel and Frederick Green were released from gaol, the government of the day was Lord Derby's short-lived ministry, dismissingly nicknamed the 'Who? Who? Ministry' because of its members' lack of renown. (The aged Duke of Wellington thought that owing to his deafness he had mistaken the names of the cabinet ministers; his questions 'Who? Who?' were overheard and used by contemporary wits.[12]) The executive of the National Association consulted Charles Sturgeon, a Tory barrister, and together they 'drew a little bill, of nine lines in length, to explain to the Judges how they had failed to explain the views of the Legislator'.[13] After tactfully alluding to 'doubts' as to the construction of the earlier statute, the bill (in an enacting part that occupied nine lines) declared:

that masters, employers, workmen, or other persons who shall enter into any combination to advance or to lower or to fix the rate of their wages, or to lessen or alter the hours or duration of the time of their working, or to peaceably persuade or induce others to abstain from work, in order to obtain the rates of wages or the altered hours of labour so fixed or agreed upon, shall not be deemed or taken to be

[9] 22 Vict., c. 34 (1859).

[10] See 'Report of the Central Committee of United Trades on the Proceedings Connected with the "Combination of Workmen Bill" in the Parliamentary Session, 1853' (1853) (hereinafter cited as 1853 Report); 'Report of the Executive Committee of the National Association of United Trades on the Proceedings Connected with the Combination of Workmen Bill, 1859' (1859). The copy of the latter pamphlet in the Kress Collection, Graduate School of Business Administration, Harvard Univ., is autographed by Thomas Winters, an officer of the National Association and another defendant in Rowlands's Case (against whom charges were eventually dropped). See also indexes to *Hansard*, 3rd ser., vols. 125–9, 152–3; *Commons Journal*, vols. 108, 114; *Lords Journal*, vols. 85, 91.

[11] See e.g. Henry H. Slesser and Charles Baker, *Trade Union Law* (3rd edn., London, 1927), 166, 181, 215; R. Y. Hedges and Allan Winterbottom, *The Legal History of Trade Unionism* (London, 1930), 41, 51; Norman Arthur Citrine, *Trade Union Law* (3rd edn., London, 1967 (ed. M. A. Hickling)); K. W. Wedderburn, *The Worker and the Law* (2nd edn., Harmondsworth, 1971), 310; Bryn Perrins, *Trade Union Law* (London, 1985), 36.

[12] See Llewellyn Woodward, *The Age of Reform, 1815–1870* (2nd edn., Oxford, 1962), 164 n. 3.

[13] Charles Sturgeon, 'Letters to the Trades' Unionists and the Working Classes on the Recent Bill Brought in to Repeal the Combination Laws, and Enslave the Working Classes, by Sir T. F. Buxton, Bart., and Mr. Young' (1868), 2. The bill so extravagantly denounced appears in *Parliamentary Papers* (1867–8), 5, 575–8. One of the legislative proposals concerning labour in the late 1860s, it soon fell by the wayside.

guilty of 'molestation' or 'obstruction' within the meaning of the said Act, and shall not therefore be subject or liable to any indictment or prosecution for conspiracy.[14]

The strategy was the familiar one from 1824–5: not to legalize the action as such but to immunize it from prosecution for criminal conspiracy. With themselves as witnesses to the expansive judicial reading of the 1825 Act and with a proposed remedy in hand, the committee was then ready to begin the next phase of its campaign: 'a quiet but persevering agitation in favour of the bill among the trades, both metropolitan and provincial'.[15] Reports and circulars were written and deputations sent out. Finally, the bill was communicated to the government, which undertook to offer no opposition.[16]

Before it could even be introduced, Derby's inglorious government had fallen, and Lord Aberdeen had formed a more substantial government of Whigs. None the less, on 16 March 1853 the Molestation of Workmen bill was given its first reading;[17] the second came on 5 April at which time there was a short debate. Henry Drummond, one of the bill's sponsors, argued that it was needed because the judges had disagreed on the meaning of key terms, while Lord Palmerston, the new Home Secretary, recorded his desire to maintain the illegality of 'that kind of molestation which, without any act of violence, would enable workmen by means of a system of intimidation which was perfectly well understood among them, to prevent members of their class, in spite of their own wish, from continuing at their employment'.[18] On 12 April the bill came before a committee of the whole House, and although the Home Secretary intimated that he would drop his opposition if suitable amendments could be agreed on,[19] no changes were made.[20] When it came time for the third and final reading on 18 April, the Attorney-General Sir Alexander Cockburn (later Lord Chief Justice) pronounced the bill unnecessary because, he said, Mr Justice Erle had stated the law correctly in Rowlands's Case. On putting the question, the bill was defeated 70 to 57. According to its sponsors, most of the Whigs were opposed, the Radicals were split, and most of the Conservatives supported it[21] (see Table 1).

When on Wednesday, 4 May, the bill's sponsors again moved the third reading, the government front bench once more went into action. This time the other law officer of the Crown, Richard Bethell, Solicitor General, spoke against it and moved that the third reading be put off six months. Since parliament would have risen well before then, this was an attempt to kill the bill by postponing it to the Greek kalends. Palmerston too spoke out:

They all knew it often happened that men who were able to abstain from work combined to do so, while there was another set of men in great distress, and who were willing to work even at a lower rate of wages, who were prevented by the

---

[14] *Parliamentary Papers* (1852–3), 1, 351.   [15] 1853 Report, 6.   [16] Ibid. 7.
[17] *Commons Journal*, 108 (1853), 342.
[18] *Hansard*, 3rd ser., vol. 125, col. 647 (5 Apr. 1853).
[19] 1853 Report, 8–10.
[20] *Commons Journal*, 108 (1853), 392.   [21] 1853 Report, 8.

TABLE 1.   Third Division on Molestation of
Workmen Bill (18 Apr. 1853)

	Yeas	Noes
Conservatives	36	8
Radicals	13	15
Whigs	8	47
Totals	57	70

Source: 'Report of the Central Committee of United
Trades on the Proceedings Connected with the
"Combination of Workmen Bill" in the Parliament-
ary Session, 1853' (1853), 8.

combination of the former from taking employment and finding the means of supporting themselves and their families.[22]

Going as usual to the heart of the matter, the Home Secretary recognized the picket as a device for enforcing solidarity among workmen in an era of surplus labour. It was, however, inconvenient for the supporters of the measure to acknowledge Palmerston's bald characterization. Montague Chambers defended the bill as a mere declaratory measure made necessary by contradictory judicial decisions: Baron Rolfe had ruled that workmen might gather to persuade others not to work, while Mr Justice Erle had ruled that it was illegal for men to agree to strike in order to force a manufacturer to alter his mode of carrying on business. The bill would simply resolve this conflict in favour of Baron Rolfe's view of the law.

As the vote drew near, the septuagenarian Joseph Hume, who thirty years earlier had worked with Francis Place for the repeal of the combination laws, moved to adjourn debate.[23] According to the bill's sponsors, Whigs and Conservatives were almost evenly divided on the motion, while most of the Radicals opposed it[24] (see Table 2). Little can be learned from the figures, however, because some of the bill's supporters favoured adjournment, while others did not. In the event, the motion was defeated 121 to 102. As a fitting conclusion to this scene of confusion, the Speaker ignored the vote and adjourned the House anyway: by its standing orders, the House rose on Wednesday at six o'clock whether it had completed its business or not.

On 1 June the question of the bill's third reading came before the House once again. Palmerston reiterated his criticism of the previous month: the bill would legalize 'that system of quiet and peaceful intimidation' by which

[22] *Hansard*, 3rd ser., vol. 126, col. 1120 (4 May 1853).
[23] 1853 Report, 9.   [24] Ibid. 10.

TABLE 2.   Adjournment Division on Molestation of Workmen Bill (4 May 1853)

	Yeas	Noes
Conservatives	82	72
Radicals	10	38
Whigs	10	11
Totals	102	121

Source: 'Report of the Central Committee of United Trades on the Proceedings Connected with the "Combination of Workmen Bill" in the Parliamentary Session, 1853' (1853), 10.

well-organized workmen could prevent others from selling their labour for less.[25] None the less, the noble lord proposed that the third reading be scheduled in two weeks, at which time amendments would also be considered. Behind Palmerston's proposal lay two months of manœuvring. Although the bill had been reported without amendment on 12 April, search for a compromise had gone on behind the scenes and explained the frequent delays.

On 15 June the House of Commons amended and passed the Molestation of Workmen bill. At the last moment agreement had been reached. The lengthened bill (its amendments indicated by italics) now declared:

that masters, employers, workmen, or other persons who shall enter into any combination to advance or to lower or to fix the rate of their wages, or to lessen or alter the hours or duration of the time of their working, or *workmen who shall by peaceable persuasion, and without any intimidation of any kind whatsoever, endeavour* to induce others to abstain from work, in order to obtain the rates of wages or the altered hours of labour so fixed or agreed upon *or to be agreed upon*, shall not be deemed or taken to be guilty of 'molestation' or 'obstruction' within the meaning of the said Act, and shall not therefore be subject or liable to any indictment or prosecution for conspiracy: *provided always, that nothing herein contained shall authorize any attempt to induce any workman to break or depart from any contract or engagement.*[26]

The new language restricted the right of peaceable persuasion to workmen, thereby excluding those volunteers ('other persons') in whose favour Mr Justice Patteson had found nothing to say,[27] and it attempted to exclude that 'system of intimidation' to which Palmerston objected. It meticulously

[25] *Hansard*, 3rd ser., vol. 127, col. 1017 (1 June 1853).
[26] *Parliamentary Papers*, Lords (1852–3), 3, 583.
[27] 5 Cox CC 492. See Chap. 5, n. 170.

made plain that it applied not only to agreements on wages and hours already concluded but also to those still in prospect ('to be agreed upon'). Finally, the proviso emphasized that Baron Rolfe's ruling was restricted to men not under contract.

Contract, the centrepiece of late nineteenth-century legal thought, made, as we have seen, a belated appearance in labour law. For centuries it had played only a supporting role in the legal scheme of things in general: Blackstone devoted less than a chapter to it in his big volume on property; in his system contract was principally a means for transferring title.[28] In the longer history of the common law its function had been to create status. The contract of marriage, which created the relationship of husband and wife, was then far closer to the centre of things. A contract of sale conferred on the purchaser what might be called the status of owner; a contract of service (in other words, an employment contract) created the relationship of master and servant. Seen in this light, there was nothing unusual about laws regulating the duties attached to this status, just as law also regulated the other 'great relations': husband and wife and parent and child.

By the mid-nineteenth century, contract was coming to play a role of its own. Creation of status was fading into the background; contract was now reconceptualized as regulating all aspects of the relationships it created. The marriage contract became an anachronism. The law of master and servant, too, seemed increasingly anomalous, but if the new legal logic undercut the law of master and servant, it bolstered the law of strikes. Strikers, unless they timed their action to coincide with the termination of their contracts, were in breach. That was bad enough. Why should they be permitted to attempt, even by peaceable persuasion, to induce others to break their own? The renovation of legal thought was far-reaching: not only was the scope of contract expanded, but contract itself was reified and became a form of property. Just as the law provided a remedy for interfering with land and chattels, so it would prevent interference with that less tangible interest. As in the earlier history of combination and conspiracy, statute and case law developed in tandem, although this time the judges finished first. Two weeks before the Molestation of Workmen bill was amended to exclude 'any attempt to induce any workman to break or depart from any contract', the judges in the landmark case of *Lumley* v. *Gye* had recognized a new common-law tort: inducing breach of contract.[29]

As amended, the bill was read for the first time in the House of Lords on 16 June. Despite the compromise with the government, it found few supporters in the upper chamber. Lord Kinnaird moved the second reading

---

[28] Blackstone, *Commentaries*, ii. chap. 30 ('Of Title of Gift, Grant and Contract').
[29] *Lumley* v. *Gye*, 2 El. & Bl. 216, 118 Eng. Rep. 749 (QB 1853). See Francis Bowes Sayre, 'Inducing Breach of Contract', 36 *Harvard Law Review* 663–703 (1922–3); 'Note', 'Tortious Interference with Contractual Relations in the Nineteenth Century: The Transformation of Property, Contract, and Tort', 93 *Harvard Law Review* 1510–39 (1980).

with reluctance, diffidently alluding to the unpropitious atmosphere produced by contemporary strikes.[30] But there had been many petitions, and, after all, the bill's object was not to change the existing law, only to explain it. In response, Lord Truro, a former Whig Lord Chancellor, denounced the bill. The National Association felt betrayed: Lord Truro had, they thought, pledged his support.[31] But worse was to come. Lord Cranworth, the present Lord Chancellor, rose to speak. His remarks were eagerly awaited because he was, in fact, the former Baron Rolfe, ennobled in 1850. After first denying any difference between himself and Mr Justice Erle, he attacked the proposed act: 'It is not illegal at present to use "peaceable persuasion"; but for a body of men to combine together to ask another to join with them was not "peaceable persuasion", and it was difficult to say that there could be any "peaceable persuasion" without some kind of molestation.'[32] The Lord Chancellor's intervention signalled defeat. Though he announced that he was prepared to amend the bill further, it was apparent that no amendments acceptable to him would be worth while for the sponsors. In the face of overwhelming opposition, Lord Kinnaird withdrew the bill. Influential Whig leaders were adamantly opposed to it, and they were to remain in power for five more years. In fact, in 1855 Palmerston succeeded Aberdeen as prime minister.

In February 1858 Lord Derby returned to power. With the advent of the Conservatives, hopes for the Molestation of Workmen bill revived. None the less, a year passed before it began its second parliamentary career. On 8 March 1859, the bill was introduced by Thomas Duncombe.[33] Dismissed by the Webbs as 'the aristocratic demagogue of the period', Duncombe was himself a past president of the National Association of United Trades.[34] After reciting that 'different decisions' had been given on the construction of the 1825 Act, the new bill, based on the amended 1853 version, provided:

that no workman or other person, whether actually in employment or not, shall, by reason merely of his entering into an agreement with any workman or workmen, or other person or persons, for the purpose of fixing or endeavouring to fix the rate of wages or remuneration at which they or any of them shall work, or by reason merely of his endeavouring peaceably, and without threat or intimidation, direct or indirect, to persuade others to cease or abstain from work, in order to obtain the rate of wages or the altered hours of labour so fixed or agreed upon or to be agreed upon, shall be deemed or taken to be guilty of 'molestation' or 'obstruction', within the meaning of the said Act, and shall not therefore be subject or liable to any prosecution or indictment for conspiracy: provided always, that nothing herein contained shall authorize any workman to break or depart from any contract or

[30] *Hansard*, 3rd ser., vol. 129, col. 1322 (16 June 1853).
[31] 1853 Report, 15.
[32] *Hansard*, 3rd ser., vol. 129, col. 1324.
[33] *Commons Journal*, 114 (1859), 98.
[34] Sidney Webb and Beatrice Webb, *The History of Trade Unionism* (rev. edn., London, 1920), 187 n. 2.

authorize any attempt to induce any workman to break or depart from any contract.[35]

This bill sailed through the House without debate. The second reading was on 6 April, the third on 8 April.

The Lords acted promptly on the matter. After a first reading on 11 April, the bill was given its second reading the next day. At that time Lord Airlie, who sponsored the bill, explained that 'there had been some doubt as to what constituted an obstruction within the meaning of the [1825] act; and, indeed, there had been contradictory decisions upon the matter'.[36] Lord Donoughmore, president of the Board of Trade, made no objection: 'It was only fair', he thought, 'that workmen should know distinctly what was penal and what was not'.[37] On 14 April the bill was referred to a committee of the whole House. On resuming, their lordships made the following amendment: after the words 'endeavouring peaceably' they inserted the words 'and in a reasonable manner'.[38] As amended, the bill passed the Lords on 15 April. On 18 April the Commons accepted the amendment, and the next day the royal assent converted the bill into 22 Victoria, c. 34.

More than seven years had passed since William Peel and Frederick Green had been released from gaol. These years of lobbying had produced a very small act indeed. Between its passage in 1859 and its repeal in 1871, the Molestation of Workmen Act provided the legal basis for picketing. Its terms were obviously restricted: aside from the proviso against inducing breach of contract, the amended act confined a picket to 'endeavouring peaceably, and in a reasonable manner, and without threat or intimidation, direct or indirect, to persuade others to cease or abstain from work'. None the less, trade union officers like Peel and Green, persons not 'actually in employment', were protected by the statute as it was finally adopted. As in the 1825 Act, however, legal agreements could concern wages and hours only. Ironically, pickets protesting at a master's use of apprentices, such as those in Selsby's Case (1847), were not included.

In the history of trade unionism, the Molestation of Workmen Act serves as a reminder of the continuing vitality of the National Association of United Trades throughout the 1850s. While labour historians have noticed the wound inflicted by the prosecution in Rowlands's Case (1851), they have ignored the National Association's gallant counterattack.[39] It is

---

[35] *Parliamentary Papers* (1859) (Sess. 1), 1, 303.

[36] *Hansard*, 3rd ser., vol. 153, col. 1624 (12 Apr. 1859).   [37] Ibid.

[38] *Lords Journal*, 91 (1859), 208.

[39] The pattern was set by George Howell, himself a trade union leader, albeit a 'respectable' one. 'Trades' Union Congresses and Social Legislation', *Contemporary Review*, 56 (1889), 401–2 ('In 1846 another attempt was made to found a federation of labour, by the inauguration of the "National Association of Organized [sic] Trades", on March 25th of that year. This association was very active during the first two years of its history, but it subsequently lost its influence, though it continued in existence down to 1861'). The Webbs were a bit more explicit on the date of decline (*History of Trade Unionism*, 195: 'The later

necessary to recognize the at least partial success of this campaign and the conditions that made it possible. Politically the act was the product of a mid-Victorian flirtation between labour and the Conservative Party. As Charles Sturgeon later recalled with the foreshortening of hindsight: 'After fighting hard against the great Liberal party for between four and five years, we passed our little Bill (22 Vic., c. 34), to the great joy of the Working Classes and chagrin of the Manchester Radicals.'[40] This rallying of Conservatives and skilled workmen foreshadowed their fruitful co-operation in the mid-1870s. Before Lord Salisbury's discovery of middle-class Toryism in the 1880s, the Conservative Party was the party of the landed interest,[41] and the landed interest (barring the organization of agricultural labourers) was not necessarily hostile to labour. The Whigs in alliance with manufacturers and Manchester Radicals could ill afford to countenance strikes, while the Conservatives, without any immediate interest in the outcome, could indulge labour in the definition of a couple of words. As late as 1906, despite the sea change in English politics, the Conservatives were still claiming credit for the Molestation of Workmen Act: 'In 1859 Lord Derby's Conservative Government passed an Act further confirming the freedom of labour and liberty of combination.'[42]

In the history of English law, the Molestation of Workmen Act occupies a deservedly minor place; it is none the less true that it enjoyed momentary greatness. In his original survey of the development of English law during the nineteenth century, A. V. Dicey dated the close of the 'period of liberal (individualist) legislation' concerning the right of association at 1859. The age of Bentham, so Dicey told the audience at his 1898 Harvard lectures,[43] ended ingloriously with that small statute. Among the readings on this topic that the lecturer recommended was John Stuart Mill's famous essay *On Liberty*, first published in 1859. In the year of the Molestation of Workmen Act, Mill had elaborated on a theme from Adam Smith; in his attempt to persuade the public of the illegitimacy of interference in 'private concerns',

history of the association is obscure . . . But it ceases after 1851 to exercise any influence or play any important part in the Trade Union Movement'). This pattern has survived. See e.g. W. Hamish Fraser, *Trade Unions and Society: The Struggle for Acceptance, 1850–1880* (Totowa, NJ, 1974), 43 ('Although [the National Association] continued in existence until the mid-sixties, it was of little importance after 1851'), and E. H. Hunt, *British Labour History, 1815–1914* (Atlantic Highlands, NJ, 1981), 204 ('There was one further attempt to launch a general union—the National Association of United Trades for the Protection of Labour (1845)—but it received very little support and soon became transformed into a modest pressure group seeking better industrial relations through conciliation').

[40] Sturgeon, 'Letters to the Trades' Unionists', 2.

[41] See James P. Cornford, 'The Transformation of Conservatism in the Late Nineteenth Century', *Victorian Studies*, 7 (1963–4), 35–66.

[42] Conservative Party, Scotland, *Campaign Guide* (1906), 255. I am indebted for this reference to G. R. Rubin of Darwin College, Univ. of Kent.

[43] See the syllabus for those lectures, 'Development of English Law during the Nineteenth Century in Connection with the Course of Public Opinion in England' (1898), 4, preserved in the Harvard Law Library.

the essayist had appealed to his readers' preconceptions about the labouring classes:

It is known that the bad workmen who form the majority of the operatives in many branches of industry are decidedly of opinion that bad workmen ought to receive the same wages as good, and that no one ought to be allowed, through piecework or otherwise, to earn by superior skill or industry more than others can without it. And they employ a moral police, which occasionally becomes a physical one, to deter skilful workmen from receiving, and employers from giving, a larger remuneration for a more useful service. If the public have any jurisdiction over private concerns, I cannot see that these people are in fault, or that any individual's particular public can be blamed for asserting the same authority over his individual conduct which the general public asserts over people in general.[44]

Dicey agreed with Mill and saw at first the fearsome dawn of the age of collectivism in the passage of this little bill. A few years' reflection, however, convinced Dicey that he had antedated England's fall from grace. In his published lectures, he moved the opening of the last phase of English legal history to coincide with the far greater labour legislation of the 1870s.[45] The lecturer's second thought was undoubtedly the better one: the 1859 Act opened no new era. The language of the earlier legislation had been vague, perhaps intentionally so, and the judges construed it according to their own 'judicial opinion'. The affected segment of the public used what little political influence it had in an effort to try to impose a favourable reading.

In 1859 the law of strikes was settled, seemingly for years to come, in a manner acceptable to labour. Violence in industrial relations, as in all other relations, was impermissible; on this rule of civilized life, labour's leaders had come to agree. Threats and intimidation were also impermissible because of their close connection with bodily harm. Molestation and obstruction, whatever they meant, sounded undesirable; labour could accept their outlawry so long as they could not be used by hostile judges as a pretext for punishing peaceable persuasion. Using any of these means to affect economic behaviour was criminal under the 1825 Act; conspiring to use them for the same ends was criminal at common law. Breaking one's contract or inducing another to break his was not authorized, but the restraint implied was not in practice very serious because many employment contracts were terminable at will, by either side without notice. Where notice was required, the period was typically short, no more than two weeks

---

[44] John Stuart Mill, *On Liberty* (1859), (Indianapolis, Ind., 1978), 85–6 chap. 4. See also, to similar effect, Mill's *Principles of Political Economy* (6th edn., 1865), bk. v, chap. 10, § 5. For Adam Smith's observation, see Chap. 2, n. 66.

[45] A. V. Dicey, *Lectures on the Relation between Law and Public Opinion in England during the Nineteenth Century* (1st ed., 1905; 2nd edn., 1914). There is likewise no mention of the Molestation of Workmen Act in the article that intervened between the Harvard lectures and the published ones: 'The Combination Laws as Illustrating the Relation between Law and Opinion in England during the Nineteenth Century', 17 *Harvard Law Review* 511–32 (1903–4).

in most cases, and employers of skilled labour, particularly where it was well organized, would have required more time to mobilize replacements in order to avoid a costly disruption of production. Labour had reached an accommodation, however awkward, with the regnant political economy, and it seemed ready to settle down and live with the rules of economic warfare it had helped to shape.[46] But the legal structure, which was so carefully proportioned, was soon to be modified by the judiciary, who would add during the decade of the 1860s a bewildering arrangement of technicalities and ill-defined dogmas. Later, after labour had joined land and capital in the political life of the nation, parliament would be forced to demolish the judges' handiwork and replace it with a more durable structure.

Litigation supplies the building blocks for judicial construction, and cases concerning strikes reached the common-law courts in increasing numbers in the 1860s. While parliament was considering the Molestation of Workmen bill for the second time, one of the most important disputes of mid-century was erupting in London. The builders demanded a nine-hour working day, the masters refused, and the men went on strike.[47] Fondly believing that they could defeat the union once and for all, the masters banded together—'combined' with dubious legality[48]—and agreed that they would never again hire unionists in their trade. Any workman seeking employment would be required to make the following declaration:

I declare that I am not now, nor will I during my engagement with you become, a member of, or support, any society which directly or indirectly interferes with the arrangements of this or any other establishment, or the hours or terms of labour, and that I recognize the right of employers and employed individually to make any trade engagements on which they may choose to agree.[49]

This was, of course, the 'document', notorious in British labour history; in America it went by the more colourful name of 'yellow-dog contract'. Whatever it was called, the declaration should be seen for what it was: a contract in defence of freedom of contract, an attempt to do by private agreement what had once been done by criminal law. Half a century earlier the Combination Act (1800) had outlawed all contracts of employment except those 'between any master and his journeyman or manufacturer, for

[46] See Roger V. Clements, 'British Trade Unions and Popular Political Economy, 1850–1875', *Economic History Review*, 2nd ser., 14 (1961–2), 93–104; Irving Garbati, 'British Trade Unionism in the Mid-Victorian Era', *University of Toronto Quarterly*, 20 (1950–1), 69–84; Trygve R. Tholfsen, *Working-Class Radicalism in Mid-Victorian England* (New York, 1976).

[47] See Raymond W. Postgate, *The Builders' History* (London, 1923), 167–76; Richard Price, *Masters, Unions and Men: Work Control in Building and the Rise of Labour, 1830–1914* (Cambridge, 1980), 39–54.

[48] It was later held that an agreement by masters not to employ any workman who is a member of a trade union was not an offence against the 1825 Act. *R. v. Mitchell*, 4 Cox Mag. C. 448 (Nisi Prius 1867) (mistakenly referring to 6 Geo. 4, c. 25, rather than to 6 Geo. 4, c. 129).

[49] Quoted in *Walsby v. Anley*, 3 El. & El. 517, 121 Eng. Rep. 536 (QB 1861).

or on account of the work or service of such journeyman or manufacturer with whom such contract may be made'.[50] By mid-century the rule was simply *pacta sunt servanda* ('contracts are to be kept').[51] Although the law by that time permitted workmen to combine in pursuit of better wages or hours—in the sense of exempting them from prosecution for criminal conspiracy—there was nothing to prevent them from agreeing to forgo the opportunity.

During the builders' strike the employers faced only one obstacle, albeit an insurmountable one: no more than a handful of men could be found willing to enter into this particular pact. One employer named Anley, for instance, who normally had a hundred men working for him, found only two who would make the required declaration.[52] In time, therefore, Anley and his fellow employers had to discard the document; the men, for their part, proved unable to make good their demand for a nine-hour day. The strike ended in a draw, but hard feelings remained. The unionists resented the strike-breakers, whom they called knobsticks (nobs) and blacklegs. Shortly after the strike ended, a workman named Walsby handed Anley a copy of a resolution signed by about thirty men stating that unless he fired the two strike-breakers, the signatories would quit. Anley refused, and the men left.

Like many middle-class persons then and now, Anley felt that what Walsby had done was wrong: it was unfair to Anley, and it was unfair to the two men who had made the declaration. There ought to be a law against this kind of thing. In fact, the Combination Act (1800) had included the offence of refusing to work with other workmen, unless for 'just or reasonable cause', but since 1825 the statutory crimes had been tied to the five impermissible means: violence, threats, intimidation, molestation, or obstruction (the latter two 'explained' by the Molestation of Workmen Act). There was no violence or threat of violence in the case, yet Anley knew that an attempt had been made to put him in fear, if not of bodily harm then of economic injury, which might be worse. By charging Walsby with a violation of the 1825 Act, rather than with a conspiracy to violate it, he could get the benefit of the speedier and less costly procedure laid down in the statute. Since the charged offence had been committed within the London metropolitan area, he could take advantage of the Metropolitan Police Courts Act (1839)[53] and bring his summary action before one stipendiary magistrate, rather than two justices of the peace. Within a month of handing over the offending resolution, Walsby was convicted of

[50] 39 & 40 Geo. 3, c. 106, § 1 (1800). See Chap. 4, n. 56.

[51] *Restatement (Second) of Contracts* (1981), chap. 11, introductory notes. Cf. Herbert Broom, *A Selection of Legal Maxims* (7th edn., 1874), 698 ('*Pacta conventa quae neque contra leges neque dolo malo inita sunt omni modo observanda sunt*' 'Agreements which are not contrary to the laws nor entered into with a fraudulent design are in all respects to be observed') (quoting *Code of Justinian* 2.3.29).

[52] 3 El. & El. 517, 121 Eng. Rep. 536.   [53] 2 & 3 Vict., c. 71 (1839).

using threats in order to force his employer to discharge certain workmen— in violation of the third branch of the crime created in 1825—and was sentenced to one month at hard labour. In Selsby's Case (1847), a case involving the first branch of the penal section of the 1825 Act—threats to prevent workmen from accepting employment—Baron Rolfe had ruled that an attempt to persuade a workman that it was not in his interest to work under certain conditions was not an illegal threat. In the present case it was arguable that all that was involved was an attempt to persuade the employer to discharge the strike-breakers or take the consequences. No threat of bodily harm was involved. Whether the police magistrate did not know of Baron Rolfe's ruling or simply chose to ignore it is not known.

Whatever the reasoning in the inferior tribunal, Walsby had grounds for hope that his conviction would be overturned on appeal. When Walsby's 'case stated' reached the Court of Queen's Bench in early 1861, the issue was whether the magistrate had erred in finding that Walsby had delivered an unlawful threat. In short order the court affirmed the conviction and made plain the irrelevance of the Molestation of Workmen Act. Applying only to the offences of molestation and obstruction, it left unaffected the law of threats, and that law would not after all be confined to threats of bodily harm. Lord Chief Justice Cockburn, former Attorney-General in Lord Palmerston's government, prefaced his opinion with seemingly generous remarks about the rights of labour: workmen have a right, he said, to put the employer the alternative of retaining their service or discharging those obnoxious to them. But, in marked opposition to Baron Rolfe's summing up in Selsby's Case, the Lord Chief Justice continued: 'if they go further, and, not content with simply putting the alternative to the employer, combine to coerce him, by threats of jointly doing something which is likely to operate to his injury, into discharging the obnoxious persons, I think that they may properly be said to bring themselves within the scope of [the 1825 Act]'.[54]

For the rest of the decade the law of strikes was vexed by the uncertain definition of threats. *Walsby* settled that it meant more than the Blackstonian minimum of 'menaces of bodily hurt' but left uncertain how much more. Three of the judges of Queen's Bench agreed at one point that what was threatened had to be an illegal act, but they immediately proceeded to expand the definition of illegality to include wrongful expulsion from a trade union and combined action respecting employment, so the scope of the offence was not noticeably narrowed.[55] Yet *Walsby* also made clear that there were some communications in the context of industrial disputes that were not threats, that were merely 'putting the alternative'. If, for example, men left their employment and, when asked for

---

[54] 3 El. & El. 522, 121 Eng. Rep. 538.
[55] *O'Neill and Galbraith v. Longman*, 4 B. & S. 387, 122 Eng. Rep. 505 (QB 1863) (Cockburn, CJ, and Wightman and Mellor, JJ).

an explanation, replied that they would not work with certain other men, they were not threatening; they were simply explaining a *fait accompli*.[56] If, on the contrary, men went first to their employer and announced their present intention of leaving in the future unless certain other men were discharged, then they were threatening.[57] The distinction is a logical one, and something may even be said for it: if workmen felt so strongly about not associating with certain of their fellows that they were willing to depart at once and face permanent loss of employment with that employer, then they should not be punished for it, even if the employer should subsequently decide that it was in his interest to regain their services at the expense of their unlucky fellow servants. However logical, the distinction was impractical. Even the aristocracy of labour was not so well organized and counselled that it could reasonably be said to choose one course over another in the heat of industrial dispute. Whether one set of men left quietly or volubly threatened to leave depended in large measure on the organization of the industry, the momentary stage in the trade cycle, and the hotheadedness of their leaders.

In trade union law the age of collectivism, as Dicey was to call it, did not arrive until the 1870s. In 1867 the faith of the waning age of Benthamism was given forceful judicial expression by Baron Bramwell, 'that sturdy individualist', as Holdsworth named him.[58] The turbulent tailors of London, with whom the story of combination and conspiracy began, had struck for higher wages and had organized the now familiar picket. Strike-breakers had been followed and had been called cowards and—a word with a particular meaning in the trade—'dungs'. (The division of tailors into 'flints', the organized workmen who maintained apprenticeship and prided themselves on their skill and respectability, and 'dungs', who were supposed to be the reverse, dated from at least the mid-eighteenth century.[59]) An indictment was presented against Druitt, the president of the tailors' trade union, and two other union leaders. Rather than proceed on the statute or at common law for conspiracy to violate the statute, the prosecutors chose to revive the earlier practice and proceed at common law for conspiracy pure and simple. Updating Hawkins, the indictment laid a conspiracy 'to restrain the freedom of trade',[60] signalling the final reification of that concept. Summing up at trial, Baron Bramwell animadverted on conspiracies against 'liberty of mind and freedom of will'. It was, he said, an indictable offence

---

[56] See e.g. *Wood and Barrow* v. *Bowron*, 10 Cox CC 344 (QB 1866); *O'Neill and Galbraith* v. *Kruger*, 4 B. & S. 389, 122 Eng. Rep. 505 (QB 1863).

[57] See e.g. *Shelbourne* v. *Oliver*, 13 L. T. Rep. N. S. 630 (QB 1866); *Skinner* v. *Kitch*, 10 Cox CC 493 (QB 1867).

[58] William S. Holdsworth, *A History of English Law* (London, 1903–76), xv. (1965), ed. A. L. Goodhart and H. G. Hanbury, 71; see also ibid. 500–2.

[59] See Frank W. Galton (ed.), *Select Documents Illustrating the History of Trade Unionism*, i. *The Tailoring Trade* (1896), pp. xl–xlii, lxxxiv–lxxxv.

[60] *R.* v. *Druitt*, 10 Cox CC 593.

for two or more persons to agree to interfere with that liberty by means of coercion and compulsion, terms he vaguely defined as anything that was 'unpleasant and annoying to the mind operated upon'. While briefly acknowledging the Molestation of Workmen Act, he instructed the jury none the less to convict defendants if the picketing 'though not carried beyond watching and observation, was still so serious a molestation and obstruction as to have an effect upon the minds of the workpeople'.[61] So instructed, the jury found Druitt and his co-conspirators guilty as charged, although it recommended them to mercy.

Bramwell's statement of the law was quickly hailed as 'authoritative' by Vice-Chancellor Malins who departed on the strength of it from the equitable tradition against enjoining crimes in order to restrain trade union officials from using placards and advertisements to notify workmen of the existence of a dispute.[62] Not all of Bramwell's contemporaries, however, were equally enthusiastic: James Fitzjames Stephen, the historian of the criminal law and its would-be codifier, thought the law was laid down 'far too widely'.[63] Stephen's cousin, A. V. Dicey, on the other hand, found it in harmony with Mill's essay *On Liberty*, which he eulogized as 'the final and authoritative apology for the Benthamite faith in individual freedom'.[64] A modern scholar, echoing that view, pleaded extenuating circumstances: judges, who reflect the best thinking of their day are 'surely not to be criticized'.[65] Both comments are beside the point. Only eight years earlier parliament had expressly declared that 'no . . . person . . . by reason merely of his endeavouring peaceably . . . to persuade others to cease or abstain from work in order to obtain the rate of wages . . . agreed upon . . . shall be deemed . . . guilty of "molestation" or "obstruction" . . . and shall not therefore be subject . . . to any prosecution . . . for conspiracy'.[66] Surely the endeavour to persuade entails the attempt to have an effect on the minds of the others.

Although the 1825 and 1859 Acts remained on the books until 1871, their days were necessarily numbered after 1867. Not only were the trade

---

[61] Ibid. 602.

[62] *Springhead Spinning Co. v. Riley*, LR 6 Eq. 551 (Eq. 1868). See Anon., 'Trades Unions in Chancery', *Solicitors Journal*, 12 (1867–8); 907–8. See also A. W. J. Thomson, 'The Injunction in Trades Disputes in Britain before 1910', *Industrial and Labour Relations Review*, 19 (1965–6); 213–23.

[63] James Fitzjames Stephen, *A History of the Criminal Law of England* (1883), iii. 222.

[64] Dicey, *Law and Opinion*, 200–1.

[65] A. H. Manchester, *A Modern Legal History of England and Wales, 1750–1950* (London, 1980), 346. See also P. S. Atiyah, *The Rise and Fall of Freedom of Contract* (Oxford, 1979), 532 ('the ideals which the judges were trying to uphold do not seem to have been so reprehensible'); W. L. Burn, *The Age of Equipoise: A Study of the Mid-Victorian Generation* (New York, 1965), 69 ('There could be no more honest, perhaps no more convincing, statement of the dominant creed'); Holdsworth, *History of English Law*, xv. 502 ('it seems to me that in one of the spheres in which this problem is pressing—the sphere of industrial disputes—Bramwell's mode of dealing with the problem is the right mode').

[66] 22 Vict., c. 34 (1859).

unions antagonized by Baron Bramwell's contributions to the law of strikes, they also had to endure in the same year the even more ominous decision in *Hornby* v. *Close*, the Boilermakers' Case, that trade unions were conspiracies in restraint of trade and could not therefore protect their funds in court. These decisions, which seemed to labour nothing less than judicial aggressions, occurred at precisely the moment in history when labour was at last beginning to gain admittance to political power by the Second Reform Act.[67] The reform (that is, the extension of the franchise) was the product of partisan politics that had developed in England since the First Reform Act (1832) a generation earlier. Whatever its remote causes, the proximate cause was Disraeli's ambition to 'dish the Whigs'.[68] Once labour joined land and capital in the political life of the nation, the law of strikes (as well as labour law generally) was marked for revision. As we have seen, a temporary Master and Servant Act was adopted within days of franchise reform, and the more difficult legal problems raised by the decision in *Hornby* were solved in part and in part postponed by statutes in the next two parliamentary sessions.

The broader issues implicated in the inevitable reform of trade union legislation were further complicated by the popular furore aroused by contemporary events in Sheffield. In the early morning of 8 October 1866 some workmen threw a can of gunpowder down the chimney of the house of a fellow workman as punishment for an infraction of union rules. The building was extensively damaged, although no one was injured. While similar to earlier incidents, this one attained national notoriety as the most infamous of the Sheffield Outrages.[69] So outrageous were they that they were accorded the full honours of the Victorian age: a royal commission[70] was appointed to write a blue book on the subject,[71] and a popular author fictionalized it in a three-volume novel.[72] By adroit political management labour leaders, notably Robert Applegarth of the Amalgamated Society of

---

[67] 30 & 31 Vict., c. 102 (1867).

[68] The famous remark ('We have dished the Whigs') is attributed to Lord Derby. William Flavelle Monypenny and George Earle Buckle, *The Life of Benjamin Disraeli* (London, 1910–20), iv. 551. But it encapsulates Disraeli's ambition in the complex parliamentary manœuvring of 1867. See Maurice Cowling, *1867: Disraeli, Gladstone and Revolution: The Passing of the Second Reform Bill* (Cambridge, 1967); contrast Royden Harrison, *Before the Socialists: Studies in Labour and Politics, 1861–1881* (London, 1965). See also Gertrude Himmelfarb, 'The Politics of Democracy: The English Reform Act of 1867', *Journal of British Studies*, 6 (1966–7), 97–138.

[69] See Sidney Pollard, 'The Ethics of the Sheffield Outrages', *Transactions of the Hunter Archaeological Society*, 7 (1951–7), 118–39. See also Pollard's Introduction to the 1971 reprint of *The Sheffield Outrages: Report Presented to the Trades Unions Commissioners in 1867*.

[70] Although parliamentary select committees such as those appointed in 1824 and 1825 to study repeal of the combination laws continued to be appointed, royal commissions not limited to members of parliament became more common in the mid-nineteenth century. Their reports bound in blue covers form a remarkable series of critical self-examinations.

[71] *Parliamentary Papers* (1867), 32, 297–865.

[72] Charles Reade, *Put Yourself in his Place* (1870).

Carpenters and Joiners, turned even this occasion to advantage.[73] Although Sir William Erle, erstwhile Chief Justice of Common Pleas and presiding judge in Rowlands's Case (1851), was chosen to chair the commission, some commissioners sympathetic to labour were appointed, among them Frederic Harrison. When the commission reported in 1869, the majority report was less unfavourable than had been expected, while the minority report, inspired by Harrison, was an extremely skilful statement of the trade union case.[74] By that time the first election had been held under the new franchise, and middle-class observers like Walter Bagehot were alarmed at the spectacle of competition between the established parties for the labour vote.[75] The labour laws were bound to end up on the table.

[73] See Asa Briggs, *Victorian People: A Reassessment of Persons and Themes, 1851–67* (Harmondsworth, 1954), chap. 7.

[74] *Parliamentary Papers* (1867), 32, 1–396; (1867–8), 39, 1–570; (1868–9), 31, 235–361. See H. W. McCready, 'British Labour and the Royal Commission on Trade Unions, 1867–1869', *University of Toronto Quarterly*, 24 (1954–5), 390–409. See also Martha S. Vogeler, *Frederic Harrison: The Vocations of a Positivist* (Oxford, 1984), chap. 3.

[75] Walter Bagehot, *The English Constitution* (2nd edn., 1872), introduction.

9
After 1871: Employers and Workmen

The first duty of a lawyer about to discuss the legal framework of industrial relations is to warn his readers not to overestimate its importance . . . There is, perhaps, no major country in the world in which the law has played a less significant role in the shaping of these relations than in Great Britain and in which to-day the law and the legal profession have less to do with labour relations.

Otto Kahn-Freund (1954)

Legislation in the 1870s, amended and supplemented in 1906, closed the era opened by the first tailors' combination act (1721). Through the eighteenth century wages were still, in legal theory, set by the justices of the peace. In fact, wage regulation largely petered out, although (as Adam Smith observed) parliament made occasional efforts to restore it in particular trades and places. Negotiation between masters and men was perforce increasingly resorted to. In various trades, scattered throughout England, workmen combined to increase their bargaining power, but parliament outlawed combination in regulated trades, and the judges entertained prosecutions of the fledgling unions for conspiracy. At the end of the eighteenth century England's rulers abandoned this *ad hoc* policy in favour of a general proposition. Negotiation, which had developed in default of regulation, was embraced, but it was to be every man for himself. All employment contracts were made criminal and void by the Combination Act (1800) except those 'between any master and his journeyman or manufacturer, for or on account of the work or service of such journeyman or manufacturer with whom such contract may be made'.[1] Negotiation, as it turned out, was here to stay, but the ban on combination eroded during the next seventy-five years. In 1824–5 parliament repealed the combination laws and permitted common action in pursuit of common claims for wages and hours, and in 1859 what Karl Marx called 'certain beautiful fragments of the old statute' were rearranged.

---

[1] 39 & 40 Geo. 3, c. 106, § 1 (1800). See Chap. 4, n. 56.

In the 1870s the logic of negotiation was finally if grudgingly accepted, and the state closed its eyes to the aggregates involved on either side: on the one hand the employer, whether a small master or a large joint-stock company; on the other the workman, whether a solitary operative or a member of a disciplined and affluent trade union. In 1906 late-nineteenth-century judicial developments that had curtailed union bargaining power were eliminated: in the law of strikes the right of peaceful picketing was again guaranteed, and in the law of torts inducement to breach of contract and civil conspiracy were excluded from trade disputes. Of even more moment, trade unions were granted complete immunity in tort. The legislation of the 1870s and 1906 set the legal framework for industrial relations for years to come; for almost a century trade union law was to be largely a commentary on these basic texts. About this law, in contrast to what went before, many books have been written,[2] despite the conceded fact that the law's role in shaping these relations has not been great, and the spectacular legal contest leading up to the 1906 legislation has generated its own impressive literature.[3] But here it is fitting to treat these developments as an end rather than a beginning and to emphasize those sections that closed the old era rather than those that opened the new.

By the time the royal commission that was appointed in the wake of the Sheffield Outrages filed its final report on trade unions in 1869, the great Liberal Party under Gladstone was firmly seated in power. Returned in the first election conducted on the recently reformed franchise by an ill-assorted coalition of landed Whigs, capitalists, and workmen, the party was united behind a programme of classical liberalism. After dealing with the Church,[4] elementary education,[5] married women's property,[6] and the universities,[7] the Liberals faced the labour problem. Their response to the royal commission's report was the passage of two statutes in 1871: the Trade Union Act,[8] which dealt with the legal status of trade unions, and the Criminal Law Amendment Act,[9] which restated the law of strikes.

---

[2] See e.g. R. Y. Hedges and Allan Winterbottom, *The Legal History of Trade Unionism* (London, 1930), 65–166 (covering 1871–1929); Norman Arthur Citrine, *Trade Union Law* (3rd edn., London, 1967 (ed. M. A. Hickling)); Kahn-Freund, *Labour and the Law* (3rd edn., London, 1983 (ed. Paul Davies and Mark Freedland)); Bryn Perrins, *Trade Union Law* (London, 1985).

[3] See e.g. Frank W. Bealey and Henry M. Pelling, *Labour and Politics, 1900–06* (London, 1958); Hugh A. Clegg, Alan Fox, and A. F. Thompson, *A History of British Trade Unions since 1889*, i. *1889–1910* (Oxford, 1964); John Saville, 'Trade Unions and Free Labour: The Background to the Taff Vale Decision', in Asa Briggs and John Saville (eds.), *Essays in Labour History* (London, 1960), 317–50; Michael J. Klarman, 'The Judges Versus the Unions: The Development of British Labor Law, 1867–1913', 75 *Virginia Law Review* 1487–1602 (1989).

[4] 32 & 33 Vict., c. 42 (1869).   [5] 33 & 34 Vict., c. 75 (1870).

[6] 33 & 34 Vict., c. 93 (1870).   [7] 34 & 35 Vict., c. 26 (1871).

[8] 34 & 35 Vict., c. 31 (1871) (short title in § 1).

[9] 34 & 35 Vict., c. 32 (1871) (no official short title). The absence of an official short title may be explained by the fact that what became the Criminal Law Amendment Act had originally been drafted as part of the Trade Union Act.

Though logically and legally separate, the two acts formed parts of one whole and must be read together; indeed, the government had originally planned only one act, but labour's lobby complained about the criminal provisions, so it was agreed to divide the bill into two for separate treatment.[10] First, they wiped the legal slate clean by repealing many of the basic statutes. The Criminal Law Amendment Act repealed the 1825 Act.[11] It was no longer true, as it had been earlier, that the repeal of a repealing act would revive the once-repealed legislation: the ghost of the eighteenth-century combination acts was well and truly laid. By a simple statute reforming parliamentary procedure in 1850 the old presumption in favour of revival had been reversed.[12] (By the same statute all acts were declared public acts unless the contrary was expressly stated.[13]) In addition to the 1825 Act, the Criminal Law Amendment Act also repealed the Molestation of Workmen Act (1859),[14] as well as the special crime of assault committed in pursuance of an unlawful combination or conspiracy, last codified in 1861.[15]

The Trade Union Act repealed the Trades Unions Funds Protection Act (1869),[16] which would have expired in any event. (The Master and Servant Act (1867), which was also an annual act, was merely continued from year to year,[17] in effect leaving it for repeal later.) Finally, the common law of criminal conspiracy was cut sharply back: 'The purposes of any trade union shall not, by reason merely that they are in restraint of trade, be deemed to be unlawful so as to render any member of such trade union liable to criminal prosecution for conspiracy or otherwise.'[18] Furthermore, the Trade Union Act declared: 'The purposes of any trade union shall not, by reason merely that they are in restraint of trade, be unlawful so as to render void or voidable any agreement or trust.'[19] *Hornby* v. *Close* (1867) had rested on the notion that trade unions typically had purposes in restraint of trade, and the new legislation, by relieving unions of the legal consequences, tacitly accepted that premiss. Although now enabled to protect their funds in court, trade unions were not thereby empowered to enforce contracts generally. The Trade Union Act expressly declared unenforceable contracts between members of trade unions concerning conditions of employment, contracts by members to pay dues or penalties, contracts by trade unions to pay benefits, and contracts between trade unions. Bonds to secure performance, such as had sometimes been used by employers' associations,

[10] See H. W. McCready, 'British Labour's Lobby, 1867–1875', *Canadian Journal of Economics and Political Science*, 22 (1956), 146–7.
[11] 34 & 35 Vict., c. 32, § 7 and schedule.
[12] 13 & 14 Vict., c. 21, § 5 (1850).   [13] Ibid. § 7.
[14] 34 & 35 Vict., c. 32, § 7 and schedule.   [15] Ibid.
[16] 34 & 35 Vict., c. 31, § 24.
[17] 31 & 32 Vict., c. 111 (1868); 32 & 33 Vict., c. 85 (1869); 33 & 34 Vict., c. 103 (1870); 34 & 35 Vict., c. 95 (1871); 35 & 36 Vict., c. 88 (1872); 36 & 37 Vict., c. 75 (1873); 37 & 38 Vict., c. 76 (1874).
[18] 34 & 35 Vict., c. 31, § 2.   [19] Ibid. § 3.

were also declared unenforceable,[20] codifying the result in *Hilton* v. *Eckersley* (1855). Trade unions remained what they had been in the beginning, voluntary associations; the agreements holding them together were still void and unenforceable, although no longer criminal. Contracts between trade unions and employers, the products of collective bargaining, went unmentioned; no attempt was made to make them legally binding.

Having wiped the legal slate largely clean, the acts then granted trade unions a limited legal status. A registry of trade unions was created, and registered unions were permitted to hold property in the names of trustees.[21] For the first time 'trade union' received an official definition (of sorts):

The term 'trade union' means such combination, whether temporary or permanent, for regulating the relations between workmen and masters, or between workmen and workmen, or between masters and masters, or for imposing restrictive conditions on the conduct of any trade or business, as would, if [the Trade Union Act] had not passed, have been deemed to have been an unlawful combination by reason of some one or more of its purposes being in restraint of trade.[22]

Two provisos were added, explicable in the light of legal history. 'Trade union' did not include 'any agreement in consideration of the sale of goodwill of a business or of instruction in any profession, trade, or handicraft'.[23] Here we catch an echo of the original meaning of restraint of trade. Long before trade unions, as we have seen, agreements in restraint of trade had been included in conveyances of business property: the seller would convey his business and promise not to compete with the buyer. In striking contrast to judicial attitudes towards labour combinations, the judges were sympathetic to these agreements in restraint of trade and enforced them if they were reasonable. A second proviso exempted from the definition of trade union 'any agreement between an employer and those employed by him as to such employment'.[24] This was the saving clause, first seen in the Combination Act (1800), by which contracts of employment were recognized. (A third proviso exempted partnership agreements: 'any agreement between partners to their own business'.[25])

As Mark Twain's Connecticut Yankee had predicted, 'combine' at last yielded, however grudgingly, to the new phrase trade union.[26] In fact, the term had first appeared in the middle third of the nineteenth century,[27] making its way even into official publications: we have seen it in the terms

[20] Ibid. § 4.
[21] Ibid. §§ 6–18.
[22] Ibid. § 23.   [23] Ibid.   [24] Ibid.   [25] Ibid.
[26] Mark Twain, *A Connecticut Yankee in King Arthur's Court* (1889) (New York, 1963), 239 (general epigraph of this book).
[27] Sidney and Beatrice Webb found no instance of workmen calling their associations 'trade unions' in the first third of the nineteenth century. (*The History of Trade Unionism* (rev. edn., London, 1920), 113). See also *Oxford English Dictionary* (1st edn., 1884–1928), s.v. 'trade union, trades union' (earliest example from *The Times* (18 Jan. 1831)).

of reference of an 1838 parliamentary select committee.[28] By 1871 it was in common use, although not yet standardized.[29] The parliamentary draftsman only two years earlier had opted for 'trades union', while Marx's translators in 1867 had chosen the plural possessive, 'trades' union'. It is, of course, possible that some distinction was intended, at least at first, between a union of workmen in one trade and a union comprising workmen from two or more trades. Such distinction, if any, was certainly not drawn in the legislation of the 1870s; in fact, the 1871 Act with its official short title and legal definition may have helped secure currency for the modern form. (Curiously, the act's long title was 'An Act to Amend the Law Relating to Trades Unions'.)

The Criminal Law Amendment Act codified the law of strikes. Each crime was carefully analysed into two elements, an act and an intent. The illegal acts were the familiar five, traceable to 1825: violence, threats, intimidation, molestation, and obstruction. With respect to threats and intimidation it was provided that they had to be such 'as would justify a justice of the peace, on complaint made to him, to bind over the person so threatening or intimidating to keep the peace'.[30] The effect was to limit the criminal acts to threats of personal violence, thus adopting Baron Rolfe's ruling in Selsby's Case (1847). Even these acts, however, were not punishable under the statute unless done with an illegal intent, defined as an intent to coerce a person

[1.] being a master to dismiss or to cease to employ any workman, or being a workman to quit any employment or to return work before it is finished;

[2.] being a master not to offer or being a workman not to accept any employment or work;

[3.] being a master or workman to belong or not to belong to any temporary or permanent association or combination;

[4.] being a master or workman to pay any fine or penalty imposed by any temporary or permanent association or combination;

[5.] being a master to alter the mode of carrying on his business, or the number or description of any persons employed by him.[31]

The status of the person coerced became almost an element of the crime. In other words, to be punishable under the statute a certain act had to be done to a person of a certain status (master or workman) with the intention of coercing him to do a certain act.

The Criminal Law Amendment Act maintained the criminality of

---

[28] *Commons Journal*, 93 (1837–8), 271. See Chap. 7, n. 17.

[29] See W. Hamish Fraser, *Trade Unions and Society: The Struggle for Acceptance, 1850–1880* (Totowa, NJ, 1974), 235 n. 98 ('There was, in the mid-nineteenth century, no consistency in the use of the terms "trade union", "trades unions", "trades' union" or even "trade's union". Each was used by unionists and middle-class commentators alike seemingly as the fancy took them').

[30] 34 & 35 Vict., c. 32, § 1.   [31] Ibid.

molestation and obstruction, but without the exception for peaceful persuasion, once secured by the Molestation of Workmen Act (1859). Instead, a statutory definition of the illegal act was provided:

A person shall, for the purposes of this Act, be deemed to molest or obstruct another person in any of the following cases; that is to say,
[1.] if he persistently follow such person about from place to place:
[2.] if he hide any tools, clothes, or other property owned or used by such person, or deprive him of or hinder him in the use thereof:
[3.] if he watch or beset the house or other place where such person resides or works, or carries on business, or happens to be, or the approach to such house or place, or if with two or more other persons he follow such person in a disorderly manner in or through any street or road.[32]

Offenders under the act were liable to imprisonment with or without hard labour for up to three months.

Continuing the tradition of earlier legislation, the Criminal Law Amendment Act provided for summary proceedings. Rather than spell out the process in detail, however, the act merely incorporated by reference the provisions of the Summary Jurisdiction Acts, defined as Jervis's Act (1848) and any amendments thereto.[33] None the less, special provisions were included concerning the persons who determined the matter at first instance: one metropolitan police magistrate, one stipendiary magistrate, or two justices of the peace. (In the City of London the mayor or any alderman could act.) To guarantee a disinterested magistrate or justice, a disqualifying clause was included that actually took a step backward towards Francis Place's sweeping exclusion in 1824: 'a person who is a master, father, son, or brother of a master in the particular manufacture, trade, or business in or in connexion with which any offence under this Act is charged to have been committed shall not act.'[34] As in the past, appeal lay to quarter sessions, the appellant being required to enter into a recognizance for £10 with two sureties for an additional £10.[35] Special recognition was made of the distinctive legal institutions of Scotland and, to a lesser degree, Ireland.

By 1872 the Liberal Party had enacted its programme, and the government front bench reminded Disraeli of 'a range of exhausted volcanoes'.[36] But labour, as we have seen, was not wholly satisfied with the government's exertions on its behalf. The Trade Union Act marked a clear advance, but the Criminal Law Amendment Act was of uncertain benefit. What had been gained in clarity with regard to threats and intimidation had

---

[32] Ibid. Subsection 2 defined and outlawed a form of coercion popularly known as 'rattening', a practice especially common in Sheffield.
[33] Ibid. § 6.   [34] Ibid. § 5. See Chap. 5, n. 83.
[35] 34 & 35 Vict., c. 32, § 3.
[36] Quoted in William Flavelle Monypenny and George Earle Buckle, *The Life of Benjamin Disraeli* (London, 1910–20), v. 191 (speech of 3 Apr. 1872).

been lost again with regard to those perennial problem words, molestation and obstruction. Outlawing watching and besetting, reminiscent of Baron Bramwell's sweeping dictum in *Druitt* (1867) about 'watching and observation',[37] seemed also to outlaw picketing.

As if to demonstrate that nothing had in fact changed, a conviction was handed down on 16 December 1872 in *Regina* v. *Bunn*,[38] the Gas Stokers' Case. The workmen had struck in protest over the dismissal of one of their number, despite the fact that they were under contract and had not given the necessary notice. Justice Brett ruled that, in addition to civil liability for breach of contract, the workmen were indictable for criminal conspiracy. In response to the argument that the recently enacted Trade Union Act had exempted workmen from prosecution for conspiracy in restraint of trade, the learned judge pointed out that the alleged conspiracy was not only in restraint of trade but was also an interference with the employer's free will, echoing Bramwell's charge concerning conspiracies against 'liberty of mind and freedom of will'.[39] Ironically, by incorporating the current understanding of what made trade unions conspiracies, that they operated in restraint of trade, the legislation seemed to permit the generative forces of common law to work in other directions. Hearkening back to William Hawkins's eighteenth-century notion that 'all confederacies whatsoever, wrongfully to prejudice a third person, are highly criminal at common law',[40] Brett's ruling threatened to reignite common-law development outside the statute. The jury in *Bunn* found the defendants guilty as charged, while recommending them to mercy 'on account of their great ignorance and being misled, and their previous good character'.[41] Notwithstanding, Brett sentenced them to twelve months' hard labour, four times the maximum for the recently defined statutory offence. In the event, Her Majesty on the advice of the Home Secretary reduced their sentences to four months.[42]

In part with the help of labour, the Conservative Party won the next general election.[43] Once in office Disraeli wanted something to be done for labour and deputed R. A. Cross, the Conservative Home Secretary, to do it.[44] After buying time with another royal commission, Cross ignored its modest proposals[45] and brought in the sweeping bills that became the

---

[37] 10 Cox CC 602. See Chap. 8, n. 61.

[38] 12 Cox CC 316 (Cent. Crim. Ct. 1872).

[39] *R.* v. *Druitt*, 10 Cox CC 602. See Chap. 8, n. 61.

[40] William Hawkins, *A Treatise of the Pleas of the Crown* (7th edn., 1795 (ed. Thomas Leach)), bk. 1, chap. 72, sect. 2 (1st edn., 1716). See Chap. 3, n. 7.

[41] 12 Cox CC 351.

[42] Ibid. 351 (a).

[43] See H. W. McCready, 'The British Election of 1874: Frederic Harrison and the Liberal–Labour Dilemma', *Canadian Journal of Economics and Political Science*, 20 (1954), 166–75, and 'British Labour's Lobby, 1867–1875', ibid. 22 (1956), 141–60.

[44] See Paul Smith, *Disraelian Conservatism and Social Reform* (London, 1967), 215–18.

[45] *Parliamentary Papers* (1874), 24, 391–556; (1875), 20, 1–162.

Conspiracy and Protection of Property Act (1875)[46] and the Employers and Workmen Act (1875).[47]

The Conspiracy and Protection of Property Act repealed the recently enacted Criminal Law Amendment Act, the Master and Servant Act (1867) which had been continued from year to year, what remained of the Statute of Artificers (1563), and all other laws that made breach of contract criminal.[48] It embraced the principle that contracts of employment were purely civil affairs. Criminal sanctions were to be available only in exceptional cricumstances, such as for breach of contract causing interruption of gas or water supplies[49]—ironically, the exception covered the gas stokers prosecuted in *Bunn*—or involving injury to persons or property[50] (giving colour to the Protection of Property emblazoned on its title). Once more, criminal conspiracy was ousted, this time more compendiously than in 1871: 'An agreement or combination by two or more persons to do or procure to be done any act in contemplation or furtherance of a trade dispute between employers and workmen shall not be indictable as a conspiracy if such act committed by one person would not be punishable as a crime.'[51] No mention was made of restraint of trade. At last, R. S. Wright's assertion that conspiracy was tied to crime, while wishful thinking, as a historical proposition, became true by legislation, at least in a trade dispute.

Once more, the law concerning strikes was codified. This time the illegal intention was more simply stated: 'to compel any other person to abstain from doing or to do any act which such other person has a legal right to do or abstain from doing'.[52] Breaking with the time-hallowed phrases, the Conspiracy and Protection of Property Act defined anew the illegal acts: when a person

[1.] uses violence to or intimidates such other person or his wife or children, or injures his property; or,

[2.] persistently follows such other person about from place to place; or,

[3.] hides any tools, clothes, or other property owned or used by such other person, or deprives him of or hinders him in the use thereof; or,

[4.] watches or besets the house or other place where such other person resides, or works, or carries on business, or happens to be, or the approach to such house or place; or,

---

[46] 38 & 39 Vict., c. 86 (1875) (short title in § 1 where it appears as the 'Conspiracy, and Protection of Property Act').

[47] 38 & 39 Vict., c. 90 (1875) (short title in § 1). Derek Beales erroneously refers to 'three Acts of 1875': the Employers and Workmen Act, the Conspiracy and Protection of Property Act, and a third measure that 'repealed the Criminal Law Amendment Act' (*From Castlereagh to Gladstone, 1815–1885* (New York, 1969), 259).

[48] 38 & 39 Vict., c. 86, § 17.

[49] Ibid. § 4. Interruption of the supply of electricity was added to the list in 1919, 9 & 10 Geo. 5, c. 100, § 31.

[50] 38 & 39 Vict., c. 86, § 5.

[51] Ibid. § 3.

[52] Ibid.

[5.] follows such other person with two or more other persons in a disorderly manner in or through any street or road.[53]

For the first time in fifty years the troublesome words threats, molestation, and obstruction dropped out of labour law. While retaining much of the substance of its Liberal predecessor, the Conservative legislation nevertheless managed to mark a new beginning. To counteract the fears of labour that the new watching and besetting would take the place of the old molesting and obstructing, an explicit exception was included for 'attending at or near the house or place where a person resides, or works, or carries on business, or happens to be, or the approach to such house or place in order merely to obtain or communicate information'.[54] For what it was worth, Baron Rolfe's dictum, uttered before his ennoblement as Lord Cranworth (and apparent change of heart), was given statutory form. As a practical matter the exception was to be worth very little because a couple of years before the Conservative legislation the nation's economy slipped into the depression, known to contemporaries as 'great', that was to darken most of the last quarter of the nineteenth century.[55] When strikes resumed late in the century, the judges determined that the law was not so clear as it appeared, and further legislation was required.

Offenders under the Conspiracy and Protection of Property Act were liable to a fine of not more than £20 or alternatively to imprisonment with or without hard labour for up to three months. Summary proceedings were retained, but the accused could object to a summary trial and insist upon the full panoply of indictment and trial by jury.[56] The Whiggish complaint eloquently voiced by Lord Holland in 1799 was at last satisfied, ironically by a Tory government; juries, though, remained as they had been, largely closed to workmen by high property qualifications. Presumably because of this option, however, no justice was automatically disqualified despite his, or his family's connection with trade. In case of trial by summary procedure and conviction appeal lay to quarter sessions. In contrast to the earlier Liberal legislation the required recognizance did not necessarily include a penal sum nor were sureties always demanded.[57] As before, procedures were accommodated to those in Scotland and Ireland.

The second Conservative statute, the Employers and Workmen Act (1875), empowered the County Courts which had been created in 1846[58] to settle industrial disputes if asked.[59] Last but not least, this statute began the slow process of changing legal language: what had been the law of master

---

[53] 38 & 39 Vict., c. 86, § 7.

[54] Ibid.

[55] See A. E. Musson, 'The Great Depression in Britain, 1873–1896: A Reappraisal', *Journal of Economic History*, 19 (1959), 199–228, and id., 'British Industrial Growth during the "Great Depression": Some Comments', *Economic History Review*, 2nd ser., 15 (1962–3), 529–33.

[56] 38 & 39 Vict., c. 86, § 9.   [57] Ibid. § 12.

[58] 9 & 10 Vict., c. 95 (1846).   [59] 38 & 39 Vict., c. 90, § 3.

and servant was now to be the law of employers and workmen (although lawyers have clung tenaciously to the older usage). In the Employers and Workmen Act 'master' was used to refer only to the dwindling class who took apprentices; a workman, in contrast, was one who worked 'under a contract with an employer'.[60] Whereas the Liberal legislation had still spoken stridently of masters and workmen, the Conservative acts were largely peopled by classless 'persons'. Formal legal equality, the desideratum of the nineteenth century as due process had been of the eighteenth, was at last achieved in labour law.

All that seemed to be left was a certain amount of legal tidying up. In 1876 the Trade Union Act Amendment Act[61] provided for some insignificant cases, such as a union's change of name or an amalgamation of unions. Finally, the legal definition of trade union was amended. More than a century earlier Dr Johnson had reminded Englishmen that '[i]t is one of the maxims of the civil law, that *definitions are hazardous*'.[62] In 1871 the Liberals had seemed to equate trade unions with conspiracies in restraint of trade, while denying the consequences of that equation. In 1876 the Conservatives denied the equation altogether, while slipping the masters back into the picture:

The term 'trade union' means any combination, whether temporary or permanent, for regulating the relations between workmen and masters, or between workmen and workmen, or between masters and masters, or for imposing restrictive conditions on the conduct of any trade or business, whether such combination would *or would not*, if [the Trade Union Act] had not been passed, have been deemed to have been an unlawful combination by reason of some one or more of its purposes being in restraint of trade.[63]

Master and servant were disappearing (despite some lapses), to be replaced by employer and workman. Criminal conspiracy no longer occupied a special place in the law of trade unions; even the legal implications of being in restraint of trade were minimized. Finally, eighteenth-century combination was gone, the word itself ceasing to be a bad name. Contract had completed its curious evolution in labour law: from being principally regarded as the tie that bound workmen together,[64] it became the nexus between capital and labour. Contract no longer created status; it made promises of service enforceable.

The pre-modern period in the legal history of labour was not, however, quite over. Starting in 1889 during a break in the Great Depression, 'new

---

[60] Ibid. § 10.
[61] 39 & 40 Vict., c. 22 (short title in § 1). With the Trade Union Act (1871) the act could be cited as the Trade Union Acts (1871 and 1876).
[62] *Rambler*, 125 (28 May 1751) (emphasis in original) (referring to *Digest* 50.17.202: '*Omnis definitio in jure civili periculosa est; parum est enim, ut non subverti possit*').
[63] Ibid. § 16 (italics added).
[64] See P. S. Atiyah, *The Rise and Fall of Freedom of Contract* (Oxford, 1979), 533.

unionism', appealing to unskilled workmen hitherto largely unorganized, led to a wave of strikes that fired the ingenuity of employers' lawyers. To defeat the new unions, employers drew on the reserves of unskilled labour still unaffiliated with trade unions, known (in a phrase chosen for its popular appeal but having a curious undertone) as 'free' labour. In response to union threats to strike against employers using free labour, prosecutions were mounted for criminal intimidation under the Conspiracy and Protection of Property Act, threats as such being no longer an offence. The legal question was the familiar one from Selsby's Case (1847): did the crime encompass every communication of untoward consequences, or was it limited to announcement of impending violence? The Criminal Law Amendment Act (1871) had answered the question by defining illegal intimidation as such 'as would justify a justice of the peace . . . to bind over the person so . . . intimidating to keep the peace',[65] that is, putting in fear of violence. But this provision had been repealed (along with the rest of the act) in 1875, and no comparable provision had been re-enacted, presumably through inadvertence. None the less it was true that the Conspiracy and Protection of Property Act had verbally coupled violence with intimidation: the crime in question was committed by a person who, in order to compel someone to do something, 'uses violence to or intimidates such other person or his wife or children, or injures his property'.[66] Although it had first been held that a threat to picket, followed by peaceful picketing, constituted wrongful intimidation,[67] this approach was finally rejected in 1891 by the Queen's Bench division.[68] 'Looking at the course of legislation', Lord Chief Justice Coleridge said, 'and keeping in mind the changing temper of the times on this subject', the court confined intimidation to putting in fear of bodily harm.[69] Baron Rolfe's opinion in Selsby's Case, as ratified by legislation in 1871, was still intact.

The employers' next step, as might be guessed, was to test the reach of watching and besetting, the latest form of those time-honoured crimes in the law of strikes, molestation, and obstruction. In 1896 in *J. Lyons & Sons* v. *Wilkins*,[70] this approach met with success. In a suit for an injunction to restrain admittedly peaceful picketing, it was held that the attempt to

---

[65] 34 & 35 Vict., c. 32, § 1.   [66] 38 & 39 Vict., c. 86, § 7.

[67] *Judge* v. *Bennett*, 4 T.L. Rep. 75 (QB 1887).

[68] The Queen's (King's) Bench division, which had been created by another piece of Liberal legislation, the Supreme Court of Judicature Act (1873), 36 & 37 Vict., c. 66, exercised the jurisdiction formerly exercised by the common-law court of Queen's (King's) Bench. In 1881 the Common Pleas division and the Exchequer division, successors to the other two common-law courts, were merged in the Queen's Bench division. The Judicature Act also merged the administration of law and equity and created the Court of Appeal, which succeeded to the jurisdiction (among others) of the Court of Exchequer Chamber and the equity courts of the county palatine of Lancaster.

[69] *Gibson* v. *Lawson*, [1891] 2 QB 559. See also S. H. Leonard, 'Wrongful Intimidation', 7 *Law Quarterly Review* 375–8 (1891). This reading was subsequently codified in the Trade Disputes and Trade Unions Act, 17 & 18 Geo. 5, c. 22, § 3 (1927).

[70] [1896] 1 Ch. 811.

persuade workmen to withhold their labour in order to injure the employer was still criminal. While the Conspiracy and Protection of Property Act explicitly permitted picketing 'to obtain or communicate information',[71] it did not in so many words permit peaceful persuasion to withhold labour. Something much closer to the repealed Molestation of Workmen Act (1859) was required. That act, we may recall, had protected from prosecution a workman who was 'endeavouring peaceably, and in a reasonable manner, and without threat or intimidation, direct or indirect, to persuade others to cease or abstain from work, in order to obtain the rate of wages or the altered hours of labour so fixed or agreed upon'.[72]

Thus far, legal actions against trade unions, win and lose, had taken familiar forms. What workmen could threaten, what pickets could do; these questions ran throughout the legal history of labour. At the very end of our story, however, new themes briefly appeared. Rather than from criminal law, which had provided the bulk of the law on combination and conspiracy, the new developments stemmed from civil law, principally tort but also contract. Hitherto tort law had made only one brief appearance, as the source of the restrictive definition of threats: 'menaces of bodily hurt, through fear of which a man's business is interrupted'.[73] Contract, as we have seen, migrated from being the essence of the crimes of combination and conspiracy to being the basis of the employment relationship.

Once located at the source of employment, contract had a different bearing on the law of strikes. By a proviso added to the Molestation of Workmen Act in the wake of *Lumley* v. *Gye* (1853), the case which recognized the tort of inducing breach of contract, strikers were expressly denied authority to make 'any attempt to induce any workman to break or depart from any contract'.[74] Conceptually, as we have seen, contract had gone beyond being merely an agreement enforceable between the parties to being a thing in itself, a form of property, good against all the world. Once contract was equated with property, interference with it became a tort. Ignored in the legislation of the 1870s, inducement to breach of contract was inevitably to figure in the new round of labour litigation. After some initial hesitation,[75] it was settled by the House of Lords in 1905 in *South Wales Miners' Federation* v. *Glamorgan Coal Co.*[76] that inducement to breach labour contracts was a tort for which damages to the employer were recoverable. In the past, when employment was thought of in terms of status, the law of master and servant had meted out criminal punishments

[71] 38 & 39 Vict., c. 86, § 7. [72] 22 Vict., c. 34 (1859).
[73] William Blackstone, *Commentaries on the Laws of England* (1765–9), iii. 120.
[74] 22 Vict., c. 34 (1859).
[75] Cf. *Temperton* v. *Russell*, [1893] 1 QB 715 (CA) (holding malicious inducement of breach of contract actionable) with *Allen* v. *Flood*, 1898 AC 1 (HL) (holding malice alone not sufficient to render otherwise lawful conduct actionable). See also *Quinn* v. *Leathem*, 1901 AC 495 (HL) (restricting *Allen*).
[76] 1905 AC 239 (HL).

for leaving work unfinished, and the law of strikes had added some supplementary provisions. With the repeal of the master and servant law and the reconceptualization of the employment relationship in terms of contract, tort took the place of crime, and civil liability proved far more punitive than imprisonment.

Tort law had also a generative potential all its own, wholly apart from contract. We have seen the criminal law of conspiracy wrestling with the problem of combined action: how could it be that what one could do lawfully several could not do together? Lord Denman had sought to resolve the problem with his famous antithesis: 'The indictment ought to charge a conspiracy, either to do an unlawful act, or a lawful act by unlawful means.'[77] Attention then turned to whether unlawful necessarily meant criminal. The debate was ended in labour law by the Conspiracy and Protection of Property Act: 'An agreement or combination by two or more persons to do or procure to be done an act in contemplation or furtherance of a trade dispute between employers and workmen shall not be indictable as a conspiracy if such act committed by one person would not be punishable as a crime.'[78] Combination was no longer the gist of the offence, although it could increase its seriousness, and 'unlawful' was confined to 'criminal'. While criminal law was occupied with public wrongs, tort concerned private wrongs. Although the earths had been stopped in one area, perhaps they remained open in the other.

In 1901 in *Quinn* v. *Leathem*[79] the House of Lords upheld a judgment against trade union officers for civil conspiracy. Defendants had threatened to strike against an employer's business customers in order to induce the employer to fire non-union workmen, a practice known today as a 'secondary strike', that is, a strike against an employer not directly involved in the dispute in order to pressure the primary employer to make concessions. There was no indictment for criminal conspiracy in *Quinn* and no question of fine or imprisonment; the Conspiracy and Protection of Property Act foreclosed that possibility. Instead, there was an ordinary civil action for damages—tort not crime. Lawyers had long known that in certain cases it was advisable to waive the tort and sue in *assumpsit*;[80] employers had just learned to waive the crime and sue in tort. Key to success was the notion that an act lawful for one could be actionable if performed by many acting together. In addition to accepting that proposition, the House of Lords in *Quinn* also held that trade unionists' motives to raise wages did not privilege them to combine to injure an employer, even though it had held in an earlier case that a cartel of businessmen (a trade union of a

---

[77] *R.* v. *Jones*, 4 B. & Ad. 349, 110 Eng. Rep. 487 (KB 1832). See Chap. 3, n. 84.

[78] 38 & 39 Vict., c. 86, § 3.

[79] 1901 AC 495 (HL).

[80] For a brief explanation of this legal manœuvre, see J. H. Baker, *An Introduction to English Legal History* (2nd edn., London, 1979), 310–12.

different sort) could injure a competitor with impunity so long as they were motivated by a desire to improve their own economic position.[81]

The final development in the evolution of tort law in this area came in another case in 1901, the well-known *Taff Vale Railway Co.* v. *Amalgamated Society of Railway Servants*.[82] Although its political and social impact was immense, the Taff Vale Case involved only one small step in legal doctrine: if trade unionists were liable for carrying out trade union policy, then the trade union itself was also liable. However small in abstract terms the step from individual to collective liability, it was of the greatest practical importance. Workmen, including trade union officers, were usually impecunious, but by the turn of the century trade unions—at least some of them like the Amalgamated Society of Railway Servants—were downright wealthy. If a wrong were done, the union could be mulcted in damages. Union liability was bad enough; added to the earlier rulings on the narrow scope of protected picketing and the torts of inducing breach of contract and civil conspiracy, it was potentially disastrous.

So serious was the threat seen to be by trade unions that they committed their awesome political power to eliminating it. The victory of the trade unions in the 1870s had been not merely a legal development; it had also marked 'an important turning-point in English social history'.[83] Not only was labour mobilized in trade unions, it increasingly found expression in political action as well, eventually forming a great political party all its own. Britain had attained nearly universal manhood suffrage by the Third Reform Act (1884),[84] and even the Conservative Party, by then well on its way to becoming the party of property, recognized the need to do something for labour. The Workmen's Compensation Act (1897)[85] provided for recovery in case of industrial accidents, reducing the effect of the fellow-servant rule, which had for so long insulated employers from liability for work-related injuries. But labour was alienated from the party in power by the judicial decisions referred to above and contributed to the Liberal landslide in the epochal election of 1906.[86] The Liberal Party, now ready to advance beyond Gladstonianism, embraced a policy of social welfare legislation, including a more comprehensive Workmen's Compensation Act (1906),[87] old-age pensions,[88] the first labour exchanges,[89] an end to

---

[81] *Mogul Steamship Co.* v. *McGregor, Gow & Co.*, 1892 AC 25 (HL).

[82] 1901 AC 426 (HL).

[83] Asa Briggs, 'Social Background', in Allan Flanders and Hugh A. Clegg (eds.), *System of Industrial Relations* (Oxford, 1954), 16.

[84] 48 Vict., c. 3 (1884).

[85] 60 & 61 Vict., c. 37 (1897). See David G. Hanes, *The First British Workmen's Compensation Act, 1897* (New Haven, Conn., 1968). There had been an earlier, largely ineffectual Employers' Liability Act, 43 & 44 Vict., c. 42 (1880).

[86] See Alan K. Russell, *Liberal Landslide: The General Election of 1906* (Hamden, Conn., 1973).

[87] 6 Edw. 7, c. 58 (1906).

[88] 8 Edw. 7, c. 40 (1908).

[89] 9 Edw. 7, c. 7 (1909).

'sweated labour' (by means of the Trade Boards Act[90]), and national insurance against sickness and unemployment.[91] But labour demanded before all else redress of its legal grievances and promptly secured the Trade Disputes Act (1906),[92] each of the four substantive sections of which reversed one of the major judicial developments in trade union law.

The first two sections amended the Conspiracy and Protection of Property Act. Section 1 added a sentence: 'An act done in pursuance of an agreement or combination by two or more persons shall, if done in contemplation or furtherance of a trade dispute, not be actionable unless the act, if done without any such agreement or combination, would be actionable.'[93] The new sentence, doing away with the tort of civil conspiracy in trade disputes, complemented the old provision against criminal conspiracy. Not only was the agreement not 'indictable' (as a crime), the act was not 'actionable' (as a tort). *Quinn* v. *Leathem* was overruled. Section 2 amended the definition of watching and besetting:

It shall be lawful for one or more persons, acting on their own behalf or on behalf of a trade union or of an individual employer or firm in contemplation or furtherance of a trade dispute, to attend at or near a house or place where a person resides or works or carries on business or happens to be, if they so attend merely for the purpose of peacefully obtaining or communicating information, or of peacefully persuading any person to work or abstain from working.[94]

Peaceful persuasion, once permitted by the Molestation of Workmen Act, was again part of the law of strikes. *J. Lyons & Sons* v. *Wilkins* was overruled. Both sections were intended to restore the status quo ante.

The next two sections broke new ground. Section 3 addressed the tort of inducing breach of contract: 'An act done by a person in contemplation or furtherance of a trade dispute shall not be actionable on the ground only that it induces some other person to break a contract of employment or that it is an interference with the trade, business, or employment of some other person, or with the right of some other person to dispose of his capital or his labour as he wills.'[95] The policy behind the proviso in the Molestation of Workmen Act against inducing breach of contract in a trade dispute was now abandoned. *South Wales Miners' Federation* v. *Glamorgan Coal Co.* was overruled. In addition, a more general tort of interference with economic relations (apart from inducing breach of contract) was denied effect in so far as a trade dispute was concerned, and Baron Bramwell's dictum in the context of a criminal prosecution about conspiracies against 'liberty of mind or freedom of will'[96] was precluded from germinating in

---

[90] 9 Edw. 7, c. 22 (1909).   [91] 1 & 2 Geo. 5, c. 55 (1911).
[92] 6 Edw. 7, c. 47 (1906).   [93] Ibid. § 1 (amending 38 & 39 Vict., c. 86, § 3).
[94] 6 Edw. 7, c. 47, § 2 (amending 38 & 39 Vict., c. 86, § 7).
[95] 6 Edw. 7, c. 47, § 3.
[96] *R.* v. *Druitt*, 10 Cox CC 602. See Chap. 8, n. 61.

civil law. Finally, section 4 conferred absolute immunity in tort on trade unions: 'An action against a trade union, whether of workmen or masters, or against any members or officials thereof on behalf of themselves and all other members of a trade union in respect of any tortious act alleged to have been committed by or on behalf of a trade union, shall not be entertained by any court.'[97] For the first time in labour law something more than an exemption was procured: the courts were positively stripped of jurisdiction. *Taff Vale Railway Co.* v. *Amalgamated Society of Railway Servants* was decisively rejected. Unions could not be sued directly, nor could the ban be evaded by a 'representative action', that is, a suit against members or officers 'on behalf of themselves and all other members of a trade union'. To the legal pundits section 4 was a grievous breach of the rule of law. Holdsworth styled it an 'enormous injustice' and thought the law had lost its way under the influence of *laissez-faire*,[98] while Dicey saw it as proof positive of the triumph of collectivism.[99] Labour had certainly abandoned its earlier goal of equal treatment and had demanded—and achieved—a special status. Whether the courts would have respected anything less, and whether it was, as labour's apologists claimed, no more in practice than capital had long enjoyed, may be left for consideration elsewhere.

It is noteworthy that the blanket immunity of section 4 was not even limited to acts done 'in contemplation or furtherance of a trade dispute', as was the case in the other substantive sections. That phrase, which had first appeared in the Conspiracy and Protection of Property Act—in the section providing immunity from criminal conspiracy, from which it was presumably copied—received its first statutory definition in the Trade Disputes Act: 'the expression "trade dispute" means any dispute between employers and workmen, or between workmen and workmen, which is connected with the employment or non-employment, or the terms of the employment, or with the conditions of labour, of any person.'[100] For trade unionists much hinged on this definition; while their unions were immune from tort regardless of context, individual immunity with respect to criminal and civil conspiracy, certain forms of picketing, and inducing breach of contract was limited to 'trade disputes'. Labour now had a vital interest in the scope of this definition. When in the aftermath of the 1926 General Strike new legislation was enacted outlawing sympathy strikes, that is, strikes in one trade or industry in support of the demands of workmen in another, it was done by limiting protected trade disputes to those 'connected with the employment or non-employment, or the terms of the employment, or with

---

[97] 6 Edw. 7, c. 47, § 4.
[98] William S. Holdsworth, *A History of English Law* (London, 1903–72), xi. 500; xv. (1965), ed. A. L. Goodhart and H. G. Hanbury, 86.
[99] A. V. Dicey, *Lectures on the Relation between Law and Public Opinion in England during the Nineteenth Century* (2nd edn., London, 1914), pp. xliv–xlvii.
[100] 6 Edw. 7, c. 47, § 5 (3).

the conditions of labour, of persons *in that trade or industry*'.[101] Even immunity has its costs. Labour was committed ever after to regaining what it had lost[102] and extending its gains if possible,[103] while its opponents were equally determined to teach it a lesson in the hazards of legal definitions.[104]

In the legislation of 1906 labour secured what it had been seeking since 1859: the right to be left alone in the exercise of its economic power. With respect to the legal area once comprehended by combination and conspiracy, it was to be for long a satisfied power, defending its position. In response to what it perceived as later aggressions, it would demand further legislation, aimed always at restoring the status quo ante. When in 1909 the Osborne Judgment[105] prohibited trade unions from spending money to secure parliamentary representation, on the ground that it was a function not within the statutory definition of a trade union (another hazardous definition), labour secured the Trade Union Act (1913),[106] which permitted political spending. When in 1971 labour's political opponents repealed the legislation dating back a century and sought to construct a new regime in trade union law,[107] it dedicated itself to setting back the clock. But labour's victory in 1974[108] was to prove almost equally short-lived; another turn of Fortune's wheel brought a new government to power in 1979, more determined than ever to resettle the law. Whether the new arrangement with its detailed regulation of trade unions will prove as enduring as the legislation that ushered in labour law's modern era belongs obviously not to legal history but to legal future.

---

[101] 17 & 18 Geo. 5, c. l22, § 1 (1927) (Trade Disputes and Trade Unions Act) (emphasis added).

[102] See 9 & 10 Geo. 6, c. 52 (1946) (Trade Disputes and Trade Unions Act) (repealing 17 & 18 Geo. 5, c. 22 (1927)).

[103] 1965, ch. 48 (Trade Disputes Act) (threat to breach contract of employment or to induce breach of such contract not actionable).

[104] For recent curtailment of the definition of trade disputes, see Employment Act, 1980, c. 42, §§ 16–17, and Employment Act, 1982, c. 46, §§ 13–14, 18. The latter act eliminated entirely the trade unions' immunity in tort. (1982, c. 46, § 15).

[105] *Amalgamated Society of Railway Servants* v. *Osborne*, 1910 AC 87 (HL 1909). See Michael J. Klarman, 'Osborne: A Judgment Gone Too Far?' *English Historical Review*, 103 (1988), 21–39, and 'The Trade Union Political Levy, the *Osborne* Judgment (1909), and the South Wales Miners' Federation', *Welsh History Review*, 15 (1990), 34–57.

[106] 2 & 3 Geo. 5, c. 30 (1913) (Trade Union Act) (reserving for trade unionists a right to contract out of the political levy). See Michael J. Klarman, 'Parliamentary Reversal of the *Osborne* Judgment', *Historical Journal*, 32 (1989), 893–924; Keith D. Ewing, *Trade Unions, the Labour Party and the Law: A Study of the Trade Union Act, 1913* (Edinburgh, 1982).

[107] 1971, c. 72 (Industrial Relations Act).

[108] 1974, c. 52 (Trade Union and Labour Relations Act).

10

Conclusion

[W]hat's past is prologue.
Shakespeare, *Tempest*, II. i. 243.

Trade unions were not created by law; they originated in the felt needs of
workmen in industrial society. Unlike business associations, trade unions
existed before law took any notice of them (or even knew what to call
them). Indeed, the first statutes concerning labour organizations, the
combination acts, were criminal laws, aimed at their suppression. The legal
problems of capital and labour were in consequence quite distinct, almost
opposite in fact. Labour wore down the opposition to trade unions,
eventually winning a place for them, while capital sought, not recognition of
a right to organize (that was conceded without question), but more efficient
means thereto. Registering their victory in literal terms, trade unions were
finally offered registered status, not incorporation.

Labour's place in the legal scheme of things was based on a series of
exceptions. The *laissez-faire* ideologues who relieved labour of some of its
restraints in 1824–5 unwittingly set a precedent that was to outlast the
nineteenth century. Labour's freedom to organize was defined in narrow
exemptions from prosecution for criminal conspiracy. With the lobbying
campaign of the National Association of United Trades in the 1850s,
workmen adopted the middle-class strategy as their own, the limit of their
ambition being to whittle away at the statutory crimes created in 1825. The
legislation of the 1870s, both Liberal and Conservative, made the pattern
permanent, and in 1906, when labour's political might earned it *carte
blanche*, it could think of asking for nothing more than a still greater
exception. Ever since then, being left alone has been one of labour's central
demands.

When regulation yielded to negotiation as the preferred means for setting
wages, contract moved inevitably to the fore. The decision to leave wages to
bargaining between the parties proved agreeable to many groups other than
capital and labour: ideologically sound, it also comported well with the
administrative weakness of the state. The ever-growing size of the factory
inspectorate suggested the scale of the problem. Contract had to grow to fill
its new role. When wages were set by officers of the state, whether national

or local, the contract of service had merely inducted workmen into the scheme; the law of master and servant supplied the missing terms. Later, when agreement became the source of all obligation, the contract was treated as executory (that is, not fully performed) while the relationship lasted, and it was scrutinized for terms, express or implied.

Once contract was put in the centre of things, all the other pieces had accordingly to be rearranged. Setting wages by contract affirmed the formal indifference of the state. Labour wholeheartedly embraced the new regime, preferring to rely on its own economic power rather than on the goodwill of officialdom. It was labour that drew the line on the advancing law of contract: individual contracts of employment were well enough, but making the collective agreement legally enforceable threatened too much involvement with the courts. Had patterns of wage-setting been established after the triumph of democracy had assured labour a powerful say in affairs of state, its attitude towards government interference in wages might well have been different.

Despite the primacy of negotiation, the state could not remain completely indifferent to industrial conditions. Factory acts, truck acts, hours legislation, workmen's compensation—all testified to continuing official interest even in the nineteenth century, the heyday of *laissez-faire*. Regulations multiplied in the twentieth century, covering far more ground, albeit in different directions, than the law of master and servant ever had. But regulation in the interest of health and safety was always, at least in theory, on the fringes; the central area, however much it dwindled, remained the domain of free collective bargaining. Labour, like many other interests, embraced the exception as well as the rule and used its political strength to build the welfare state, all the while zealously preserving its own privileges and immunities.

Parliamentary action was well rooted in labour's experience. From complaints about eighteenth-century legislation, to petitions against details of the 1799 Combination Act, to those in favour of reform in 1824, through the lobbying that produced the Molestation of Workmen Act (1859), to political jockeying in the 1870s, to the famous victory in 1906, labour had learned to ask and receive. Workmen shared in small but significant measure in the eighteenth-century victory of due process, giving them valuable common ground with their political masters. But labour could never fully accept the transformation of due process into a rule of formal legal equality. In a world of gross disparities, why should single workmen and giant companies be treated alike? In time, labour came to view its position as exceptional; advancing democracy made it only more likely to get its way with the statute book.

With the common-law courts, on the other hand, labour's experience had not been so happy. At first the courts merely kept pace, more or less, with parliamentary developments. The Cambridge Tailors' Case (1721) came within months of the first tailors' combination act (1721); the common law of criminal conspiracy developed in tandem with parliament's groping for a general proposition on combination. With the rise of contract, inducement to its breach struck court and legislature alike as a bad thing. Judicial reaction to the Molestation of Workmen Act (1859), however, signalled greater problems to come. That small act had been speedily relegated to insignificance, foreshadowing judicial developments at the end of the nineteenth century that jeopardized the hard-won gains of the 1870s. Accelerated legal developments in the 1890s seemed designed to dramatize judicial power and unpredictability. New legal doctrines, however well grounded in the rapidly growing science of the law, struck practical workmen as betrayals of traditional fair play. Surpassing parliament as the chief threat to labour, the courts had to be sidelined if not defeated. The lesson labour learned from its history was to see the common law as inherently hostile to its organizational aspirations and to use its parliamentary power to avoid as much as possible the law and the legal profession.

Appendix I

Comparison of the 1800 Act with the 1799 Act

Section of 1800 Act	Summary of Section in 1800 Act	Comparison with 1799 Act	Comparable Section of 1799 Act
1	preamble; repeal of 1799 Act (anything done under Act valid); definition of illegal contract (excluding individual employment contract)	preamble; definition of illegal contract	1
2	*crime*: making contract; *punishment*: up to 3 months in common gaol or up to 2 months at hard labour in house of correction; *limitation of actions*: 3 months; trial by 2 justices of the peace; conviction must be supported by confession or 1 witness	same crime, punishment, and limitation of actions; trial by 1 justice of the peace; same evidence	2
3	*crimes*: combining for any purpose contrary to act, 'wilfully and maliciously' endeavouring to prevent workman from accepting or continuing work, 'wilfully and maliciously' preventing master from employing whomever he thinks proper, 'without' any just or reasonable cause' refusing to work	*crimes*: combining for any purpose contrary to act, 'directly or indirectly' endeavouring to prevent workman from accepting or continuing work, 'directly or indirectly' preventing master from employing whomever he thinks proper, refusing to work with any other workman; same	3

Section of 1800 Act	Summary of Section in 1800 Act	Comparison with 1799 Act	Comparable Section of 1799 Act
	with any other workman; *punishment*: up to 3 months in common gaol or up to 2 months at hard labour in house of correction; *limitation of actions*: 3 months; trial by 2 justices of the peace; conviction must be supported by confession or 1 witness	punishment and limitation of actions; trial by 1 justice of the peace; same evidence	
4	*crimes*: attending meeting to make illegal agreement or to form an illegal combination, endeavouring to induce workman to attend such meeting or to join illegal combination, collecting or paying money for illegal purposes; *punishment*: up to 3 months in common gaol or up to 2 months at hard labour in house of correction; *limitation of actions*: 3 months; trial by 2 justices of the peace; conviction must be supported by confession or 1 witness	*crimes*: attending meeting to make illegal agreement or to form an illegal combination, 'directly or indirectly' endeavouring to induce workman to attend such meeting or to join illegal combination or to leave work, collecting or paying money for illegal purposes; same punishment and limitation of actions; trial by 1 justice of the peace; same evidence	4
5	*crimes*: 'wilfully' paying expenses of any person violating act, supporting any workman that refuses to work, collecting or receiving money in such circumstances; *punishment*: for paying or supporting, fine of up to £10, for collecting or receiving, fine of up to £5; trial by 2 justices of the	same crimes (although 'wilfully' omitted) and punishment; trial by 1 justice of the peace; same evidence; fine to Crown; if fine not paid, distress and sale; if inadequate, imprisonment in common gaol or house of correction for 2 to 3 months	5

Section of 1800 Act	Summary of Section in 1800 Act	Comparison with 1799 Act	Comparable Section of 1799 Act
	peace; conviction must be supported by confession or 1 witness; fine divided half to Crown, quarter each to informer and poor of parish; if fine not paid, distress and sale; if inadequate, imprisonment for up to 3 months in common gaol or up to 2 months at hard labour in house of correction		
6	money collected must be returned within 3 months of passage of act or it shall be forfeited, as also all money collected in future; forfeitures divided half to Crown, half to whomever shall sue for it	identical	6
7	Attorney-General or informer may prefer information in court of equity against person holding money collected for illegal purposes; that person shall be obliged to answer	identical	7
8	person holding money collected for illegal purposes shall be discharged from penalty and suits by private parties by paying money into court of equity; person answering information indemnified against prosecution	identical but without indemnification	8
9	witness may be compelled to testify even though he may have offended against act; such witness immune from prosecution	similar	9

Section of 1800 Act	Summary of Section in 1800 Act	Comparison with 1799 Act	Comparable Section of 1799 Act
10	on complaint and information on oath 1 justice of the peace to summon offender; summons to be served personally or left at usual place of abode at least 24 hours before trial; if person summoned fails to appear or if 2 justices of the peace think fit, 2 justices of the peace may issue warrant for arrest; when accused is present or upon proof that accused absconded, trial by 2 justices of the peace; conviction must be supported by confession or 1 witness; *limitation of actions*: 3 months	on complaint and information on oath 1 justice of the peace to summon offender; summons to be served personally or left at usual place of abode; if person summoned fails to appear or if 1 justice of the peace thinks fit, 1 justice of the peace may issue warrant for arrest; when accused is present, trial by 1 justice of the peace; same evidence and limitation of actions	10
11	at request in writing 2 justices of the peace shall summon witness; summons may be served personally or left at usual place of abode at least 24 hours before trial; if witness refuses to appear or testify, 2 justices of the peace shall issue warrant to imprison witness until he shall answer	at request in writing 1 justice of the peace shall summon witness; summons may be served personally or left at usual place of abode; if witness refuses to appear or testify, 1 justice of the peace shall issue warrant to imprison witness until he shall answer	11
12	convictions and commitments to be drawn up in form set forth in schedule or in another form to same effect	identical	12
13	form of conviction shall be transmitted to next quarter sessions; quarter sessions to hear and determine any appeal	form of conviction shall be transmitted to next quarter sessions; quarter sessions to hear and finally determine any appeal; 'no *certiorari* shall be granted'	13

Section of 1800 Act	Summary of Section in 1800 Act	Comparison with 1799 Act	Comparable Section of 1799 Act
14	act does not limit powers of justices of the peace under other statutes	identical	15
15	act does not empower master to employ otherwise illegal workmen; however, 1 justice of the peace may issue written licence permitting master to employ illegal workmen if qualified workmen usually employed obstruct ordinary course of trade	identical	16
16	no master in the trade involved shall act as justice of the peace	no counterpart	—
17	*crime*: master's entering into illegal agreement; *punishment*: fine of £20; *limitation of actions*: 3 months; trial by 2 justices of the peace; conviction must be supported by confession or 1 witness; fine divided half to Crown, quarter each to informer and poor of parish; if fine not paid, distress and sale; if inadequate, imprisonment in common gaol or house of correction for 2 to 3 months	no counterpart	—
18 19 20 21 22	arbitration sections	no counterpart	—
23	offender may appeal to quarter sessions; judgment appealed from suspended if appellant enters into recognizance himself for £10 with 2 sureties for £5	offender may appeal to quarter sessions; judgment appealed from suspended if appellant enters into recognizance with 2 sureties in penalty of £20;	14

Section of 1800 Act	Summary of Section in 1800 Act	Comparison with 1799 Act	Comparable Section of 1799 Act
	each; if appeal fails, appellant to pay 'just and reasonable' costs; in case of failure to pay, imprisonment	same provision for costs	
24	despite repeal of 1799 Act all proceedings under it were valid	no counterpart	
25	action against anyone enforcing act must be brought within 3 months; if defendant prevails, plaintiff must pay full costs	identical except if defendant prevails, plaintiff must pay treble costs	17
1st schedule	forms* (1) of conviction and commitment, (2) of conviction in a pecuniary penalty, (3) of commitment of a person summoned as a witness	comparable forms	schedule
2nd schedule	forms for use in arbitration	no counterpart	—

*Errors were left in each of these forms. Although the error in the third form (describing the act as 'made in the thirty-ninth year of the reign of His present Majesty') seems never to have been corrected, the errors in the first two were rectified by 41 Geo. 3, c. 38 (1801).

Appendix II

Statutes Repealed by Name in 1824 and 1825

ENGLAND

Citation	Title	Extent of Repeal	Order in which Named
33 Edw. 1, st. 2 (1304)	Who be Conspirators	in so far as relates to conspiracies to alter wages, hours, or quantity of work or to control management	1
3 Hen. 6, c. 1 (1424)	Masons shall not confederate themselves in Chapiters and Assemblies	in so far as relates to annual congregations of masons (in 1824 wholly repealed)	2
2 & 3 Edw. 6, c. 15 (1548)	The Bill of Conspiracies of Victuallers and Craftsmen	whole	4
13 & 14 Car. 2, c. 15 (1662)	An Act for regulating the Trade of Silk Throwing	in so far as prohibits Corporation of Silk Throwers from setting wages	11
7 Geo. 1, st. 1, c. 13 (1721)	Tailors' Combination Act I	whole, except in so far as relates to recovery of wages or to refusal of work	12
12 Geo. 1, c. 34 (1726)	Weavers' Combination Act	in so far as prohibits such workmen from entering into agreements	13
22 Geo. 2, c. 27 (1749)	Omnibus Combination Act	in so far as extends 12 Geo. 1, c. 34 (1726)	16
29 Geo. 2, c. 33 (1756)	Weavers' Act II	in so far as relates to assessment of wages*	17

* The sections concerning wage regulation had been previously repealed by 30 Geo. 2, c. 12 (1757).

Citation	Title	Extent of Repeal	Order in which Named
8 Geo. 3, c. 17 (1768)	Tailors' Combination Act II	whole	20
13 Geo. 3, c. 68 (1773)	Spitalfields Act I	in so far as relates to regulation of wages and to combination of workmen[†]	23
17 Geo. 3, c. 55 (1777)	Hatters' Combination Act	in so far as relates to combination of workmen	24
32 Geo. 3, c. 44 (1792)	Spitalfields Act II	in so far as extends 13 Geo. 3, c. 68 (1773)[†]	29
36 Geo. 3, c. 111 (1796)	Papermakers' Combination Act	whole	30
39 & 40 Geo. 3, c. 106 (1800)	1800 Combination Act	whole, except in so far as relates to arbitration and to repeal of 1799 Combination Act	32

SCOTLAND

Citation	Title	Extent of Repeal	Order in which Named
5 Parl. Jac. 1, c. 78 (1426)	Of the Fees of Craftsmen, and the Price of their Worke	whole	5
5 Parl. Jac. 1, c. 79 (1426)	Of the Fees of Workmen	whole	6
5 Parl. Jac. 1, c. 80 (1426)	Of Writches and Masones	whole	7
7 Parl. Jac. 1, c. 102 (1427)	The Price of Silk Workmanshippe	whole	8
5 Parl. Mar., c. 23 (1551)	The Price of Craftesmenne's Wark, of Meate and Drinke in Tavernes	whole	9
7 Parl. Jac. 6, c. 121 (1581)	Anent the setting of Ordour and Price in all Stuffe	whole	10
39 Geo. 3, c. 56 (1799) (passed by union parliament)	An Act to explain and amend the Laws relative to Colliers in that Part of *Great Britain* called *Scotland*	in so far as relates to fixing hire and wages	31

[†] Repealed *in toto* by 5 Geo. 4, c. 66 (1824).

Citation	Title	Extent of Repeal	Order in which Named

IRELAND

Citation	Title	Extent of Repeal	Order in which Named
33 Hen. 8, st. 1, c. 9 (1542)	An Act for Servants' Wages	whole	3
3 Geo. 2, c. 14 (1729)	An Act to prevent unlawful Combinations of Workmen, Artificers, and Labourers . . . and for the better Payment of their Wages . . .	in so far as prohibits Irish workmen from entering into agreements	14
17 Geo. 2, c. 8 (1743)	An Act for continuing several Statutes now near expiring, and for amending other Statutes . . .	in so far as prohibits Irish combinations	15
3 Geo. 3, c. 17 (1763)	An Act for continuing and amending certain temporary Statutes heretofore made, for the better Regulation of the City of *Cork* . . .	in so far as relates to combination of workmen	18
3 Geo. 3, c. 34 (1763)	An Act for the better Regulation of the Linen and Hempen Manufactures	in so far as relates to combination of workmen	19
11 & 12 Geo. 3, c. 18 (1771)	An Act for the Regulation of the City of *Cork*, and for other Purposes therein mentioned relative to the said City	in so far as relates to combination of workmen, to refusal of work, and to ascertainment of wages	21
11 & 12 Geo. 3, c. 33 (1772)	An Act for regulating the Journeymen Tailors and Journeymen Shipwrights of the City of *Dublin* and the Liberties thereof, and of the County of *Dublin*	in so far as relates to combination of workmen, to refusal of work, and to regulation of wages and hours	22
19 & 20 Geo. 3, c. 19 (1780)	An Act to prevent Combinations, and for the further Encouragement of Trade	in so far as declares that combinations are public nuisances	25

Citation	Title	Extent of Repeal	Order in which Named
19 & 20 Geo. 3, c. 24 (1780)§	An Act for the better Regulation of the Silk Manufacture	in so far as relates to wages and to combinations	26
19 & 20 Geo. 3, c. 36 (1780)	An Act for regulating the curing and preparing Provisions, and for preventing Combinations among the several Tradesmen and other Persons employed in making up such Provisions . . .	in so far as relates to combination of workmen	27
25 Geo. 3, c. 48 (1785)	An Act for granting the Sums of £20,000 . . . to certain Trustees, and for promoting the several Manufactures therein named	in so far as relates to ascertainment of wages	28
43 Geo. 3, c. 86 (1803) (passed by union parliament)	An Act to prevent unlawful Combinations of Workmen, Artificers, Journeymen, and Labourmen, in *Ireland* . . .	in so far as outlaws combinations	33
47 Geo. 3, st. 1, c. 43 (1807) (passed by union parliament)	An Act to declare that the Provisions of an Act, made in the Parliament of *Ireland* in the Thirty-third year of King *Henry* the Eighth [st. 1, c. 9, see above] . . . shall extend to all Counties of Cities and Counties of Towns in *Ireland*	whole	34

§ The Irish parliament modelled 19 & 20 Geo. 3, c. 24 on the Spitalfields Act I. The English parliament extended it by the Spitalfields Act II. Ironically, all three had been wholly repealed by 5 Geo. 4, c. 66.

Citation	Title	Extent of Repeal	Order in which Named

SCOTLAND AND IRELAND

57 Geo. 3, c. 122 (1817) (passed by union parliament)	An Act to extend the Provisions of an Act of the Twelfth Year of His late Majesty King *George* the First [c. 34, see above], and an Act of the Twenty-second Year of His late Majesty King *George* the Second [c. 27, see above] . . . to Labourers employed in the Collieries . . . in the United Kingdom . . . and for extending the Provisions of the said Acts to *Scotland* and *Ireland*	in so far as extends the Acts to Scotland and Ireland	35

Appendix III

Key for Comparing the 1824 Act
with the 1800 Act

Section(s) of 1824 Act	Section(s) of 1800 Act
1	1
2	—
3	—
4	1
5 and 6	1, 2–5, 17
7 and 13	10
8	16
9	11
10	9
11	12
12	23
14	25
schedule	1st schedule

Appendix IV

Comparison of the 1825 Act with the 1824 Act

Section of 1825 Act	Summary of Section in 1825 Act	Comparison with 1824 Act	Comparable Section(s) of 1824 Act
1	preamble; repeal of 1824 Act	preamble; repeal of statutes against combination [see App. II]	1
2	repeal of statutes against combination [see App. II]		
3	*crimes*: by violence, threats, intimidation, molesting, or obstructing, forcing or endeavouring to force workmen to stop work, or not to accept work, or to join any club, or to make any contribution, or to pay any fine for not having complied with orders as to wages, hours, or working conditions; by violence, threats, intimidation, molesting, or obstructing, forcing or endeavouring to force master to alter his mode of carrying on business or to limit number of apprentices or number or description of workmen; *punishment*: up to 3 months in prison with or without hard labour	*crimes*: by violence, threats, or intimidation 'wilfully or maliciously' forcing workman to stop work before the end of his service or to spoil work, or not to accept work; 'wilfully or maliciously' using violence, threats, or intimidation towards a workman for not having complied with orders as to wages, hours, or working conditions; by violence, threats, or intimidation 'wilfully or maliciously' forcing master to alter his mode of carrying on business; *punishment*: up to 2 months in prison with or without hard labour (same punishment if crime committed by combination)	5 and 6
4	no one shall be liable to any prosecution or penalty, 'any law or statute to the contrary notwithstanding',	workmen shall not be liable to indictment or for conspiracy 'or to any other criminal information or	2

Section of 1825 Act	Summary of Section in 1825 Act	Comparison with 1824 Act	Comparable Section(s) of 1824 Act
	for meeting with others for sole purpose of agreeing on wages and hours to be demanded	punishment whatever, under the common or the statute law' for entering into any combination to raise wages, to lessen hours, to decrease quantity of work, to induce a workman to stop work, to induce a workman not to accept work, or to regulate mode of carrying on any business	
5	no one shall be liable to any prosecution or penalty, 'any law or statute to the contrary notwithstanding', for meeting with others for the sole purpose of agreeing on wages and hours to be offered	masters shall not be liable to indictment for conspiracy 'or to any other criminal information or punishment whatever, under the common or the statute law' for entering into any combination to lower wages, to increase hours, to increase quantity of work, or to regulate mode of carrying on any business	3
6	witness may be compelled to testify even though he may have offended against act; such witness indemnified against prosecution	substantially the same	10
7	on complaint and information on oath 1 justice of the peace to summon offender; summons to be served personally or left at usual place of abode at least 24 hours before trial; if person summoned fails to appear or if 2 justices of the peace think fit, 2 justices of the peace may issue warrant for arrest; when accused is present or upon proof that	on complaint and information on oath 1 justice of the peace to summon offender; summons to be served personally or left at usual place of abode at least 24 hours before trial; if person summoned fails to appear or if 2 justices of the peace think fit, 2 justices of the peace may issue warrant for arrest; when accused is present, trial by 2 justices of	7 and 13

Section of 1825 Act	Summary of Section in 1825 Act	Comparison with 1824 Act	Comparable Section(s) of 1824 Act
	accused absconded, trial by 2 justices of the peace; conviction must be supported by confession or 1 witness; *limitation of actions*: 6 months	the peace; trial to be held as near as may be to place where offence committed; conviction must be supported by confession or 2 witnesses; same limitation of actions	
8	at request in writing 2 justices of the peace shall summon witness; summons may be served personally or left at usual place of abode at least 24 hours before trial; if witness refuses to appear or testify, 2 justices of the peace shall issue warrant to imprison witness for 3 months or until he shall answer	at request in writing 1 justice of the peace shall summon witness; summons may be served personally or left at usual place of abode at least 24 hours before trial; if witness refuses to appear or testify, 2 justices of the peace shall issue warrant to imprison witness for 2 months or until he shall answer (if trial held without witness, then witness must serve full term)	9
9	convictions and commitments to be drawn up in form set forth in schedule or in another form to same effect	identical	11
10	form of conviction shall be transmitted to next quarter sessions; quarter session to hear and determine any appeal	no counterpart	—
11	in Scotland prosecutions initiated by public prosecutor, may be judged by 2 justices of the peace or by sheriff	no counterpart	—
12	offender may appeal to quarter sessions; judgment appealed from suspended if appellant enters into recognizance himself for £10 with 2 sureties for £10	no appeal allowed	12

Section of 1825 Act	Summary of Section in 1825 Act	Comparison with 1824 Act	Comparable Section(s) of 1824 Act
13	no master in the trade involved shall act as justice of the peace	no master or father or son of a master in any trade shall act as a justice of the peace	8
—	no counterpart	penal proceedings under any repealed statute or for any act exempted from punishment shall become null and void	4
—	no counterpart	if defendant prevails in an action brought for enforcing act, plaintiff must pay full costs	14
schedule	forms (1) of conviction and commitment, (2) of commitment of a person summoned as a witness	comparable forms	schedule

Bibliography

I. PRIMARY SOURCES

Note: Citations to cases and statutes are in their respective tables.

A. Contemporary Documents

(Collections of Contemporary Documents are listed in section B, below, arranged alphabetically by editor's surname.)

[ALISON, ARCHIBALD], 'Practical Working of Trades' Unions', *Blackwood's Edinburgh Magazine*, 43 (1838), 281–303. (Attribution in Walter E. Houghton (ed.), *Wellesley Index to Victorian Periodicals* (Toronto, 1966–72), ii. 56.)

[——], 'Trades' Unions and Strikes', *Edinburgh Review*, 67 (1838), 209–59. (Attribution in Walter E. Houghton (ed.), *Wellesley Index to Victorian Periodicals* (Toronto, 1966–72), i. 485. Reviewing report of trial of Glasgow cotton spinners; see s.n. Thomas Hunter, *et al.*, defendants. Author was Sheriff of Glasgow (1834–67).)

ALLEN, L. B., *Brief Considerations on the Present State of the Police of the Metropolis* (1821).

Anon., 'Rules Adopted by the Journeymen Millwrights, for the Well-Governing of their Society' (1801).

—— 'Critique of a Speech by Francis Jeffrey in Praise of Joseph Hume, 18 November 1825, Edinburgh', *Monthly Review*, 3rd ser., 1 (1826), 1–9. For the text of the speech, see s.n. Francis Jeffrey.

—— 'Combinations and Combination Laws', *Law Magazine*, 11 (1834), 143–80.

—— 'The Case of the Dorsetshire Labourers', *Law Magazine*, 11 (1834), 460–72. The case is *R. v. Loveless* (Tolpuddle Martyrs).

—— 'The Dorsetshire Labourers', *Westminster Review*, 21 (1834), 52–62.

—— 'Trades'-Union and Strikes', *Edinburgh Review*, 59 (1834), 341–59. Reviewing, *inter alia*, [Edward Carleton Tufnell], *Character, Object, and Effects of Trades' Unions* (1834).

—— 'Strikes: Their Tendencies and Remedies', *Westminster Review*, NS 18 (1860), 1–23. Reviewing, *inter alia*, Francis D. Longe, *An Inquiry into the Law of 'Strikes'* (1860).

ARCHBOLD, JOHN FREDERICK, *Criminal Pleading, Evidence, and Practice* (1st edn., 1822; 40th edn., 1979 (ed. S. Mitchell)).

—— *The Justice of the Peace and Parish Officer*, 4 vols. (1st edn., 1840; 4th edn., 1854–5).

—— *Jervis's Acts, 11 & 12 Victoria, cc. 42, 43 and 44; Relating to the Duties of Justices of the Peace* (1st edn., 1848; 3rd edn., 1851).

ATKINSON, EDWARD, *et al.*, defendants, *An Account of the Rise and Progress of the*

Dispute between the Masters and Journeymen Printers, Exemplified in the Trial at Large (1799).

AUSTIN, JOHN, *Lectures on Jurisprudence, or the Philosophy of Positive Law*, 2 vols. (3rd edn., 1869 (ed. Robert Campbell)). (*The Province of Jurisprudence Determined*, rev. and repr. in vol. i., was first published in 1832.)

BAGEHOT, WALTER, *The English Constitution* (2nd edn., 1872; repr. with introd. by R. H. S. Crossman, Ithaca, NY, 1963).

BECCARIA, CESARE BONESANA, Marchese de, *On Crimes and Punishments* (1st (Italian) edn., 1764; trans. Henry Paolucci, Indianapolis, 1963).

BEESLY, EDWARD SPENCER, 'Trades' Unions', *Westminster Review*, NS 20 (1861), 510–42 (reviewing, *inter alia*, T. J. Dunning, *Trades' Unions and Strikes* (1860), and National Association for the Promotion of Social Science report on *Trades' Societies and Strikes* (1860)).

—— 'The Trades' Union Commission', *Fortnightly Review*, NS 2 (1867), 1–18.

BENTHAM, JEREMY, *An Introduction to the Principles of Morals and Legislation* (1789), ed. J. H. Burns and H. L. A. Hart, London, 1970).

[BIRD, JAMES BARRY], *The Laws Respecting Masters and Servants; Articled Clerks, Apprentices, Journeymen and Manufacturers* (1st edn., 1795; 2nd edn., *c*.1797). (Attribution in Harvard Law Library catalogue.)

BLACKSTONE, WILLIAM, *Commentaries on the Laws of England*, 4 vols. (1765–9).

[BRENTANO, LUDWIG JOSEPH], 'On the History and Development of Gilds, and the Origin of Trade-Unions', in Toulmin Smith (ed.), *English Gilds* (1870), pp. xlix–cxcix.

—— 'The Growth of a Trades-Union', *North British Review*, 53 (1870–1), 59–114. (Attribution ('probable') in Walter E. Houghton (ed.), *Wellesley Index to Victorian Periodicals* (Toronto, 1966–72), i. 695. The union is the Journeymen Steam Engine and Machine Makers Friendly Society (the 'Engineers').)

BURN, RICHARD, *The Justice of the Peace and Parish Officer*, 4 vols. (1st edn., 1755; 19th edn., 1800 (ed. John Burn)).

BURTON, JOHN HILL (ed.), *Benthamiana: or, Select Extracts from the Works of Jeremy Bentham* (1843).

CAMPBELL, LORD, *Lives of the Lord Chancellors of England*, 3 vols. (1845–7). (Concludes with dismissal of Lord Brougham in 1834. Vol. iv, published posthumously, completed the life of Brougham and added the life of Lyndhurst.)

—— *Lives of the Chief Justices of England*, 3 vols. (1849–57). (Concludes with death of Lord Tenterden (Charles Abbott) in 1832. The author went on to be Chief Justice himself from 1850 until 1859 when he became Lord Chancellor.)

CARSON, HAMPTON, L., *The Law of Criminal Conspiracies and Agreements, As Found in the American Cases* (1887) (bound with R. S. Wright's book with the same main title).

CHITTY, JOSEPH, *A Practical Treatise on the Law Relative to Apprentices and Journeymen, and to Exercising Trades* (1812).

—— *A Treatise on the Laws of Commerce and Manufactures*, 4 vols. (1820–4).

—— *A Practical Treatise on the Criminal Law*, 4 vols. (2nd edn., 1826).

COHEN, HERMAN, 'Total Immunity of Trade Union Funds', *Fortnightly Review*, NS 80 (1906), 925–41.

—— and HOWELL, GEORGE, *Trade Union Law and Cases: A Text Book Relating to Trade Unions and to Labour* (1901) (2nd edn., 1907; 3rd edn., 1913).

COKE, EDWARD, *Institutes of the Laws of England*, 4 vols. (1628–41).

COMYNS, JOHN, *A Digest of the Laws of England* (1st (French) edn., 1762–7; 4th edn., 1800 (ed. Samuel Rose)).

Conservative Party, Scotland, *Campaign Guide* (1906).

CUMMINGS, EDWARD, 'A Collectivist Philosophy of Trade Unionism', *Quarterly Journal of Economics*, 13 (1898–9), 151–86.

CUNNINGHAM, T., *The Law of Simony* (1784). (Includes report of *Bishop of London v. Ffytche* (HL 1783).)

DICEY, A. V., 'The Legal Boundaries of Liberty', *Fortnightly Review*, NS 3 (1868), 1–13.

—— 'Development of English Law during the Nineteenth Century in Connection with the Course of Public Opinion in England', syllabus for lectures delivered at the Harvard Law School (1898).

—— 'The Combination Laws as Illustrating the Relation between Law and Opinion in England during the Nineteenth Century', 17 *Harvard Law Review* 511–32 (1903–4).

—— *Lectures on the Relation between Law and Public Opinion in England during the Nineteenth Century* (1st edn., 1905; 2nd edn., 1914).

DUNCKLEY, H., *'Strikes' Viewed in Relation to the Interests of Capital and Labour* (1853).

DUNNING, T. J., *Trades' Unions and Strikes: Their Philosophy and Intention* (1860). (Dunning was secretary of the Consolidated Society of Bookbinders. For review, see s.n. Edward Spencer Beesly.)

EDEN, WILLIAM, *Principles of Penal Law* (1771).

[ELLIS, WILLIAM], 'Art. 5', *Westminster Review*, 3 (1825) 386–94. (Attribution in Frank W. Fetter, *Journal of Political Economy*, 70 (1962), 584.)

ENGELS, FRIEDRICH, *The Condition of the Working Class in England* (1st (German) edn., 1845), ed. and trans. W. O. Henderson and W. H. Chaloner (Stanford, Calif., 1958).

ERLE, WILLIAM, *The Law Relating to Trade Unions* (1869). (Originally prepared as a memorandum for the royal commission on trade unions, 1867–9, which Erle chaired; repr. from the *Parliamentary Papers* (1868–9), 31, pp. 235–361. For reviews, see s.n. [G. K. Rickards] and *Law Times*, 46 (1869), 283–4, 303, 322, 342–3, 362 (anon.).)

ERSKINE MAY, THOMAS, *A Practical Treatise on the Law, Privileges, Proceedings and Usage of Parliament* (1844).

FIELDING, HENRY, *An Enquiry into the Causes of the Late Increase of Robbers* (1751).

FOSS, EDWARD, *The Judges of England*, 9 vols. (1848–64).

GELDART, W. M., 'The Report of the Royal Commission on Trade Disputes', *Economic Journal*, 16 (1906), 189–211.

HALDANE, R. B., 'The Labourer and the Law', *Contemporary Review*, 83 (1903), 362–72.

Hansard's Parliamentary Debates, 1st ser. (1803–20); 2nd ser. (1820–30); 3rd ser. (1830–91).

HANSON, JOSEPH, defendant, *The Whole Proceedings on the Trial of an Indictment against Joseph Hanson Esq. for a Conspiracy to Aid the Weavers of Manchester in Raising their Wages* (1809).

HARRISON, FREDERIC, 'The Trades-Union Bill', *Fortnightly Review*, NS 6 (1869), 30–45. (The author served on the royal commission on trade unions, 1867–9.)

HAWKINS, WILLIAM, *A Treatise of the Pleas of the Crown*, 4 vols. (1st edn., 1716–21; 7th edn., 1795 (ed. Thomas Leach, 1795)).

[HODGSKIN, THOMAS], *Labour Defended against the Claims of Capital* (1825) (3rd edn., with introd. by G. D. H. Cole, London, 1922).

House of Commons Journal.

House of Lords Journal.

HOWARD, JOHN, *The State of the Prisons in England and Wales* (1777).

HOWELL, GEORGE, *A Handy-book of the Labour Laws, Being a Popular Guide* (1st edn., 1876; 3rd, rev. edn., 1895).

—— 'Trades' Union Congresses and Social Legislation', *Contemporary Review*, 56 (1889), 401–20.

—— *Labour Legislation, Labour Movements and Labour Leaders* (1902).

HUME, DAVID, *Commentaries on the Law of Scotland, Respecting Crimes*, 2 vols. (4th edn., 1844). (Originally published as two separate works, one on criminal law (1797), the other on criminal procedure (1800). Nephew of the famous philosopher of the same name, the author was professor of Scots Law in the Univ. of Edinburgh from 1786 until 1822 when he became a baron of the Scottish Court of Exchequer.)

HUNTER, THOMAS, *et al.*, defendants, *Report of the Trial of Thomas Hunter, Peter Hacket, Richard M'Niel, James Gibb, and William M'Lean, Cotton-Spinners in Glasgow* . . . by Archibald Swinton (1838). (For review, see s.n. [Archibald Alison].)

—— *Trial of Thomas Hunter, Peter Hacket, Richard M'Niel, James Gibb, and William M'Lean, the Glasgow Cotton Spinners* . . . reported by James Marshall (1838).

ILBERT, COURTENAY, *Legislative Methods and Forms* (1901).

JEFFREY, FRANCIS, 'Combinations of Workmen: Substance of the Speech of Francis Jeffrey . . . at the Public Dinner Given at Edinburgh to Joseph Hume, Esq. M.P. on Friday the 18th of November 1825' (1825). (At the time of the speech, Jeffrey was editor of the *Edinburgh Review*; in 1830 he became Lord Advocate of Scotland and in 1834 a judge of the Court of Session. For an anonymous critique of this speech, see *Monthly Review*, 3rd ser., 1 (1826), 1–9.)

JEVONS, WILLIAM S., *The State in Relation to Labour* (1882).

JOHNSON, SAMUEL, *Dictionary* (1755).

JUNIUS (pseud.), *Letters*, ed. John Cannon (Oxford, 1978). (Originally appeared in the *Public Advertiser* (Jan. 1769–Jan. 1772). Letter 41 (14 Nov. 1770) was addressed to Lord Mansfield.)

KENYON, GEORGE T., *Life of Lord Kenyon* (1873).

LEONARD, S. H., 'Wrongful Intimidation', 7 *Law Quarterly Review* 375–8 (1891).

LONGE, FRANCIS D., *An Inquiry into the Law of 'Strikes'* (1860). (An abridged version was included in the National Association for the Promotion of Social Science report on *Trades' Societies and Strikes* (1860). Reviewed anonymously in *Westminster Review*, 18 (1860), 1–23.)

LOVELESS, GEORGE, *The Victims of Whiggery, being a Statement of the Persecutions Experienced by the Dorchester Labourers* (1837) (repr. Communist Party, London, 1969). (By the principal Tolpuddle Martyr.)

[LOWE, ROBERT], 'Trades' Unions', *Quarterly Review*, 123 (1867), 351–83. (Attribution in Walter E. Houghton (ed.), *Wellesley Index to Victorian Periodicals* (Toronto, 1966–72), i. 750. The author reviewed, *inter alia*, the first report of the royal commission on trade unions (1867).)

LUDLOW, J. M. and JONES, LLOYD, *Progress of the Working Class, 1832–1867* (1867). (An abridged version was included in *Questions for a Reformed Parliament* (1867).)

[McCULLOCH, J. R.], 'Combination Laws—Restraints on Emigration, etc.', *Edinburgh Review*, 39 (1824), 315–45. (Attribution in Walter E. Houghton (ed.), *Wellesley Index to Victorian Periodicals* (Toronto, 1966–72), i. 465.)

—— *An Essay on the Circumstances which Determine the Rate of Wages and the Condition of the Labouring Classes* (1826). (Later edns. (in which *Treatise* replaces *Essay* in the title) were published in 1851, 1854, and 1868.)

MALTHUS, THOMAS ROBERT, *An Essay on the Principle of Population* (1798), ed. Anthony Flew (Harmondsworth, 1970).

MARTINEAU, HARRIET, *History of England during the Thirty Years' Peace* (1849). (Covers 1815–45.)

[——], 'Secret Organisation of Trades', *Edinburgh Review*, 110 (1859), 525–63. (Attribution in Walter E. Houghton (ed.), *Wellesley Index to Victorian Periodicals* (Toronto, 1966–72), i. 509. The author reviewed, *inter alia*, the decision in *R. v. Duffield* (1851).)

MARX, KARL, *Capital: A Critique of Political Economy* (1st (German) edn., 1867), trans. Samuel Moore and Edward Aveling, ed. Friedrich Engels (1887).

MAYHEW, HENRY, *London Labour and the London Poor*, 4 vols. (1861–2).

MENGER, ANTON, *The Right to the Whole Produce of Labour* (1st (German) edn., 1886), trans. M. E. Tanner (1899).

MILL, JOHN STUART, *Principles of Political Economy*, 2 vols. (1st edn., 1848; 6th edn., 1865).

—— *On Liberty* (1859).

National Association for the Promotion of Social Science, *Trades' Societies and Strikes* (1860). (For review, see s.n. Edward Spencer Beesly.)

National Association of United Trades, 'Report of the Central Committee of United Trades on the Proceedings Connected with the "Combination of Workmen Bill" in the Parliamentary Session, 1853' (1853).

—— 'Report of the Executive Committee of the National Association of United Trades on the Proceedings Connected with the Combination of Workmen Bill, 1859' (1859).

NORTH, J., 'State of the Poor in the Parish of Ashdon, Essex', *Annals of Agriculture*, 35 (1800), 459–73. (The author was rector of Ashdon. *Annals* was edited by the pioneer investigator Arthur Young.)

PALEY, W., *The Law and Practice of Summary Convictions on Penal Statutes by Justices of the Peace* (1814).

Parliamentary Papers,
    (1824), 5, 'Artizans and Machinery'.
    (1825), 4, 'Combination Laws'.
    (1837–8), 8, 'Combination of Workmen'.
    (1841), 10, 'Hand-Loom Weavers'.
    (1867), 32, 'Organization and Rules of Trade Unions and other Associations'.

(1867–8), 39, 'Organization and Rules of Trade Unions (cont.)'.

(1868–9), 31, 'Organization and Rules of Trade Unions (cont.)'.

(1874), 24, 'Master and Servant Act (1867) and the Criminal Law Amendment Act (1871) (Labour Laws Commission)'.

(1875), 30, 'Labour Laws Commission (cont.)'.

(1892), 34–6, 'Labour'.

(1893–4), 32–9, 'Labour'.

(1894), 35, 'Labour'.

(1906), 56, 'Trade Disputes and Trade Combinations'.

Parliamentary Register; or, History of the Proceedings and Debates of the Houses of Lords and Commons.

PEEL, ROBERT, *From his Private Papers*, 3 vols., ed. Charles Stuart Parker (1891–9).

[PLACE, FRANCIS], 'Observations on Mr. Huskisson's Speech' (1825). (The speech in question appears in *Hansard*, 2nd ser., vol. 12, cols. 1290–301. Attribution in Harvard Law Library catalogue.)

—— *The Autobiography of Francis Place (1771–1854)*, ed. Mary Thale (Cambridge, 1972).

Questions for a Reformed Parliament (1867). (Includes Godfrey Lushington, 'Workmen and Trade Unions'.)

RICARDO, DAVID, *On the Principles of Political Economy and Taxation* (1817), ed. R. M. Hartwell (Harmondsworth, 1971).

[RICKARDS, G. K.], 'Trades' Unions', *Edinburgh Review*, 126 (1867), 415–57. (Attribution in Walter E. Houghton (ed.), *Wellesley Index to Victorian Periodicals* (Toronto, 1966–72), i. 516.)

—— 'Thornton on Labour', *Edinburgh Review*, 130 (1869), 390–417. (Attribution in Walter E. Houghton (ed.), *Wellesley Index to Victorian Periodicals* (Toronto, 1966–72), i. 518. Reviewing, *inter alia*, William Erle, *The Law Relating to Trade Unions* (1869). The author served as counsel to the Speaker of the House of Commons.)

[——], 'The Combinations', *Blackwood's Edinburgh Magazine*, 18 (1825), 463–78. (Attribution in Walter E. Houghton (ed.), *Wellesley Index to Victorian Periodicals* (Toronto, 1966–72), i. 18.)

[ROBINSON, DAVID], 'The Repeal of the Combination Laws', *Blackwood's Edinburgh Magazine*, 18 (1825), 20–31. (Attribution in Walter E. Houghton (ed.), *Wellesley Index to Victorian Periodicals* (Toronto, 1966–72), i. 17.)

[ROSS, CHARLES], 'Artizans and Machinery', *Quarterly Review*, 31 (1825), 391–419.

RUSKIN, JOHN, *'Unto This Last': Four Essays on the First Principles of Political Economy* (1862). (Originally appeared in *Cornhill Magazine* (1860).)

SCARLETT, PETER CAMPBELL, *A Memoir of . . . James, First Lord Abinger* (1877). (Includes autobiography of James Scarlett, Lord Abinger (1769–1844).)

SELSBY, HENRY, *et al.*, defendants, *The Trial of the Mechanics at Liverpool*, ed. W. P. Roberts (1847). (Roberts (1806–71), known as the 'miners' attorney-general', served militant trade unions.)

SENIOR, NASSAU W., *Historical and Philosophical Essays*, 2 vols. (1865).

SMILES, SAMUEL, *Self-Help with Illustrations of Conduct and Perseverance* (1859), centenary edn., with introd. by Asa Briggs (1958).

SMILES, SAMUEL, 'Strikes', *Quarterly Review*, 106 (1859), 485–522. (Attribution in Walter E. Houghton (ed.), *Wellesley Index to Victorian Periodicals* (1966–72), i. 742.)

SMITH, ADAM, *An Inquiry into the Nature and Causes of the Wealth of Nations* (1776), ed. Edwin Cannan (New York, 1937).

STEPHEN, HENRY JOHN, *New Commentaries on the Laws of England*, 4 vols. (4th edn., 1858 (ed. James Stephen); 21st edn., 1951). (The author was the uncle of James Fitzjames Stephen and Leslie Stephen (the father of Virginia Woolf).)

STEPHEN, JAMES FITZJAMES, *A History of the Criminal Law of England*, 3 vols. (1883). (Brother of Leslie Stephen, the author was a judge of the Queen's Bench Division from 1879 to 1891.)

STURGEON, CHARLES, 'Letters to the Trades' Unionists and the Working Classes on the Recent Bill Brought in to Repeal the Combination Laws, and Enslave the Working Classes, by Sir T. F. Buxton, Bart., and Mr. Young' (1868). (The bill in question appears in *Parliamentary Papers* (1867–8), 5, 575–8.)

[TUFNELL, EDWARD CARLETON], *Character, Object, and Effects of Trades' Unions; with some Remarks on the Law Concerning Them* (1834), repr. s.n. *Trades Unionism a Hundred Years Ago* (1933). (Reviewed anonymously in *Edinburgh Review*, 59 (1834), 341–59.)

WALLACE, JOHN WILLIAM, *The Reporters* (4th edn., Boston, 1882 (ed. Franklin Fiske Heard)).

WARD, THOMAS HUMPHREY (ed.), *The Reign of Queen Victoria: A Survey of Fifty Years of Progress*, 2 vols. (1887). (Lord Bowen wrote on 'Progress in the Administration of Justice during the Victorian Period' (i. 281–329), while A. J. Mundella and George Howell contributed the article on 'Industrial Association' (ii. 43–82).)

WELCH, SAUNDERS, *Observations on the Office of Constable* (2nd edn., 1758).

WENTWORTH, JOHN, *A Complete System of Pleading: Comprehending the Most Approved Precedents and Forms of Practice*, 10 vols. (1797–9). (Vols. iv and vi cover criminal cases. The 'precedents' of the title are forms of indictments and pleadings 'approved' by the courts.)

[WHITE, GEORGE] (comp.), *Combination and Arbitration Laws, Artizans and Machinery* (1824). (Attribution in Judith Blow Williams, *A Guide to the Printed Materials for English Social and Economic History* (Columbia, 1926), ii. 313.) (Includes: (1) an address to the working people by George White, (2) a letter to the Glasgow weavers by Joseph Hume, (3) parliamentary proceedings, 12 Feb. 1824, including speeches by Hume and Huskisson, (4) membership and witnesses for select committee, (5) abstract of acts, (6) resolutions of select committee.)

[—— and HENSON, GRAVENER], *A Few Remarks on the State of the Laws, at Present in Existence, for Regulating Masters and Work-People* (1823). (Attribution in catalogue of Kress Collection, Graduate School of Business Administration, Harvard Univ.)

WILSON, ROLAND KNYVET, *History of Modern English Law* (1875).

WRIGHT, R. S., *Law of Criminal Conspiracies and Agreements* (1873). (American repr. in 1887 bound with Hampton L. Carson's survey of American cases.)

B. Collections of Contemporary Documents

ASPINALL, ARTHUR (ed.), *The Early English Trade Unions: Documents from the Home Office Papers in the Public Record Office* (London, 1949). (Documents from 1791 to 1825.)

CARPENTER, KENNETH E. (comp.), *British Labour Struggles: Contemporary Pamphlets, 1727–1850*, 32 vols. (New York, 1975). (Pamphlets from the Kress Collection, Graduate School of Business Administration, Harvard Univ.)

COLE, G. D. H., and FILSON, A. W. (eds.), *British Working Class Movements: Select Documents, 1789–1875* (London, 1951). (Companion to Cole's *Short History*.)

COMMONS, JOHN R., *et al.* (eds.), *A Documentary History of American Industrial Society*, 10 vols. (New York, 1910–11). (Vols. iii–iv on 'Labor Conspiracy Cases' ed. by Commons and Eugene A. Gilmore.)

FROW, EDMUND, and KATANKA, MICHAEL (eds.), *1868, Year of the Unions: A Documentary Survey* (London, 1968).

GALTON, FRANK W. (ed.), *Select Documents Illustrating the History of Trade Unionism, i. The Tailoring Trade* (London, 1896).

JEFFERYS, JAMES B. (ed.), *Labour's Formative Years, 1849–1879, History in the Making*, ii. (London, 1948).

MANCHESTER, A. H. (ed.), *Sources of English Legal History, 1750–1950* (London, 1984). (Companion to Manchester's *Modern Legal History*.)

MILNE-BAILEY, W. (ed.), *Trade Union Documents* (London, 1929).

MORRIS, MAX (ed.), *From Cobbett to the Chartists, 1815–1848, History in the Making*, i. (London, 1948).

OLDHAM, JAMES (ed.), *Unpublished Legal Papers of Lord Mansfield* (Chapel Hill, NC, forthcoming).

Trade Unions in the Victorian Age: Debates on the Issue from Nineteenth-Century Critical Journals, 4 vols. (Farnborough, 1973). (Articles from the *Edinburgh Review*, the *Westminster Review*, the *Quarterly Review*, *Blackwood's*, and *Fraser's*.)

II. SELECTED SECONDARY SOURCES

ABEL-SMITH, BRIAN, and STEVENS, ROBERT, with the assistance of BROOKE, ROSALIND, *Lawyers and the Courts: A Sociological Study of the English Legal System, 1750–1965* (Cambridge, Mass., 1967).

ALLEN, V. L., *Trade Unions and the Government* (London, 1960).

—— 'Valuations and Historical Interpretation: A Case Study', *British Journal of Sociology*, 14 (1963), 48–58. The case study referred to is Beatrice Webb's and Sidney Webb's work as trade union historians.

—— 'The Origins of Industrial Conciliation and Arbitration', *International Review of Social History*, 9 (1964), 237–54.

AMULREE, LORD, *Industrial Arbitration in Great Britain* (London, 1929).

ANDERSON, ALAN, 'The Political Symbolism of the Labour Laws', *Bulletin of the Society for the Study of Labour History*, 23 (Autumn 1971), 13–15. (Summary of conference paper.)

ARMYTAGE, W. H. G., *A. J. Mundella, 1825–1897: The Liberal Background to the Labour Movement* (London, 1951).

ASHTON, T. S., *The Industrial Revolution, 1760–1830* (Oxford, 1948).

ATHERLEY-JONES, L. A., 'Labour Disputes', *Fortnightly Review*, NS 720 (1926), 757–67. (The author was a judge and former Liberal MP.)

ATIYAH, P. S., *The Rise and Fall of Freedom of Contract* (Oxford, 1979).

ATLAY, JAMES B., *The Victorian Chancellors*, 2 vols. (London, 1906–8).

AVERY, DIANE, 'Images of Violence in Labor Jurisprudence: The Regulation of Picketing and Boycotts, 1894–1921', 37 *Buffalo Law Review* 1–117 (1988–9). (On American labour.)

BAGWELL, PHILIP S., *Industrial Relations. Government and Society in Nineteenth Century Britain: Commentaries on British Parliamentary Papers* (Dublin, 1974).

BAKER, J. H., *An Introduction to English Legal History* (2nd edn., London, 1979).

BATT, JOHN, ' "United to Support but not Combined to Injure": Public Order, Trade Unions and the Repeal of the Combination Acts of 1799–1800', *International Review of Social History*, 31 (1986), 185–203.

BEALEY, FRANK W., and PELLING, HENRY M., *Labour and Politics, 1900–06* (London, 1958).

BEATTIE, J. M., *Crime and the Courts in England, 1660–1800* (Princeton, NJ, 1985).

BECKER, CRAIG, 'Property in the Workplace: Labor, Capital, and Crime in the Eighteenth-Century British Woolen and Worsted Industry', 69 *Virginia Law Review* 1487–515 (1983).

BEHAGG, CLIVE, 'Custom, Class and Change: The Trade Societies of Birmingham', *Social History*, 4 (1979), 455–80.

BELLAMY, JOYCE M., and SAVILLE, JOHN, *Dictionary of Labour Biography*, 8 vols. to date (London, 1972–87).

BERCUSSON, BRIAN, 'One Hundred Years of Conspiracy and Protection of Property: Time for a Change', 40 *Modern Law Review* 268–92 (1977).

BERESFORD, MAURICE W., 'The Common Informer, the Penal Statutes and Economic Regulation', *Economic History Review*, 2nd ser., 10 (1957–8), 221–38.

BERG, MAXINE, HUDSON, PAT, and SONENSCHER, MICHAEL (eds.), *Manufacture in Town and Country before the Factory* (Cambridge, 1983).

BINDOFF, S. T., 'The Making of the Statute of Artificers', in S. T. Bindoff, J. Hurstfield, and C. H. Williams (eds.), *Elizabethan Government and Society: Essays Presented to Sir John Neale* (London, 1961), 56–94.

BOHSTEDT, JOHN, *Riots and Community Politics in England and Wales, 1790–1810* (Cambridge, Mass., 1983).

BRAND, CARL F., 'The Conversion of the British Trade-Unions to Political Action', *American Historical Review*, 30 (1924–5), 251–70.

BRANTLINGER, PATRICK, 'The Case against Trade Unions in Early Victorian Fiction', *Victorian Studies*, 13 (1969–70), 37–52.

BREBNER, J. B., '*Laissez-faire* and State Intervention in Nineteenth Century Britain', *Journal of Economic History*, 8, supp. (1948), 59–73.

BREWER, JOHN, and STYLES, JOHN (eds.), *An Ungovernable People: The English and their Law in the Seventeenth and Eighteenth Centuries* (London, 1980).

BRIGGS, ASA, *Victorian People: A Reassessment of Persons and Themes, 1851–67* (Harmondsworth, 1954).

—— and SAVILLE, JOHN (eds.), *Essays in Labour History* (London, 1960).

—— and —— (eds.), *Essays in Labour History, 1886–1923* (Hamden, Conn., 1971).

BROWN, E. H. PHELPS, *The Growth of British Industrial Relations: A Study from the Standpoint of 1906–14* (London, 1959).

BROWN, KENNETH D. (ed.), *Essays in Anti-Labour History: Responses to the Rise of Labour in Britain* (Hamden, Conn., 1974).

BRYAN, JAMES WALLACE, *The Development of the English Law of Conspiracy* (Baltimore, 1909).

BUCHANAN, R. A., 'Trade Unions and Public Opinion, 1850–1875', Ph.D. thesis (Cambridge Univ., 1957).

BURGESS, KEITH, *The Origins of British Industrial Relations: The Nineteenth-Century Experience* (London, 1975).

—— *The Challenge of Labour: Shaping British Society, 1850–1930* (London, 1980).

CHALONER, W. H., *The Skilled Artisans during the Industrial Revolution, 1750–1850* (London, 1969).

CITRINE, NORMAN ARTHUR, *Trade Union Law* (3rd edn., London, 1967 (ed. M. A. Hickling)). (Continues Henry H. Slesser and Charles Baker's text of the same name.)

CLAPHAM, JOHN H., 'The Spitalfields Acts, 1773–1824', *Economic Journal*, 26 (1916), 459–71.

—— *An Economic History of Modern Britain*, 3 vols., i. *The Early Railway Age, 1820–50* (2nd edn., Cambridge, 1950); ii. *Free Trade and Steel, 1850–86* (2nd edn., Cambridge, 1951); iii. *Machines and National Rivalries, 1887–1914* with an *Epilogue, 1914–29* (2nd edn., Cambridge, 1952).

CLARK, ELAINE, 'Medieval Labor Law and English Local Courts', *American Journal of Legal History*, 27 (1983), 330–53.

CLEGG, HUGH A., FOX, ALAN, and THOMPSON, A. F., *A History of British Trade Unions since 1889*, i. *1889–1910* (Oxford, 1964).

CLEMENTS, ROGER V., 'British Trade Unions and Popular Political Economy, 1850–1875', *Economic History Review*, 2nd ser., 14 (1961–2), 93–104.

COATES, WILLSON H., 'Benthamism, Laissez-faire and Collectivism', *Journal of the History of Ideas*, 11 (1950), 357–63.

COCKBURN, J. S. (ed.), *Crime in England, 1550–1800* (Princeton, NJ, 1977).

COLE, G. D. H., 'Some Notes on British Trade Unionism in the Third Quarter of the Nineteenth Century', *International Review for Social History*, 2 (1937), 1–22. (Review not to be confused with *International Review of Social History*.)

—— *Persons and Periods: Studies* (London, 1938). (Includes 'A Study in Legal Repression (1789–1834)'.)

—— *British Working Class Politics, 1832–1914* (London, 1941).

—— *A Short History of the British Working-Class Movement, 1789–1947* (rev. edn., London, 1948). (For a companion volume of documents see Cole and Filson in I. B above.)

—— *Attempts at General Union: A Study in British Trade Union History, 1818–1834* (London, 1953).

COLEMAN, D. C., *The British Paper Industry, 1495–1860: A Study in Industrial Growth* (Oxford, 1958).

COOKE, COLIN A., *Corporation, Trust and Company: An Essay in Legal History* (Manchester, 1950). (Ends with the Companies Act (1862).)

CORNFORD, JAMES P., 'The Transformation of Conservatism in the Late Nineteenth Century', *Victorian Studies*, 7 (1963–4), 35–66.

CORNISH, W. R., HART, JENIFER, MANCHESTER, A. H., and STEVENSON, J., *Crime and Law in Nineteenth Century Britain*. Government and Society in Nineteenth Century Britain: Commentaries on British Parliamentary Papers (Dublin, 1978).

COSGROVE, RICHARD A., *The Rule of Law: Albert Venn Dicey, Victorian Jurist* (Chapel Hill, NC, 1980). (Reviewed by John V. Orth, 80 *Michigan Law Review* 753–64 (1982).)

COWDEN, MORTON H., 'Early Marxist Views on British Labor, 1837–1917', *Western Political Quarterly*, 16 (1963), 34–52.

COWLING, MAURICE, *1867: Disraeli, Gladstone and Revolution: The Passing of the Second Reform Bill* (Cambridge, 1967).

DANGERFIELD, GEORGE, *The Strange Death of Liberal England* (New York, 1936).

DAVIES, MARGARET G., *The Enforcement of English Apprenticeship: A Study in Applied Mercantilism, 1563–1642* (Cambridge, Mass., 1956).

DEANE, PHYLLIS, and COLE, W. A., *British Economic Growth, 1688–1959: Trends and Structure* (2nd edn., Cambridge, 1967).

DERRY, T. K., 'Repeal of the Apprenticeship Clauses of the Statute of Apprentices', *Economic History Review*, 1st ser., 3 (1931–2), 67–87.

DICKSON, RALPH, 'The Tolpuddle Martyrs: Guilty or Not Guilty?' *Journal of Legal History*, 7 (1986), 178–87.

DOBSON, C. R., *Masters and Journeymen: A Prehistory of Industrial Relations, 1717–1800* (London, 1980).

DUMAN, DANIEL, *The Judicial Bench in England, 1727–1875: The Reshaping of a Professional Élite* (London, 1982).

EWING, KEITH D., *Trade Unions, the Labour Party and the Law: A Study of the Trade Union Act, 1913* (Edinburgh, 1982).

FETTER, FRANK W., 'The Authorship of Economic Articles in the *Edinburgh Review*, 1802–47', *Journal of Political Economy*, 61 (1953), 232–59.

—— 'The Economic Articles in the *Quarterly Review* and their Authors, 1809–1852', *Journal of Political Economy*, 66 (1958), 47–64, 154–70.

—— 'The Economic Articles in *Blackwood's Edinburgh Magazine* and their Authors, 1817–1853', *Scottish Journal of Political Economy*, 7 (1960), 85–107, 213–31.

—— 'Economic Articles in the *Westminster Review* and their Authors, 1824–1851', *Journal of Political Economy*, 70 (1962), 570–96.

—— 'Economic Controversy in the British Reviews, 1802–1850', *Economica*, NS 32 (1965), 424–37.

FIFOOT, C. H. S., *Judge and Jurist in the Reign of Victoria* (London, 1959).

FLANDERS, ALLAN, and CLEGG, HUGH A. (eds.), *The System of Industrial Relations in Great Britain: Its History, Law, and Institutions* (Oxford, 1954).

FLETCHER, GEORGE P., 'The Metamorphosis of Larceny', 89 *Harvard Law Review* 469–530 (1976).

FORBATH, WILLIAM E., 'The Ambiguities of Free Labor: Labor and the Law in the Gilded Age', 1985 *Wisconsin Law Review* 767–817. (On American labour.)

FOSTER, JOHN, *Class Struggle and the Industrial Revolution: Early Industrial Capitalism in Three English Towns* (London, 1974).

FOX, ALAN, 'Industrial Relations in Nineteenth-Century Birmingham', *Oxford Economic Papers*, NS 7 (1955), 57–70.

FRASER, W. HAMISH, 'Trade Unions, Reform and the Election of 1868 in Scotland', *Scottish Historical Review*, 50 (1971), 138–57.

—— *Trade Unions and Society: The Struggle for Acceptance, 1850–1880* (Totowa, NJ, 1974).

FREESTONE, DAVID, and RICHARDSON, J. C., 'The Making of English Criminal Law, Part 7: Sir John Jervis and his Acts', 1980 *Criminal Law Review* 5–16.

FROW, R., FROW, E., and KATANKA, MICHAEL, *The History of British Trade Unionism: A Select Bibliography* (London, 1969).

GARBATI, IRVING, 'British Trade Unionism in the Mid-Victorian Era', *University of Toronto Quarterly*, 20 (1950–1), 69–84.

GATRELL, V. A. C., LENMAN, BRUCE, and PARKER, GEOFFREY (eds.), *Crime and the Law: The Social History of Crime in Western Europe Since 1500* (London, 1980).

GAYER, ARTHUR, ROSTOW, W. W., and SCHWARTZ, ANNA, *The Growth and Fluctuation of the British Economy, 1790–1850*, 2 vols. (Oxford, 1953).

GELDART, W. M., 'The Status of Trade Unions in England', 25 *Harvard Law Review* 579–601 (1911–12).

GEORGE, M. DOROTHY, *London Life in the Eighteenth Century* (New York, 1925).

—— 'The Combination Laws Reconsidered', *Economic Journal* (Supp.), Economic History Ser., 2 (May 1927), 214–28.

—— 'The London Coal-heavers: Attempts to Regulate Waterside Labour in the Eighteenth and Nineteenth Centuries', *Economic Journal* (Supp.), Economic History Ser., 2 (May 1927), 229–48.

—— *England in Transition: Life and Work in the Eighteenth Century* (Harmondsworth, 1931).

—— 'The Combination Laws', *Economic History Review*, 1st ser., 6 (1935–6), 172–8. (A 'revision in economic history'.)

GILBOY, ELIZABETH W., *Wages in Eighteenth Century England* (Cambridge, Mass., 1934).

GILLESPIE, FRANCES E., *Labor and Politics in England, 1850–1867* (Durham, NC, 1927).

GINSBERG, MORRIS (ed.), *Law and Opinion in England in the Twentieth Century* (London, 1959).

GLAZEBROOK, P. R. (ed.), *Reshaping the Criminal Law: Essays in Honour of Glanville Williams* (London, 1978).

GOODHART, A. L., 'The Legality of the General Strike in England', 36 *Yale Law Journal* 464–85 (1926–7).

GOSDEN, P. H. J. H., *The Friendly Societies in England, 1815–1875* (Manchester, 1961).

GRAY, J. L., 'The Law of Combination in Scotland', *Economica*, OS 8 (1928), 332–50.

HAINES, BRIAN W., 'English Labour Law and the Separation From Contract', *Journal of Legal History*, 1 (1980), 262–96.

HALÉVY, ÉLIE, *The Growth of Philosophic Radicalism* (1st (French) edn., 1901; trans. Mary Morris, Boston, 1955).

—— *Thomas Hodgskin* (1st (French) edn., 1903; trans. A. J. Taylor, London, 1956).

—— *England in 1815* (1st (French) edn., 1913; 2nd rev. edn., trans. E. I. Watkin and D. A. Barker, London, 1949).

HAMMOND, J. L., and HAMMOND, BARBARA, *The Skilled Labourer, 1760–1832* (London, 1919).

—— *The Town Labourer, 1760–1832: The New Civilization* (London, 1917).

HANES, DAVID G., *The First British Workmen's Compensation Act, 1897* (New Haven, Conn., 1968).

HANSON, C. G., *Trade Unions: A Century of Privilege?* (London, 1973).

—— 'Craft Unions, Welfare Benefits and the Case for Trade Union Law Reform, 1867–75', *Economic History Review*, 2nd ser., 28 (1975), 243–59. (For comments by Pat Thane and A. E. Musson and a reply by Hanson, see ibid., 2nd ser., 29 (1976), 617–35.)

HARDING, ALAN, *A Social History of English Law* (Baltimore, 1966).

HARRIS, JAMES RAY, 'The Trade Union Charter: A Struggle for Legal Status, 1867–1876', Ph.D. thesis (Univ. of Oklahoma, 1971).

HARRISON, DAVID, *Conspiracy as a Crime and as a Tort in English Law* (London, 1924).

HARRISON, ROYDEN, *Before the Socialists: Studies in Labour and Politics, 1861–1881* (London, 1965).

HASLAM, A. L., *The Law Relating to Trade Combinations* (London, 1931).

HATTAM, VICTORIA, 'Unions and Politics: The Courts and American Labor, 1806–1896', Ph.D. thesis (Massachusetts Inst. of Technology, 1987).

HAY, DOUGLAS, LINEBAUGH, PETER, RULE, JOHN, THOMPSON, E. P., and WINSLOW, CAL, *Albion's Fatal Tree: Crime and Society in Eighteenth-Century England* (New York, 1975).

HEATON, HERBERT, 'The Assessment of Wages in the West Riding of Yorkshire in the Seventeenth and Eighteenth Centuries', *Economic Journal*, 24 (1914), 218–35.

HEDGES, R. Y., *The Law Relating to Restraint of Trade* (London, 1932).

—— and WINTERBOTTOM, ALLAN, *The Legal History of Trade Unionism* (London, 1930).

HICKS, J. R., 'The Early Industrial Conciliation in England', *Economica*, os 10 (1930), 25–39.

HILL, L. M., 'The Two-Witness Rule in English Treason Trials: Some Comments on the Emergence of Procedural Law', *American Journal of Legal History*, 12 (1968), 95–111.

HILTON, GEORGE W., *The Truck System: Including a History of the British Truck Acts, 1465–1960* (Cambridge, 1960).

HIMMELFARB, GERTRUDE, 'The Politics of Democracy: The English Reform Act of 1867', *Journal of British Studies*, 6 (1966–7), 97–138.

HOBSBAWM, E. J., *Labouring Men: Studies in the History of Labour* (London, 1964).

—— 'Trade Union Historiography', *Bulletin of the Society for the Study of Labour History*, 8 (Spring 1964), 31–6.

—— *Worlds of Labour: Further Studies in the History of Labour* (London, 1984).

—— and RUDÉ, GEORGE, *Captain Swing* (New York, 1969).

HOLDSWORTH, WILLIAM S., *A History of English Law*, 17 vols. (London, 1903–76) (vols. xiii–xvi, published posthumously, ed. A. L. Goodhart and H. G. Hanbury; vol. xvii, a general index, prepared by John Burke).

—— 'Industrial Combinations and the Law in the Eighteenth Century', 18 *Minnesota Law Review* 369–90 (1934) (repr. with minor additions in *History of English Law*, xi. 475–501.

HOLT, WYTHE, 'Labour Conspiracy Cases in the United States, 1805–1842: Bias and Legitimation in Common Law Adjudication', 22 *Osgoode Hall Law Journal* 591–663 (1984).

HOUGHTON, WALTER E. (ed.), *Wellesley Index to Victorian Periodicals, 1824– 1900*, 2 vols. (Toronto, 1966–72).

HOVENKAMP, HERBERT, 'Labor Conspiracies in American Law, 1800–1930', 66 *Texas Law Review* 919–65 (1988).

HUME, L. J., 'Jeremy Bentham and the Nineteenth Century Revolution in Government', *Historical Journal*, 10 (1967), 361–75.

HUNT, E. H., *British Labour History, 1815–1914* (Atlantic Highlands, NJ, 1981).

HURST, GERALD B., 'The Dorchester Labourers, 1834', *English Historical Review*, 40 (1925), 54–66.

HUTCHINS, B. L., and HARRISON, A., *A History of Factory Legislation* (1903) 3rd edn., London, 1926).

HUTT, ALLEN, *British Trade Unionism: A Short History* (6th edn., London, 1975).

JEFFERYS, JAMES B., *The Story of the Engineers, 1800–1945* (London, 1946). (Commissioned by the Amalgamated Engineering Union for its 25th anniversary.)

JONES, B. M., *Henry Fielding, Novelist and Magistrate* (London, 1933).

JONES, E. L., and MINGAY, G. E. (eds.), *Land, Labour and Population in the Industrial Revolution: Essays Presented to J. D. Chambers* (London, 1967).

JONES, STEPHEN, 'Community and Organisation—Early Seamen's Trade Unionism on the North-East Coast, 1768–1844', *Maritime History*, 3 (1973), 35–66.

KAHN-FREUND, OTTO, 'The Illegality of a Trade Union', 7 *Modern Law Review* 192–205 (1944).

—— 'The Role of the Courts in the Development of English Labour Law', *Rivista di Diritto Internazionale e Comparato del Lavoro*, NS 1 (1961), 172–89.

—— 'Blackstone's Neglected Child: The Contract of Employment', 93 *Law Quarterly Review* 508–28 (1977).

—— *Labour and the Law* (3rd edn., London, 1983 (ed. Paul Davies and Mark Freedland)).

KEETON, GEORGE W., SCHWARZENBERGER, GEORG (eds.), *Jeremy Bentham and the Law: A Symposium* (London, 1948).

KERR, BARBARA, 'The Dorset Agricultural Labourer, 1750–1850', *Proceedings of the Dorset Natural History and Archaeological Society*, 84 (1962), 158–77.

KLARMAN, MICHAEL J., 'Osborne: A Judgment Gone Too Far?' *English Historical Review*, 103 (1988), 21–39.

—— 'The Judges Versus the Unions: The Development of British Labor Law, 1867– 1913', 75 *Virginia Law Review* 1487–602 (1989).

—— 'Parliamentary Reversal of the *Osborne* Judgment', *Historical Journal*, 32 (1989), 893–924.

KLARMAN, MICHAEL J., 'The Trade Union Political Levy, the *Osborne* Judgment (1909), and the South Wales Miners' Federation', *Welsh History Review*, 15 (1990), 34–57.

KNOWLES, K. G. J. C., *Strikes: A Study in Industrial Conflict* (New York, 1952).

KONEFSKY, ALFRED S., ' "As Best to Subserve their own Interests": Lemuel Shaw, Labor Conspiracy, and Fellow Servants', *Law and History Review*, 7 (1989), 219–39. (On American labour.)

KYNASTON, DAVID, *King Labor: The British Working Class, 1850–1900* (Totowa, NJ, 1976).

LANDIS, JAMES M., *Cases on Labor Law* (Chicago, 1934). (American case-book.)

LASLETT, PETER, *The World We have Lost* (3rd edn., New York, 1984).

LEVENTHAL, F. M., *Respectable Radical: George Howell and Victorian Working Class Politics* (London, 1971).

LEVY, LEONARD W., *The Law of the Commonwealth and Chief Justice Shaw: The Evolution of American Law, 1830–1860* (New York, 1957).

LEWIS, ROY, 'The Historical Development of Labour Law', *British Journal of Industrial Relations*, 14 (1976), 1–17.

LIPSON, EPHRAIM, *Economic History of England*, 3 vols., i. *The Middle Ages* (12th edn., London, 1959); ii–iii. *The Age of Mercantilism* (6th edn., London, 1956).

LOVELL, JOHN, *British Trade Unions, 1875–1933* (London, 1977).

—— and ROBERTS, B. C., *A Short History of the TUC* (London, 1968).

MCCREADY, H. W., 'The British Election of 1874: Frederic Harrison and the Liberal-Labour Dilemma', *Canadian Journal of Economics and Political Science*, 20 (1954), 166–75.

—— 'British Labour and the Royal Commission on Trade Unions, 1867–1869', *University of Toronto Quarterly*, 24 (1954–5), 390–409.

—— 'British Labour's Lobby, 1867–1875', *Canadian Journal of Economics and Political Science*, 22 (1956), 141–60.

MACDONAGH, OLIVER, 'The Nineteenth Century Revolution in Government: A Reappraisal', *Historical Journal*, 1 (1958), 52–67.

MACDONALD, DONALD FARQUHAR, *The State and the Trade Unions* (London, 1960).

MACKINNON, FRANK, 'The Law and the Lawyers', in *Johnson's England: An Account of the Life and Manners of His Age*, ed. A. S. Turberville, 2 vols. (Oxford, 1933), ii. 287–309.

MAITLAND, FREDERIC WILLIAM, *Constitutional History of England*, ed. H. A. L. Fisher (Cambridge, 1908). (Based on lectures delivered 1887–8.)

MALCOMSON, ROBERT W., *Life and Labour in England, 1700–1780* (London, 1981).

MANCHESTER, A. H., *A Modern Legal History of England and Wales, 1750–1950* (London, 1980). (For a companion volume of documents see A. H. Manchester in I. B, above.)

MARCUS, STEVEN, *Engels, Manchester and the Working Class* (New York, 1974).

MARKS, GARY, *Unions in Politics: Britain, Germany, and the United States in the Nineteenth and Early Twentieth Centuries* (Princeton, NJ, 1989).

MARLOW, JOYCE, *The Tolpuddle Martyrs* (London, 1971).

MARTIN, ROSS M., 'Legal Personality and the Trade Union', in Leicester C. Webb (ed.), *Legal Personality and Political Pluralism* (Melbourne, 1958), 93–142.

—— *TUC: The Growth of a Pressure Group, 1868–1976* (Oxford, 1980).

MARWICK, W. H., *A Short History of Labour in Scotland* (Edinburgh, 1967).

MEACHAM, S., *A Life Apart: The English Working Class, 1890–1914* (Cambridge, 1977).

MILES, DUDLEY, *Francis Place: The Life of a Remarkable Radical, 1771–1854* (New York, 1988).

MILNE-BAILEY, W., *Trade Unions and the State* (London, 1934).

MINCHINTON, W. E., 'The Petitions of the Weavers and Clothiers of Gloucestershire in 1756', *Transactions of the Bristol and Gloucestershire Archaeological Society*, 73 (1954), 216–27.

—— *Wage Regulation in Pre-Industrial England* (New York, 1972). (Other than Minchinton's title essay, this volume consists of reprints: R. H. Tawney, 'The Assessment of Wages in England by the Justices of the Peace'; R. Keith Kelsall, 'Wage Regulation under the Statute of Artificers'; and id., 'A Century of Wage Assessments in Herefordshire, 1666–1762'.

MOHER, JIM, 'From Suppression to Containment: Trade Union Law, 1799–1825', *Bulletin of the Society for the Study of Labour History*, 49 (Autumn 1984), 7–9. (Summary of conference paper.)

MORRIS, RICHARD B., 'Criminal Conspiracy and Early Labor Combinations in New York', *Political Science Quarterly*, 52 (1937), 51–85.

—— *Government and Labor in Early America* (New York, 1946).

MORTON, A. L., and TATE, GEORGE, *The British Labour Movement, 1770–1920* (London, 1956).

MUSSON, A. E., *British Trade Unions, 1800–1875* (London, 1972).

—— *Trade Unions and Social History* (London, 1974).

NELLES, WALTER, 'The First American Labor Case', 41 *Yale Law Journal* 165–200 (1931). (On the Philadelphia Cordwainers' Case (1806).)

—— 'Commonwealth v. Hunt', 32 *Columbia Law Review* 1128–70 (1931–2).

'Note', 'Tortious Interference with Contractual Relations in the Nineteenth Century: The Transformation of Property, Contract, and Tort', 93 *Harvard Law Review* 1510–39 (1980).

'Note', 'A Short History of the Right to Petition Government for the Redress of Grievances', 96 *Yale Law Journal* 142–66 (1986).

'Note', 'Law and Legitimacy in England, 1800–1832: Bringing Professors Hay and Thompson to the Bargaining Table', 68 *Boston University Law Review* 621–51 (1988).

O'HIGGINS, PAUL, and PARTINGTON, MARTIN, 'Industrial Conflict: Judicial Attitudes', 32 *Modern Law Review* 53–8 (1969). (Statistical survey of decisions by higher courts in cases concerning industrial conflict between 1871 and 1969.)

O'HIGGINS, RACHEL, 'Irish Trade Unions and Politics, 1830–1850', *Historical Journal*, 4 (1961), 208–17.

OLIVER, W. H., 'The Consolidated Trades' Union of 1834', *Economic History Review*, 2nd ser., 17 (1964–5), 77–95.

—— 'Tolpuddle Martyrs and Trade Union Oaths', *Labour History*, 10 (May 1966), 5–12 (Journal of Australian Society for the Study of Labour History).

ORTH, JOHN V., 'The British Trade Union Acts of 1824 and 1825: Dicey and the Relation between Law and Opinion', 5 *Anglo-American Law Review* 131–52 (1976).

ORTH, JOHN V., 'Combination and Conspiracy: The Legal Status of English Trade Unions, 1799–1871', Ph.D. thesis (Harvard Univ., 1977).

—— 'Doing Legal History', 14 NS *Irish Jurist* 114–23 (1979).

—— 'The Legal Status of English Trade Unions, 1799–1871', in Alan Harding (ed.), *Law-Making and Law-Makers in British History* (London, 1980), 195–207.

—— 'English Law and Striking Workmen: The Molestation of Workmen Act, 1859', *Journal of Legal History*, 2 (1981), 238–57.

—— 'The Law of Strikes, 1847–1871', in J. A. Guy and H. G. Beale (eds.), *Law and Social Change in British History* (London, 1984), 126–44.

—— 'English Combination Acts of the Eighteenth Century', *Law and History Review*, 5 (1987), 175–211. (Omitted Appendix printed ibid. 587.)

—— 'The English Combination Laws Reconsidered', in Francis Snyder and Douglas Hay (eds.), *Labour, Law, and Crime: An Historical Perspective* (London, 1987), 123–49.

—— 'Casting the Priests out of the Temple: John Austin and the Relation Between Law and Religion', in John Witte and Frank S. Alexander (eds.), *The Weightier Matters of the Law: Essays on Law and Religion* (Atlanta, 1988), 229–49.

PARK, PATRICK, 'The Combination Acts in Ireland, 1727–1825', 14 NS *Irish Jurist* 340–59 (1979).

PARRIS, HENRY, 'The Nineteenth-Century Revolution in Government: A Reappraisal Reappraised', *Historical Journal*, 3 (1960), 17–37.

PELLING, HENRY, *The Origins of the Labour Party, 1880–1900* (2nd edn., Oxford, 1965).

—— *Popular Politics and Society in Late Victorian Britain* (London, 1968).

—— *History of British Trade Unionism* (3rd edn., London, 1976).

PERKIN, HAROLD, *The Origins of Modern English Society, 1780–1880* (London, 1969).

—— 'Individualism Versus Collectivism in Nineteenth Century Britain: A False Antithesis', *Journal of British Studies*, 17 (1977–8), 105–18.

PERRINS, BRYN, *Trade Union Law* (London, 1985).

PLUCKNETT, THEODORE F. T., *A Concise History of the Common Law* (5th edn., Boston, 1956).

PLUMB, J. H., *England in the Eighteenth Century*, Pelican History of England, vii. (Harmondsworth, 1950).

PLUMMER, ALFRED, *The London Weavers' Company, 1600–1970* (London, 1972).

POLLARD, SIDNEY, 'The Ethics of the Sheffield Outrages', *Transactions of the Hunter Archaeological Society*, 7 (1951–7), 118–39.

—— Introduction to *The Sheffield Outrages: Report Presented to the Trades Unions Commissioners in 1867* (New York, 1971). (*Report* reprinted from *Parliamentary Papers*.)

POOS, L. R., 'The Social Context of Statute of Labourers Enforcement', *Law and History Review*, 1 (1983), 27–52.

PORTER, ROY, *English Society in the Eighteenth Century* (Harmondsworth, 1982).

POSTGATE, RAYMOND W., *The Builders' History* (London, 1923).

PRICE, RICHARD, *Masters, Unions and Men: Work Control in Building and the Rise of Labour, 1830–1914* (Cambridge, 1980).

—— *Labour in British Society: An Interpretative History* (London, 1986).

PRITT, D. N., *Law, Class and Society*, 4 vols. (London, 1970–2).

—— and FREEMAN, RICHARD, *The Law vs. the Trade Unions* (London, 1958).

PUTNAM, BERTHA HAVEN, *The Enforcement of the Statutes of Labourers during the First Decade after the Black Death, 1349–1359* (New York, 1908).

RADZINOWICZ, LEON, *A History of English Criminal Law and its Administration from 1750*, 5 vols. (London, 1948–86). (Vol. v co-written by Roger Hood.)

REDIKER, MARCUS, *Between the Devil and the Deep Blue Sea: Merchant Seamen, Pirates, and the Anglo-American Maritime World, 1700–1750* (Cambridge, 1987).

ROBBINS, LIONEL, *The Theory of Economic Policy in English Classical Political Economy* (London, 1952).

ROBERTS, B. C., *The Trades Union Congress, 1868–1921* (London, 1958).

ROMANES, JOHN H., 'The Evolution of the Law of Trade Unions', in *The Economic Studies of a Lawyer* (Edinburgh, 1930), 32–41.

ROSTOW, W. W., *The British Economy of the Nineteenth Century* (Oxford, 1948).

—— *The Stages of Economic Growth: A Non-Communist Manifesto* (2nd edn., Cambridge, 1971).

ROTHSCHILD, V. HENRY (II), 'Government Regulation of Trade Unions in Great Britain', 38 *Columbia Law Review* 1–48, 1335–92 (1938).

ROWE, D. J., 'A Trade Union of the North-East Coast Seamen in 1825', *Economic History Review*, 2nd ser., 25 (1972), 81–98.

—— 'Francis Place and the Historian', *Historical Journal*, 16 (1973), 45–63.

ROWLEY, CHARLES K., 'Toward a Political Economy of British Labor Law', 51 *University of Chicago Law Review* 1135–60 (1984).

RUBIN, G. R., and SUGARMAN, DAVID (eds.), *Law, Economy and Society, 1750–1914: Essays in the History of English Law* (Abingdon, 1984). (Reviewed by John V. Orth, *Law and History Review*, 4 (1986), 210–12.

RUDÉ, GEORGE, *Wilkes and Liberty: A Social Study of 1763 to 1774* (Oxford, 1962).

RULE, JOHN, *The Experience of Labour in Eighteenth-Century English Industry* (New York, 1981).

RUSSELL, ALAN K., *Liberal Landslide: The General Election of 1906* (Hamden, Conn., 1973).

SAVILLE, JOHN (ed.), *Democracy and the Labour Movement: Essays in Honour of Dona Torr* (London, 1954).

SAYRE, FRANCIS BOWES, 'Criminal Conspiracy', 35 *Harvard Law Review* 393–427 (1921–2).

—— *A Selection of Cases and other Authorities on Labor Law* (Cambridge, Mass., 1922). (American case-book.)

—— 'Inducing Breach of Contract', 36 *Harvard Law Review* 663–703 (1922–3).

SEARS, DON W., 'Legal Regulations of Labor Relations: A Comparative View of the United States and the British Isles', 55 *University of Colorado Law Review* 273–317 (1984).

SHARP, IAN G., *Industrial Conciliation and Arbitration in Great Britain* (1950).

SIMPSON, A. W. B. (ed.), *Biographical Dictionary of the Common Law* (London, 1984).

SLESSER, HENRY H., 'The Legality of Trade Unionism', in *The Art of Judgment and other Studies* (1962), pp. 87–112.

—— and BAKER, CHARLES, *Trade Union Law* (3rd edn., London, 1927). (Continued by Norman Arthur Citrine (*q.v.*). Born Schloesser, the first author changed his name during World War I. Solicitor General in Ramsay MacDonald's first Labour Government, Slesser was a judge on the Court of Appeals from 1929 to 1940.)

SMITH, PAUL, *Disraelian Conservatism and Social Reform* (London, 1967).

SNYDER, FRANCIS, and HAY, DOUGLAS (eds.), *Labour, Law, and Crime: An Historical Perspective* (London, 1987).

SPICER, ROBERT, *Conspiracy: Law, Class and Society* (London, 1981).

STEVENSON, JOHN, *Popular Disturbances in England, 1700–1870* (London, 1979).

SUTHERLAND, GILLIAN (ed.), *Studies in the Growth of Nineteenth-Century Government* (Totowa, NJ, 1972).

THOLFSEN, TRYGVE R., *Working-class Radicalism in Mid-Victorian England* (New York, 1976).

THOMAS, MAURICE WALTON, *The Early Factory Legislation: A Study in Legislative and Administrative Evolution* (Leigh-on-Sea, 1948). (Covers 1831–53.)

THOMAS, W. E. S., 'Francis Place and Working Class History', *Historical Journal*, 5 (1962), 61–70.

THOMIS, MALCOLM I., *The Luddites* (Newton Abbot, 1970).

—— 'Gravener Henson: The Man and the Myth', *Transactions of the Thoroton Society of Nottinghamshire*, 75 (1971), 91–7.

—— *The Town Labourer and the Industrial Revolution* (London, 1974).

THOMPSON, E. P., *The Making of the English Working Class* (New York, 1963).

—— 'The Peculiarities of the English', *Socialist Register 1965*, 311–62.

—— *Whigs and Hunters: The Origin of the Black Act* (New York, 1975).

THOMSON, A. W. J., 'The Injunction in Trades Disputes in Britain before 1910', *Industrial and Labor Relations Review*, 19 (1965–6), 213–23.

TOMLINS, CHRISTOPHER L., *The State and the Unions: Labor Relations, Law, and the Organized Labor Movement in America, 1880–1960* (Cambridge, 1985).

—— 'Criminal Conspiracy and Early Labor Combinations: Massachusetts, 1824–1840', *Labour History*, 28 (1987), 370.

TOWNSHEND-SMITH, RICHARD, 'Labor Law in Great Britain and America: The Similarity of the Underlying Themes', 9 *George Mason University Law Review* 245–309 (1987).

TURNER, HERBERT A., *Trade Union Growth, Structure and Policy: A Comparative Study of the Cotton Unions* (London, 1962).

VOGELER, MARTHA S., *Frederic Harrison: The Vocations of a Positivist* (Oxford, 1984).

WALLAS, GRAHAM, *The Life of Francis Place, 1771–1854* (3rd edn., New York, 1919).

WARD, J. T., *The Factory Movement, 1830–1855* (London, 1962).

WEBB, SIDNEY, and WEBB, BEATRICE, *English Local Government from the Revolution to the Municipal Corporations Act*, 9 vols. (London, 1906–29). (Covers 1688–1835.)

—— *The History of Trade Unionism* (rev. edn., London, 1920).

—— *Industrial Democracy* (rev. edn., London, 1920).

WEDDERBURN, K. W., *The Worker and the Law* (2nd edn., Harmondsworth, 1971).

WIGHAM, ERIC L., *Strikes and the Government, 1893–1974* (London, 1976).

WIGMORE, JOHN H., 'Required Number of Witnesses: A Brief History of the Numerical System in England', 15 *Harvard Law Review* 83–108 (1901–2); repr.

in id., *Wigmore on Evidence*, rev. James H. Chadbourne (Boston, 1978), § 2032.

—— 'The Privilege against Self-Crimination; Its History', 15 *Harvard Law Review* 610–37 (1901–2); repr. (with brief review of subsequent literature) in id., *Wigmore on Evidence*, rev. John T. McNaughton (Boston, 1961), § 2250.

WILLIAMS, JUDITH BLOW, *A Guide to the Printed Materials for English Social and Economic History, 1750–1850*, 2 vols. (New York, 1926).

WINFIELD, PERCY H., *The History of Conspiracy and Abuse of Legal Procedure* (Cambridge, 1921).

WOODWARD, DONALD, 'The Background to the Statute of Artificers: The Genesis of Labour Policy, 1558–63', *Economic History Review*, 2nd ser., 33 (1980), 32–44.

WRIGLEY, CHRIS (ed.), *A History of British Industrial Relations, 1875–1914* (Amherst, Mass., 1982).

ZANGERL, CARL H. E., 'The Social Composition of the County Magistracy in England and Wales, 1831–1887', *Journal of British Studies*, 11 (1971–2), 113–25.

Glossary of Legal Terms

Assizes Judicial sessions held in various towns by royal judges. Among the commissions authorizing the judges to hold assizes was the commission of *nisi prius*, q.v. Assizes were ended in 1972.

Benefit of Clergy Originally the privilege of ordained churchmen to be tried for felony (q.v.) only by church courts. By the eighteenth century, benefit of clergy meant, for felonies to which it still applied, that all persons whether in religious orders or not were exempt from capital punishment for the first offence. Felonies for which the exemption did not apply were expressly made 'without benefit of clergy'. As part of a general reform of criminal law, benefit of clergy was abolished in 1827.

Case Stated Form of appeal on points of law from justice of the peace to superior court. First authorized in 1857, the case stated is a recital of the facts plus one or more questions of law.

Certiorari Order by Court of King's (Queen's) Bench requiring that the record of a proceeding be certified and sent to it. Although not in form an appeal, *certiorari* provided a means for reviewing decisions of inferior tribunals, such as quarter sessions. In function it resembled the writ of error (q.v.) which was available to review the decisions of common-law courts.

Civil Law Used in two distinct senses: as contrasted with criminal law, the rules governing private wrongs; as contrasted with common law (q.v.), a legal system based on Roman law.

Common Gaol A public gaol, called 'common' to distinguish it from a private gaol kept by a privileged person.

Common Law Law applied by royal judges since the twelfth century, common to the whole of England. It was extended to Wales, but Scotland retained civil law, q.v. Common law was formerly called *lex non scripta* (unwritten law). In fact, it was gathered from written reports of judicial decisions in particular cases, and in consequence was also called case law as opposed to statute law. Jeremy Bentham disparagingly referred to it as judge-made law; the name has survived but the connotation is no longer negative. Common law is also contrasted with equity, q.v.

Covenant A promise or agreement in writing marked with a seal.

Equity In English law the distinctive rights and remedies administered by the Court of Chancery, as opposed to the courts of common law, q.v. The administration of law and equity were merged by the Judicature Act (1873).

Error, Writ of Order by Court of King's (Queen's) Bench requiring that the record of a proceeding in a common-law court be sent to it for review for errors of law.

Ex-Officio Oath Oath used in ecclesiastical courts requiring a person to give evidence against himself. Abuses of the oath by the Court of High Commission in the seventeenth century led to its abolition.

Felony Originally a serious crime punishable at common law with forfeiture of lands and goods. By the eighteenth century most felonies were also punishable by death, although in practice this was qualified by the benefit of clergy, q.v. In common parlance, felonies were all capital crimes below treason. In 1870 forfeiture was abolished, and in 1967 all distinctions between felony and less serious crime or misdemeanour (q.v.) were abolished.

General Issue Defendant's plea denying plaintiff's cause of action, both facts and law. The effect was to cast the whole burden of proof on the plaintiff. Originally prohibited, pleading the general issue was by the mid-eighteenth century allowed by the courts in some cases and by statutes in many more.

Habeas Corpus The name of a variety of writs ordering an officer to bring a person before a court. The most famous writ, *habeas corpus ad subjiciendum*, secured by the Habeas Corpus Act (1679), protects against unlawful confinement. (It was suspended from 1794 to 1801 during the war with France.) Other varieties provide for the production of a person, for example, to testify (*ad testificandum*) or to be prosecuted (*ad prosequendum*).

Indictment Written accusation charging a person with a crime triable by jury, the functional equivalent of an information (q.v.) for a crime triable by justices of the peace. Indictments were the subject of many, highly technical rules.

Justices of the Peace Local officials, originally unpaid, appointed by the Crown to keep the peace. They met four times annually in quarter sessions, q.v. In addition to judicial functions, justices of the peace performed numerous local governmental duties, which were transferred to elected local authorities in the nineteenth century.

Misdemeanour At common law a crime for which the punishment was less severe than that for treason or felony, q.v. In 1967 all distinctions between misdemeanour and felony were abolished.

Nisi Prius Commission authorizing trial before a single judge, usually sitting in the district in which the dispute arose. The name (in Latin, 'unless before') came from the commission literally ordering trial before the full bench at a date certain, *unless before* then a trial had been held in the district before a single judge. The commission of *nisi prius* was one of the commissions authorizing judges to hold a assizes, q.v.

Nonsuit Judicial order in favour of defendant discontinuing suit when plaintiff fails to establish a legal cause of action or to support his pleadings by admissible evidence.

Private Act A statute establishing an exception to a general rule. Unlike a public act (q.v.), a private act was not published in the Statutes at Large, and judges were not required to take notice of it unless it was specially pleaded. During its passage special fees were payable to parliamentary officers.

Public Act A statute establishing a general rule, as opposed to a private act, q.v. A public act must be observed by judges without need for special proof of its terms. Since 1850 all statutes are presumed public unless expressly labelled private.

Quarter Sessions Meetings of the justices of the peace (q.v.), held four times a year at dates determined by the Christian calendar: Michaelmas (29 Sept.), Epiphany (6 Jan.), Easter (a moveable feast between 22 Mar. and 25 Apr.), and the Translation of St Thomas (7 July). Between quarter sessions, 'petty sessions' of one or more justices met. Quarter sessions were abolished in 1971.

Qui Tam **Action** Form of action used by an informer to secure a penalty provided by statute. Since a further penalty was usually payable to the government, the plaintiff was said to sue 'as well for the King as for himself'; hence the name *qui tam*, from the Latin for 'who as well'.

Recognizance An obligation to perform some act or suffer a penalty.

Summary Procedure Expedited trial dispensing with common-law forms including indictment and jury. Statutes conferred on justices of the peace power to try minor offences by summary procedure.

Transportation A species of exile. Provided by statute as an alternative to hanging, systematic transportation began in 1717. From then until the American Revolution (1776), the destination was one of Britain's North American colonies, thereafter it was Australia. Sentences of transportation were ended in 1857.

Weekly Bills of Mortality Records of burials kept by the Company of Parish Clerks in the greater London area since the seventeenth century. As records of mortality, the bills were incomplete since they included only burials in Church of England graveyards. The area covered by the returns was referred to in legal shorthand as 'within the weekly bills of mortality'.

Table of Cases

Until 1865 English cases were reported by lawyers on a private-enterprise basis, without official status. Citations begin with the volume number, then give the name of the reporter (usually abbreviated), and conclude with the first page on which the particular case is reported. When the original report has been reprinted in the *English Reports—Full Reprint* (1900–30), I have included the parallel citation. In addition, I have added in parentheses the court that decided the case and the year of decision. Some cases were reported by more than one reporter, so multiple citations may be listed. In a few cases the only report was a newspaper account or a privately published pamphlet. After 1865 several competing series of reports were begun, many of them indicating in their title the date and/or court. Criminal cases, brought in the name of the Crown, are arranged under R. (for Rex or Regina).

Table of Statutes

Until 1962 English statutes were cited by the year of the monarch's reign in which they were adopted, together with the particular act, called a chapter (abbreviated c.), according to its numerical order. If two sessions of parliament were held during one regnal year, the particular session (misleadingly indicated st. for statute) is included. In case of private local acts the chapter number is given in lower-case Roman numerals. I have added in parentheses the calendar year given in Danby Pickering's edition of the *Statutes at Large* (i–xxiii (1762–6) (periodic volumes thereafter)), unless it would be misleading. Aside from the obvious problems involved in dating very early statutes, there remained until the mid-eighteenth century the problem that lawyers paid more attention to the regnal year that began on a different month and day for each monarch than to the calendar year. The English calendar posed problems of its own until the adoption of the Gregorian calendar in 1751: theretofore England adhered to the Julian calendar and usually began a new year on Lady Day, 25 March. Matters were further complicated by the legal rule, not altered until 1793 (33 Geo. 3, c. 13), that statutes were effective from the first day of the parliamentary session in which they were passed (unless otherwise specified). I have also added in some cases a descriptive name in parentheses. Official short titles did not appear until the last third of the nineteenth century.

UNITED KINGDOM

(Including acts of English Parliament (–1706) and Parliament of Great Britain (1707–1800).)

SCOTLAND

IRELAND

UNITED STATES

Index